T0418968

THE CONCEPT OF TRAGEDY

Events in the world today appear to be increasingly uncontrollable and unknowable. Climate change, refugee crises, and global pandemics seem to demonstrate the limits of human reason, science, and technology. In light of this, the terms "tragedy" and "tragic" have come into greater use. What does the register of the tragic do? What does its deployment in the contemporary context and other times of crisis mean? In addressing such questions, this book also argues for a "tragic vision" embedded in the history of social thought, demonstrating the relevance of the ancient tragedians and Aristotle as well as Shakespeare and modern dramatists to the most pressing questions of agency and collectivity in the social sciences. Developing a theory of "tragic social science," which is applied to topics including global inequality, celebrity culture, pandemics, and climate change, *The Concept of Tragedy* aims to restore "tragedy" as a productive analytic in the social sciences. As such, it will appeal to scholars of sociology, anthropology, social theory, media and communications, and literary criticism with interests in tragedy, suffering, and modernity.

Sam Han is Lecturer in Sociology at Brunel University, London. He is the author of *(Inter)Facing Death: Life in Global Uncertainty, Technologies of Religion: Spheres of the Sacred in a Post-Secular Modernity* and *Digital Culture and Religion in Asia* (with Kamaludeen Mohamed Nasir), and other works.

Classical and Contemporary Social Theory
Series Editor: Stjepan G. Mestrovic
Texas A&M University, USA

Classical and Contemporary Social Theory publishes rigorous scholarly work that re-discovers the relevance of social theory for contemporary times, demonstrating the enduring importance of theory for modern social issues. The series covers social theory in a broad sense, inviting contributions on both 'classical' and modern theory, thus encompassing sociology, without being confined to a single discipline. As such, work from across the social sciences is welcome, provided that volumes address the social context of particular issues, subjects, or figures and offer new understandings of social reality and the contribution of a theorist or school to our understanding of it.

The series considers significant new appraisals of established thinkers or schools, comparative works or contributions that discuss a particular social issue or phenomenon in relation to the work of specific theorists or theoretical approaches. Contributions are welcome that assess broad strands of thought within certain schools or across the work of a number of thinkers, but always with an eye toward contributing to contemporary understandings of social issues and contexts.

Titles in this series

Perspectivism
A Contribution to the Philosophy of the Social Sciences
Kenneth Smith

A Sociology of Seeking:
Portents of Belief
Kieran Flanagan

True Believers and the Great Replacement:
Understanding Anomie and Alienation
Alf Walle

The Concept of Tragedy:
Its Importance for the Social Sciences in Unsettled Times
Sam Han

For more information about this series, please visit: https://www.routledge.com/sociology/series/ASHSER1383

THE CONCEPT OF TRAGEDY

Its Importance for the Social Sciences in Unsettled Times

Sam Han

Routledge
Taylor & Francis Group

LONDON AND NEW YORK

Designed cover image: © Sam Han

First published 2023
by Routledge
2 Park Square, Milton Park, Abingdon, Oxon OX14 4RN

and by Routledge
605 Third Avenue, New York, NY 10158

Routledge is an imprint of the Taylor & Francis Group, an informa business

British Library Cataloguing-in-Publication Data
A catalogue record for this book is available from the British Library

ISBN: 978-0-367-62798-0 (hbk)
ISBN: 978-0-367-62033-2 (pbk)
ISBN: 978-1-003-11085-9 (ebk)

DOI: 10.4324/9781003110859

Typeset in Bembo
by KnowledgeWorks Global Ltd.

CONTENTS

ACKNOWLEDGMENTS

The idea for this book came right as the COVID-19 pandemic hit. Having written most of it in an isolated Western Australia, which has seen a total of 639 deaths from the coronavirus, a small sum compared to the loss of 6.6 million lives (as of this writing) around the world, I experienced the pandemic largely *through* media, as a distant spectator. Watching the tragic drama unfold from afar, especially with the United States, and my hometown of New York City, bearing the brunt of it early on, I was full of equal parts anger, pity, and helplessness. Thinking *with* and about tragedy during this time was uncanny.

A book meant to be about tragedy *in* the social sciences wound up being written during the tragedy *of* the social sciences at The University of Western Australia, which decided to dissolve its program in anthropology and sociology in 2022. I found myself writing on the value of tragic thinking while simultaneously contemplating the place of the social sciences and humanities within the context of their devaluation in universities across the world. My former colleagues at UWA deserve mention here for demonstrating solidarity, kindness, and encouragement: Farida Fozdar, Loretta Baldassar, Greg Acciaioli, Tim Winter, Glenn Savage, Martin Forsey, and Katie Glaskin. Likewise, my thanks to Ethan Blue, Kirk Essary, Yu Tao, and Jo Elfving-Hwang. My students at UWA were a tremendous source of solace and inspiration. I want to give a shout out to the members of the social thought reading group—Marinus van der Riet Schimmel, Madison Lee, India Easton, Michael West, Sophia Bartlett, Taneesha Stallbaum, Linc Murray, Ibrahim Barre, Diana Truman, Amy Vinicombe, and Katherine Ong.

The finishing touches of this book were made at a new university and in a new city. At Brunel University, I wish to thank my colleagues in Sociology, Communications, and Journalism for the warm welcome.

Ideas contained in this book were previously presented at The Australian Sociological Association annual conference in 2021, the Sociology in the West Symposium in 2021, The British Sociological Association Conference in 2022, and the Thesis Eleven/TASA Social Theory Thematic Group Workshop in 2022. I wish to express my appreciation to my interlocutors at those events.

Portions of Chapter 8 appeared as "Towards a tragic social science: Critique, translation, and performance" in a special section of *Thesis Eleven* (Vol. 1, Issue 1) edited by Andrew Gilbert, Rachel Busbridge, and Nick Osbaldiston.

At Routledge, my editor Neil Jordan (as always) gives me the trust and latitude necessary to write a book like this. My thanks to him, Alice Salt, and Gemma Rogers for their work on this manuscript.

But the greatest gratitude I wish to extend to Ruth, who was with me throughout the entire process of writing. The impact of our countless conversations on my thinking is immeasurable. I learn so much from you every single day. The fact that I get to share life's tragedies and comedies with her can only be attributed to a beautiful twist of fate.

While I received so much help and encouragement in the course of writing, the book's inevitable errors and faults are my own.

Sam Han
East London

1

INTRODUCTION

Why tragedy? Why now?

Introduction

Many aspects of the contemporary world are described as "tragic"—the massive loss of life, bungled governmental responses, the economic impact of the pandemic, the swirl of misinformation that has gotten to a fever pitch. These are but some of the facets of this multi-layered crisis that is gripping the world. Still, there are others that have been in with us for longer—colonialism, genocide, climate change, the rise of right-wing neo-fascism, and the ever-increasing gap between the rich and the poor. These, of course, have not gone away or even subsided. As Ian Goldin has put it, "Far from being a 'great equalizer,' COVID-19 has revealed and compounded existing inequalities in wealth, race, gender, age, education and geographical location" (Goldin, 2021). But the immediacy of the COVID-19 pandemic and its aftermath has seen an uptick in the evocation of "tragedy" and the tragic register to describe recent events.

We can see this quite clearly in the earliest headlines accompanying articles dealing with the global pandemic in some of the major journalistic outlets around the world. The *New York Times* sported these two:

'An incredible scale of tragedy': The U.S. records 25 million virus cases.
(Tompkins, 2021)

'A Tragedy Is Unfolding': Inside New York's Virus Epicenter
(Correal et al., 2020)

DOI: 10.4324/9781003110859-1

One of the *New Yorker*'s early articles, published in 2020, taking stock of America's response to COVID-19 was called:

> The Plague Year: The mistakes and the struggles behind America's coronavirus tragedy.
>
> (Wright, 2020)

The *Guardian* spoke of what occurred in Italy, the first hotspot outside of China, in this manner:

> 'Totally awakened': how tragedy has left Italians alert to deadly virus
>
> (Giuffrida, 2020)

Across all these headlines, this much is clear: the pandemic is tragic because of the suffering that it had caused. Beyond this, there is hardly any consistency across these various examples. For instance, in the first article listed above in the *Times*, the first utterance of the word "tragedy" is by a source, an epidemiologist at Johns Hopkins University.

> "Twenty-five million cases is an incredible scale of tragedy," said Caitlin Rivers, an epidemiologist at the Johns Hopkins Bloomberg School of Public Health, who called the coronavirus pandemic one of the worst public health crises in history.
>
> (Tompkins, 2021)

For Rivers, the quantitative scale of the number of cases is tragic. The other article in the *Times* quotes the co-director of advocacy organization focusing on working-class Latinos based in the borough of Queens in New York City. After detailing the number of immigrant taxi drivers that have died, he states, "A tragedy is unfolding," referring to "the virus's disproportionate impact on immigrant communities" (Correal et al., 2020). In this case, it was the fact that COVID-19 had affected an already vulnerable population that occasioned a tragic register.

In the case of the *New Yorker*, the handling of the pandemic specifically under the Trump administration is the tragedy. In perhaps the most authoritative recounting of the failure of the American response to the pandemic at the time, Lawrence Wright notes:

> During the transition to the Trump Administration, the Obama White House handed off a sixty-nine-page document called the Playbook for Early Response to High-Consequence Emerging Infectious Disease Threats and Biological Incidents. A meticulous guide for combatting a "pathogen of pandemic potential," it contains a directory of government

resources to consult the moment things start going haywire…The Trump Administration jettisoned the Obama playbook.

(Wright, 2020)

Meanwhile, the *Guardian* article speaks to the "horror" of the high death tolls in Italy during the early months of the pandemic:

> The lingering effects of a tough two-month lockdown and the horror experienced at the height of the emergency–when the country held one of the highest death tolls in the world–may however help to explain why Italy, the first European country to be hit by an outbreak, appears to be more successful than its neighbors in containing a resurgence.

(Giuffrida, 2020)

One could accuse the media outlets of analytic messiness at worst and unimaginative copy at best. But journalists are not alone in this confusion of what "tragic" means.

Scholars of tragedy have long debated what makes a work—whether it be a play, a poem or a novel—"tragic" (Kitto, 2011; Marshall, 2002; Orr, 1989). There are several questions around which the scholarship has organized this discussion, with the emphasis mostly on tragic *drama*. Firstly, there is the question of form. What are the components of tragedy? This line of inquiry has largely settled on plot, character, diction, thought, spectacle, and song as the constituent elements of tragedy in the theatrical sense (Critchley, 2019: 204). Second, related to the previous, is the response of the audience of tragic drama. What emotions are the audience meant to feel when viewing tragedy? While hotly contested in literary history and criticism, many scholars have landed on two key emotions—pity and fear, due in large part to Aristotle's influence (Critchley, 2019: 190). Third, there is the question of message or philosophy. What is the audience meant to think about as a result of viewing tragedy? This too has been much debated. There are some like Simon Critchley who suggest that the Attic tragedy that Aristotle had commented on had no persuasive or educational function (Critchley, 2019: 190). Others, such as Terry Eagleton, argue quite differently—that Greek tragedy was in fact a political institution in addition to an aesthetic experience. It, he argues, provided a form of "ethico-political education which helped to inculcate virtue" (Eagleton, 2020: 3). Lastly, and relatedly, there is the matter of social function. What role does tragedy have in society? Eagleton argues that the educational function of tragedy indicates a "double role," which is to both validate and call into question social institutions. It does this through the "regulation" of emotions. For Aristotle, the emotions that were most significant to regulate was pity and fear, as these could "prove disruptive if left unchecked." This "homeopathic function" was to maintain the health of the polis (Eagleton, 2020: 4).

While there has been disagreement among generations of scholars regarding the ins and outs of the components of tragic drama, there is some degree of consensus among commentators that there is a relationship between tragedy and crisis (Gilbert, 2019; Kaufmann, 1992; Szondi, 2002; Szondi and Hays, 1983). As Eagleton, perhaps the most ardent critic (and defender) of tragedy in recent decades, writes, "liminal states are the periods of major tragedy" (Eagleton, 2020: 57). For him, tragedy is especially identifiable in periods where "one way of life collides with another." In the West, he argues, tragedy is born "each time that the pendulum of civilization is halfway between a sacred society and a society built around humanity" (Eagleton, 2020: 57). Speaking of Greek tragedy in particular, Eagleton posits that it came to be in a period of "spectacular social and political turbulence, with internecine struggles between various aristocratic factions, growing popular resentment of the ruling class and the rise of popular tyrants." Specifically, however, he points to the "cultural transition" when the religious thought of old was waning but still maintained some degree of authority yet not unassailable. It is in such periods where "the old civilization is breaking up, and is palpable in its very passing" (Eagleton, 2020: 57). Put differently, what Eagleton is identifying as "transitional" is a period whereby traditional moral codes no longer provide an individual's "experience with sufficient meaning" (Eagleton, 2020: 70). Tragedy comes to fulfill this potential void but acting as one of "the various surrogates for religion in the modern period, dealing with as it does with guilt, transgression, suffering, redemption and glorification" (Eagleton, 2020: 6).

Eagleton is not alone when equating tragedy with transition. Peter Szondi argues similarly (Szondi, 2002: 49), as does Critchley when he notes that tragedy emerged at the end of the sixth-century BCE to deal with the ambiguity of transition. It was then that myth no longer had a hold on the political realities of the polity (Critchley, 2019: 41), by offering a clear vision of the distance and separation that characterizes the "proper relation between gods and mortals" (Critchley, 2019: 228). Martha Nussbaum goes back a bit further to suggest that late fifth century Athens was characterized by an "exuberant confidence in human power." Through the discovery of the concept of *technai* (human art or science), Athenians, she writes, were "more than ever gripped by the idea that the progress might bring about the elimination of ungoverned contingency from social life" (Nussbaum, 2001: 89).

Tragedy, then, is a specific sort of break with tradition, arising "at the point … when a gap opens up between the new legal and political thought of the democratic city on the one hand, and mythic and heroic traditions of the archaic past on the other" (Critchley, 2019: 46). For Critchley, tragedy is "the art form of between times," when an "old world" is passing away and a new one is "coming into being." This, Critchley claims, is true for Greek tragedy as well as Elizabethan tragedy (Critchley, 2019: 14).

While Eagleton uses the language of crisis and Critchley deploys the term "ambiguity," Jeffrey Alexander uses "fin de siècle." While it means "end of the century," fin de siècle can also denote the end of an era. For Alexander, a "transition" is made up of a clash of "unequal and contradictory systems." For instance, the shift in the mode of production from feudalism to capitalism meant an equally momentous transformation of other aspects of collective life, most notably, for him, in the conceptualization of reason.

According to Alexander, it is a mistake to view the centrality of reason in Western thought as a mere result of abstract metaprocesses such as "science, capitalism and secularism." To the contrary, religious thought, particularly in the Abrahamic tradition, had already established some sort of divine, organizing principle. The idea that the world was established according to some form of reason, albeit God's reason, had already existed. Hence, the idea of a "force" making abstract demands on human beings was not revolutionary per se. However, what the emergence of modern science and secular thought in the 16th and 17th centuries had done, he suggests, was to separate "godly reasonableness" from "earthly development." In other words, there was an ontological schism, which occurred but the idea that there was "an impersonal and objective force" that dictated earthly matters shifted from God to reason (Alexander, 1995: 1). Tragedy, then, does not only arise out of crisis but specifically one of ontology and epistemology.

Tragedy as supplement

For the critics mentioned above, tragedy is a mechanism for coping with the erosion of faith in the set of overarching symbols and values during periods of transition or crisis. In such instances, tragedy takes on the character of a Derridean "supplement" (Derrida, 1997), offering up a new "chronotope" which provides, or at least attempts to, sufficient wholeness (epistemological *and* ontological) to the populace. In classic, Bakhtinian terms, "chronotope" refers to "spatial and temporal indicators [that] are fused into one carefully thought-out concrete whole" (White, 1987: 122). This is most often in reference to literature, especially novels, in which, the argument goes, the author constructs a world that contains configurations of time and space distinct to the work. This then can serve as a heuristic device to study different genres of literature. Greek epics have a certain chronotope. Novels have their own. In the historian Hayden White's usage, a chronotope is extended beyond literary works to social relations more broadly, to bear on:

> instances of socially determining structurations of practices which set limits not only on what can possibly happen within their effective confines, but also what can be perceived and even imagined by agents acting within their constraints.
>
> (White, 1987: 122)

For White, "chronotope" sits in contradistinction to "world-view," which is "conceived as a fact of consciousness." Chronotope "directs attention to the effective conditions of possibility of both thought and action, consciousness and praxis within discrete milieux, structured as fields of institutional and productive arrangements." It sets within it, "bodies and psyches of human agents and the relations they can bear with others, whether indigenous to that space-time or only visitors to it from elsewhere, are rigidly delimited" (White, 1987: 122).

In modernity, White argues:

> [...]the chronotope is nature, more or less dominated by human agents and specific social institutions which determine the kinds of work, the forms of violence, the very possibilities of human community held open to both dominant and subordinate groups, and even the forms of alienation to which the casualties of the system may legitimately aspire. Much more "active" than what used to be called "the background" or "scene" of the action by an older criticism or what narrative historians call "the context" of the acts, agents, and events whose story they wish to tell, the chronotope lies halfway between an environment or milieux, on the one side, and the fantastic "Zeitgeist" of Hegelian historical metaphysics, on the other. For the chronotope belongs neither to nature nor to culture, but is the form that the mediation between these two orders of existence takes in discrete historical places and time periods. The chronotope must, therefore, be doubly invented: first, as a product of human labor, domination, repression, and sublimation; secondly, as a fact of consciousness, in the minds both of those who produce it and of those who reproduce it—either as a recognizable condition of possibility for their own labors or as an object of study by historians of the events that take place within its confines and are recognizable as events "belonging" to the age or period in which they occur by their concomitance with the conditions of possibility dictated by the chronotope itself.
>
> (White, 1987: 123–124)

Actor-network theory uses similar language to White, in describing modernity's onto-cosmology. Forgoing the supposedly given division of nature and culture, Bruno Latour rather famously argues that modernity arises out of a specific sort of "world" that separates "humans and nonhumans on the one hand, and between what happens 'above' and what happens 'below' on the other" (Latour, 1993: 13). In other words, modernity is primarily a result of a setup involving the locking of ontological entities and the defining of their actions into a relational axis of "transcendence and immanence" (Latour, 1993: 34), or what he more simply calls "above" and "below," in a striking resemblance to Charles Taylor's characterization of the secular age as "vertical ontology" (Taylor, 2009). In so doing, Latour points out, moderns were able to "mobilize Nature, objectify the social, and feel the spiritual presence of God, even while firmly maintaining that Nature escapes us, that Society is our own work, and that God no longer truly intervenes" (Latour, 1993: 34). In sum, the commonplace processes associated with modernity, including "the invention of humanism, ... the emergence of the sciences, ... the secularization of society, ... the mechanization of the world" are epiphenomenal. Yet, as Latour points out, we were never truly modern because the world never embodied the rules of its official "Constitution"(Latour, 1993: 369).

Nowhere is this clearer for Latour than in the ambiguous nature of the modern concept of God, which somehow could not interfere with Natural Law nor with the Laws of the Republic. It was "pushed to the sidelines," merely serving as a functionary of the modern constitution, becoming a resource for moderns to protect their own invincibility. As one interpreter of Latour puts it, the "majority religion of secular modernity," that is, the "Religion of the Moderns," can be "characterized by a religious sensibility that has been thwarted by its own religious epistemology." The modern project consists of a "search for a substance and a God not made by human hands," which by the way, "they have made the origin of all virtue" [sensibility] and "a practice that obliges them not to take that project into account" [epistemology] (Howles, 2016). The modern constitution, therefore, can be described as "tragic" in the sense that it attempts the tricky task of retaining a religious sensibility within an epistemology that also works to assert the invincibility of human beings.

Latour's "crossed-out God" is in many ways a recapitulation of the French sociologist Lucien Goldmann's concept of "*deus absconditus*," or the hidden God. (It is unclear whether Latour is directly influenced by Goldmann in his account of the modern constitution but the similarities are striking.) Goldmann suggests that tragic thought emerges from the central problem that moderns must face: "discovering whether there still was some means and some hope of reintegrating supra-individual values into" a rational universe (Goldmann, 2013: 35). "For tragic thought," Goldmann writes, "this represents an essential but constantly unrealized possibility" (Goldmann, 2013: 37). As God is no longer a guide and guardian, there is no one whom moderns can turn to for advice (Goldmann, 2013: 38). With God relegated in such a way, moderns are "alone in the face of a silent and static world of things and individuals." Goldmann's indebtedness to Georg Lukacs here is evident. In the latter's famed essay on the "metaphysics of tragedy," God is understood as having "left the stage" but "[remaining] a spectator" (Lukács, 2010: 177).

The term "deus absconditus" is from Pascal, specifically his interpretation of Isaiah 45:15. "Vere tu es Deus absconditus," or "Truly, you are a God who hidest thyself," is a verse that has been commented on by many theologians, including Luther. In Goldmann's reading, Pascal's hidden God is both present and absent. The hidden God always exists but never appears. One cannot see nor hear this God. Counterintuitively, however, it is this occlusion, according to Goldmann, that makes God "more real and more important" for moderns. A God that is empirical or perceptible would be available for feedback. Humans could look toward God for some sort of "judgement" in hopes that it will "illuminate the different struggles" in the world. But,

> the clear voice of judgement of God no longer sounds out above the march of human destiny, for the voice which once gave life to all has now fallen

silent. Man[sic] must live alone and by himself. The voice of the Judge has fallen silent forever, and this is why man will always be vanquished, doomed to destruction in victory even more than in defeat.

(Goldmann, 2013: 35–36)

Not only is the human being in the face of the hidden God one that still desires meaning and explanation but also one that "demands absolute value" yet quickly realizes that "all the possibilities offered by this world are limited and inadequate" (Goldmann, 2013: 58).

Tragedy and social science

Reckoning with the consequences of the unresponsive God does not in the least begin with Goldmann in the history of social thought. In fact, one could argue that it begins with the formation of modern social science itself, with Max Weber, who used the phrase "secular theodicy." In asking why in a world made by God there is evil, social science, as secular theodicy, "seeks to reconcile normative expectations of social life with adversities, inequalities and forms of human suffering which appear intractable to reason, justice or even hope" (Wilkinson and Kleinman, 2016: 199). In effect, Weber's work

> points to this glaring discrepancy between modernity's ideal expectations of the social world and the lived experience of its history, not just to document the consequences of suffering on people's lives, but in order to reassess the experience of modernity at the end of possibly the most disturbed and violent century the world has known.
>
> (Wilkinson and Kleinman, 2016: 201)

As Ian Wilkinson, David Morgan, Arthur Kleinman, and others argue, Weber operates out of Nietzsche's previous identification of what senseless suffering does if left unchecked, especially in the wake of the Enlightenment. What modernity and its highly rationalized order does is open up the possibility for greater "loss of selfhood, moral purpose, and social meaning" (Wilkinson and Kleinman, 2016: 117), as any sort of suffering becomes inexplicable and "senseless" (Wilkinson and Kleinman, 2016: 120). Rationalization, in particular scientific knowledge, was supposed to have "monitored, regulated and controlled" suffering. Yet, suffering, while immensely decreased, still remains. Meanwhile, our expectations and worldviews have adjusted to the promises of Progress. As we moderns grow more accustomed to living in bureaucratic machines, the more likely it is, as Wilkinson and Kleinman put it, that we are "morally unsettled and emotionally disturbed by events and experiences that painfully expose us to 'the irrationality of the world.'" In an all-too-human fashion, the existence of unfathomable suffering often drives us to "further rationalize our experience and actions." The "tragedy of modern culture" then is that we are disposed to respond to human suffering with "more refined measures of understanding to inform practices designed to 'tame' the enduring hazards of uncertainty and chance" (Wilkinson and Kleinman, 2016: 122). In other words, suffering puts pressure on the progressive narrative of modernity and runs the risk of "shattering" the "purposive-rational categories of understanding" and with it, faith in knowledge and Progress (Wilkinson and Kleinman, 2016: 124), the new Gods.

Suffering poses a crisis to modernity's self-mythology rooted in "our idea of progress and civility" (Morgan and Wilkinson, 2001: 203). But it is not just the physical pain, violence, material deprivation, destruction, and loss. Suffering, Elaine Scarry writes, "unmakes our world." Morgan and Wilkinson note, "whilst suffering appears to depend upon the need to impose meaning upon our lives, suffering is often at its most unbearable when meaning is the very thing it negates" (Morgan and Wilkinson, 2001: 203). Suffering, therefore, expresses a quest for meaning; however, when "the brute fact of its senseless irrationality" is mediatized and thus circulated, then there is too much suffering to explain (Morgan and Wilkinson, 2001: 204). It defies reason. It makes suffering "for nothing."

> The global scale of suffering appears to defy reason. In the guise of injustice, affliction, adversity and pain, suffering confronts the limits of rationality; it shatters everyday orientations to the world and impresses upon us the need for other-worldly (magical, religious, ecstatic) meanings for experiences which cannot be explained pragmatically. Hence, the unresolved problem of theodicy is that suffering exhausts the limits of practical reason: the logic of purposive explanation appears facile when confronted with the conflicts, exploitation and absurdities of suffering in a refractory world.
> (Morgan and Wilkinson, 2001: 204)

While Morgan and Wilkinson focus on matters of meaning, and whether a "coherent conception of the order" holds up, they acknowledge (albeit in a footnote) that sociodicies and theodicies are rooted in what they call "cosmology" (Morgan and Wilkinson, 2001: 207). Sociodicy in a modern context, and theodicy prior to that, is an attempt "to defend an ideal conception of the world against those experiences which threaten to destabilize the frailty of human existence." Both "seek to validate a 'cultural reality' which sustains a way of life" (Morgan and Wilkinson, 2001: 211). Here, we see the clearest expression of secular theodicy's relationship to "conceptions of order" whether they are called chronotopes or cosmologies. Social orders of all kinds have in common a requirement of the smooth-enough functioning of chronotopes and cosmologies to ensure buy-in and adherence.

Social theory has struggled with how to articulate the interlocking nature of epistemology, ontology, and ethics (if we understand this term to mean how to be in the world) since the institutional formation of the European tradition of the "human sciences" in the 19th century (Dilthey, 1989; Wagner, 2006). By the 20th century, social science had shifted the question of the human being and "spirit" [Geist] to that of agency versus structure. Today, well into the 21st century, the so-called "agency/structure debate" has been discussed ad nauseum. But despite the eye-rolling that occurs in seminars and conferences, which seemingly express its status as passe, in classrooms across the globe, the terms still seem to permeate. In my own experience of teaching sociology, anthropology, and media studies for nearly a decade and a half, questions about agency, choice, and structure still emanate from students.

This is especially so when discussing "socialization." Socialization is undoubtedly the key mechanism allowing sociologists to provide evidence of society. After all, society is hidden; and thus, membership is not evinced by some sort of license or a card. But when describing "social institutions," such as the family, schools, and jobs, as "agents of socialization" wherein one "learns" the norms and values of society, students are able to relate their own rule-following behavior, and their impulse to conform, to the larger social order. To boot, socialization is how sociologists explain the development of individuals from childhood into adulthood. It is by turning everyone into "responsible adults" that society does its work. Once responsible adults raise their own children within the norms and values of society within the confines of the institution of the family, they are, wittingly or not, then agents of socialization themselves. This is the process of social reproduction in its most basic, textbook form (Bhattacharya, 2017; Bourdieu et al., 1990). Yet, there has been a lot of contention about this regulatory function of society. After all, the image of the individual—"the agent," in sociological terms—is almost as an automaton. Its conformity is not so much a negotiation or even a process. It is simply a matter of the agent being passed one from institution to another.

This "oversocialized conception of man in modern sociology," according to Dennis Wrong, is an expression of social theory's failure to resolve the "Hobbesian question," or "the problem of order." In other words, it does not fully address "why, if man is simply a gifted animal, men refrain from unlimited resort to fraud and violence in pursuit of their ends and maintain a stable society at all" (Wrong, 1961: 185). The problematic nature of the idea so basic to sociology— the very idea of "society" in the first place—plagues social theory.

Wrong's assertion, from a highly unorthodox Freudian approach, is that contemporary social theory answers Hobbes' question in two ways, each of which "denies the reality and meaningfulness of the question." On the one hand, social norms are internalized. On the other hand, human beings are motivated by social status. "Together," he writes, "they constitute a model of human nature, sometimes clearly stated, more often implicit in accepted concepts, that pervades modern sociology" (Wrong, 1961: 185). This dominant sociological perspective, "that action follows institutionalized patterns, [which opposes] individual and common interests" is "unreal," as he puts it.

While this may be the case for many reasons, the most egregious is the misuse of the chief lesson of the Freudian concept of the superego, which is that "social norms are constitutive rather than merely regulative of human nature"(Wrong, 1961: 186). Put differently, the psychoanalytic view of the human being is "less deterministic than the sociological." Sociology has appropriated the super-ego but detached it from the id. The sociological view of the social order and human action sidesteps the Hobbesian problem altogether. Just as long as individuals "internalize the norms and conform to them in conduct, the Hobbesian problem is not even perceived as a latent reality"(Wrong, 1961: 187).

> Modern sociologists believe that they have understood these processes and that they have not merely answered but disposed of the Hobbesian question, showing that, far from expressing a valid intimation of the tensions and possibilities of social life, it can only be asked out of ignorance.
>
> (Wrong, 1961: 186)

But, as Wrong notes, "internalization" is not fully fleshed out. It is often described as "learning" or "habit formation" (Wrong, 1961: 187). He traces this back to the influence of Talcott Parsons' structural functionalism, in particular the place of Durkheimian thought in *sociological* social theory (Seidman, 1991). Parsons' Durkheim was the early Durkheim. It was the Durkheim of viewing society as "imposing constraints" through sanctions. Thus, society's task was to incorporate the individual, by which he means to regulate it.

This is unrealistic, according to Wrong, in that it makes the socialization process (and the attendant process of social reproduction) rather easy. It assumes that in nature there is "stability and built-in harmony between 'individual and common interests.'" (Wrong, 1961: 190). This emphasis on homeostasis in the social order contributes to, in mainstream sociology, the "stress of inner conflict" and the "powerful impulses" of the ideas being "[dropped] out of the picture." The Freudian view, he rightly notes, does not see this process of the internalization of norms as without conflict. To say that a norm has been internalized, Wrong states, is also to assert that the conforming person will suffer guilt. The person who conforms is "bothered." Therefore, conformity—the adherence to the social order—is not seen as "a result of coercion rather than conviction" (Wrong, 1961: 188).

It is interesting, however, that Wrong lumps in the work of Robert Merton in this regard, as Merton's strain theory famously extends Durkheim's regulatory tendency to reconceptualize social reproduction and anomie. Merton's theory specifically delinks conformity and socialization. In demonstrating the significance of the adoption of the overarching cultural goals *without* necessarily adhering to their pursuit via institutionally normalized means, he lays bare the argument that conformity (defined as both the acceptance of cultural goals and institutionalized norms) is not necessary for the maintenance of the social order. Merton's example of money-making (as the predominant cultural goal in the United States) still serves as a viable illustration for understanding a capitalist social order. The widely accepted means of achieving said goal is a job. However, there are those, in 1930s

America and today, that are more than happy to make money but will not submit to the institutionally normalized means of doing so. Instead, such as those involved in organized crime, they innovate (Merton, 1938).

Are their actions deviant? Does their behavior undermine the social order? For instance, would it be easier to bring the "innovators" in Merton's terms back into the social fold as they would simply be provided new means to attain the cultural goal of money-making than convincing those without any interest in it (whom Merton labels "retreatists") to change their value-orientation?

When Wrong writes, "All men are socialized in the latter sense, but this does not mean that they have been completely molded by the particular norms and values of their culture," and thus human beings are "social but not socialized" (Wrong, 1961: 192), it is tempting to see this as a defense of agency. However, it is more accurate to see it as a very specific reading of Freudian theory based on two assumptions. First, Wrong is pointing out the structure of the unconscious *within* the agent prior to the internalization of the norms and values of social structure. Thus, "structures" can be both internal and external to the individual. This leads on to the second reminder which is that the agent is not universal and is certainly not a blank slate. Social structures do not work on everyone in the same manner. And if the external social structures work on the internal structures of the individual, what even is the agent? Is the agency simply consciousness?

This question, by the late-20th century, had yet to be answered even within the context of the supposed "macro/micro debate" (De Landa, 2019: 4). But the issue of "oversocialization" persists. Manuel De Landa summarizes it accurately:

> The…position that has been historically adopted towards the micro–macro problem is that social structure is what really exists, individual persons being mere products of the society in which they are born. The young Durkheim, the older Marx, and functionalists such as Talcott Parsons are examples of this stance. These authors do not deny the existence of individual persons but assume that once they have been socialized by the family and the school, they have so internalized the values of the societies or the social classes to which they belong that their allegiance to a given social order may be taken for granted.
>
> (De Landa, 2019: 5)

To be fair, as De Landa details, in recent decades, there have been attempts by theorists to cut through the impasse by taking a look at the "intermediate level" between the micro and macro (De Landa, 2019: 5). We can see this in the work of Anthony Giddens and Pierre Bourdieu, who have, "in fact, proposed to frame the question of the micro-macro link in just these terms, breaking with a long tradition of privileging one of the two sides of the equation" (De Landa, 2019: 32).

Giddens' theory attempts to "transcend the duality of agency and structure by arguing for their mutual constitution." Agency, as a part of practice, "reproduces structure." Giddens conceptualizes structure as "consisting of behavioral procedures and routines, and of material and symbolic resources, neither one of which possesses a separate existence outside of their instantiation in actual practice." And thus, practices that "instantiate rules and mobilize resources" are part of a "continuous flow of action" or feedback loop. Agency and structure mutually constitute each other dialectically. This is what Giddens famously dubs "structuration" (Giddens, 2003; De Landa, 2019: 10).

Bourdieu's notion of "habitus" likewise tries to cut through the micro/macro debate. Bourdieu does so most famously through an examination of taste and social class. By focusing on *cultural* capital, including "possessing a general education or specialized technical knowledge, as well as owning the diplomas, licenses and credentials needed to profit legitimately from such knowledge" (De Landa, 2019: 63), Bourdieu complicates the macro understanding of social class by demonstrating that "different sets of objective opportunities and risks condition the day-to-day practices of groups leading to the development of a durable set of *dispositions*, tendencies to behave in certain ways and to display certain aspirations" (Bourdieu, 1977, 1984; De Landa, 2019: 64).

For De Landa, while both Giddens and Bourdieu are the best that sociology could do when it comes to the linkages between the micro and the macro, their limitations still remain. Each retains the dichotomy of micro and macro in the form of subject and object duality. While both, with different conceptual emphases, attempt to show "how individual action and structure actually presuppose one another," each still recapitulates the subjectivist and objectivist tendencies in social theory (Elliott, 2020; Mouzelis, 2000). Reflexivity (Giddens) and habitus (Bourdieu) become "master" processes (De Landa, 2019: 65). As a Deleuzian, De Landa argues for "getting rid of the idea that social processes occur at only two levels … in terms of generalities like 'the individual' and 'society as a whole'" (De Landa, 2019: 32).

While De Landa's critique stands, it is certainly not new. In fact, such an invitation is contained in one of sociology's most forceful and poetic calls for renewal, C. Wright Mills' *The Sociological Imagination*. In the opening chapter, entitled, "The Promise," Mills describes the experience of private life as "a series of traps." People seem to feel that they are unable to "overcome their troubles." What Mills notes however is that "the sense of being trapped" is due to the "impersonal changes in the very structure" of societies. Mills thus equates large-scale, structural changes with "history" (Mills, 2000: 3). "Seldom aware of the intricate connection between the patterns of their own lives and the course of world *history*," he claims, "ordinary people do not usually know what this connection means for the kinds of people they are becoming and for the kinds of *history*-making in which they might take part" (Mills, 2000: 3–4 Emphasis added). He then goes on to describe the sociological imagination as a "quality of mind essential to grasp the interplay of individuals and society, of biography and history, of self and world." When someone—anyone—embodies this form of imagination (not always a given among sociologists as Mills' classic work shows), they are able to "grasp what is going on in the world, and to understand what is happening in themselves as *minute points of the intersections of biography and history within society*" (Mills, 2000: 7 Emphasis added). It is a way of recognizing that lying behind their personal troubles are structural transformations. Or, in De Landa's terms, the sociological imagination, when exercised, is able to traverse levels, seeking connections across them rather than artifiically arriving at an intermediary midpoint. It opens up the possibility that beneath the experience of "the private" is indeed "the public." Contained within one's biography is oftentimes history.

Tragic sensibility

Going back to at least Hegel, tragedy has been seen as "the key to unlocking history," as Miriam Leonard notes (Leonard, 2012:146). For Hegel, tragedy represents the dialectical movement of historical progress. Tragedy as this kind of "metahistory" is clearly distilled in versions of Marxist historical materialism, for example (Aronowitz, 1990; White, 1975, Ch. 8). The movement from feudalism to communism is, in its cheapest version, linear and progressive. More recently, Michel Maffesoli has spoken of a "tragic mood" that has *overturned* history in postmodernity. Previously, history unfolded. Nowadays, "the event arrives." There is no capacity for expectation. Rather, events "intrude." They "startle." Modernity had a dramatic tonality in the form of "the dialectic," which postulates a solution or a possible synthesis. Today, the form that predominates is "the tragic," which Maffesoli describes as an "aporetic" (Maffesoli, 2008: 323), it is irresolvable. As the sociologists Christina Simko and Jeffrey Olick describe it:

> Modernity's legitimating narratives promised technological advancement, a profound expansion of our powers to predict and control, and, as a result, an ability to significantly ameliorate human pain and suffering. In contrast, tragedy dramatized that reality is one of enduring limitations on human agency; the intractable presence of chance, accident, and randomness; the chastening impact of unanticipated consequences; and inevitable value conflicts.
>
> (Simko and Olick, 2020: 662)

In their work on trauma and memory, they articulate a vision of social science that embraces the "notion of working through," associated with Freudian psychoanalysis, rather than "mastery" embodied by mainstream social science with its penchant for "social explanation and research-based interventions" (Simko and Olick, 2020: 652). In other words, they suggest that social science must challenge the historical narrative of modernity that consists of an understanding of the world getting better as a result of human control over it. A social science with a "tragic sensibility" would therefore approach the world's suffering as unable to be healed fully by "medicine, science, and technology" (Simko and Olick, 2020: 661).

Similarly, the present volume asserts the significance of the tragic for theorizing in the social sciences. In doing so, it does not simply argue that tragedies are worth reading. Quite frankly, the analyses of specific works of tragedy that are contained in the following chapters do not make up the core of this book. Instead, they contribute to a larger point that that tragedy (and specifically the idea of the tragic) is acutely relevant for this particular political and cultural moment. In choosing to contextualize this in terms of a "disenchanted disenchantment" (which will be explicated further below), this book deliberately points out that the social and cultural phenomena of the 21st century are signs of a crisis of the chronotope/cosmology/constitution of modernity. In other words, the book functions as notes toward an approach to the social sciences, sociology, and social theory that does not adopt wholesale the primacy of human rationality and control and also recognizes that previous transcendent figures such as God, gods, values, or structures have been pushed aside or rendered ineffective, all the while, not seeing this as problematic or debilitating. This, *The Concept of Tragedy* maintains, is more important than ever, given the uncertain times that we are living through today.

When Mills wrote of the sociological imagination in the late 1950s, he did so amid massive changes underway as well.

> In what period have so many people been so totally exposed at so fast a pace to such earthquakes of change? That Americans have not known such catastrophic changes as have the men and women of other societies is due to historical facts that are now quickly becoming "merely history." The history that now affects every individual is world history. Within this scene and this period, in the course of a single generation, one sixth of humankind is transformed from all that is feudal and backward into all that is modern, advanced, and fearful. Political colonies are freed; new and less visible forms of imperialism installed. Revolutions occur; people feel the intimate grip of new kinds of authority. Totalitarian societies rise, and are smashed to bits—or succeed fabulously. After two centuries of ascendancy, capitalism is shown up as only one way to make society into an industrial apparatus. After two centuries of hope, even formal democracy is restricted to a quite small portion of mankind. Everywhere in the underdeveloped world, ancient ways of life are broken up and vague expectations become urgent demands. Everywhere in the overdeveloped world, the means of authority and of violence become total in scope and bureaucratic in form. Humanity itself now lies before us, the super-nation at either pole concentrating its most coordinated and massive efforts upon the preparation of World War Three.
>
> (Mills, 2000: 4)

In this sea of changes, Mills notes, "the ability of people to orient themselves in accordance with cherished values" is outpaced. Plus which, he asks, "And which values?"

> Even when they do not panic, people often sense that older ways of feeling and thinking have collapsed and that newer beginnings are ambiguous to the point of moral stasis. Is it any wonder that ordinary people feel they cannot cope with the larger worlds with which they are so suddenly confronted? That they cannot understand the meaning of their epoch for their own lives? That—in defense of selfhood—they become morally insensible, trying to remain altogether private individuals? Is it any wonder that they come to be possessed by a sense of the trap?
>
> (Mills, 2000: 5)

Mills seems to be describing "a sense of the trap" that results from a very specific crisis of values—that of a globalized world where modernity has run out of steam, and where a sense of History is missing.[1]

This volume works to bring back "the tragic" as a productive analytic without being overly prescriptive about defining tragedy. In this regard, it follows the scholars who have turned their attention away from content (e.g., suffering) and form (e.g., Aristotle) of tragedy to its philosophy (i.e., the idea of the tragic). In large part, referring back to German Romanticism, these scholars have identified a way of "drifting free of the genre of tragedy." To speak of a "tragic mode" as opposed to a "tragic genre" offers a "general theoretical salience and metaphorical power as prism though which to grasp the antinomies of the human condition" (Felski, 2008: 3). In effect, what Rita Felski, among others, has suggested is that the shift to the "adjectival usage" allows for an "emancipation" from the "prescriptive taxonomies in literary criticism" when analyzing the tragic (Felski, 2008: 14). More specifically, it encourages us to move beyond the "formal particulars of sadness" of tragedy such as plot, structure, characters, and language and focus on how it bears on everyday life.

The Concept of Tragedy asserts the significance of tragedy and the tragic through an expansive view in two parts. First, it will explore the history of the tragedy in order reintroduce it to readers that may not be familiar with it or need a refresher, drawing on literary history, literary criticism, classics, and theology. It argues that tragedies have embodied the sociological imagination in the sense that it brought forth the tension between overarching forces and the human individual. In addition, the book also demonstrates tragedy's ongoing entanglement with the social sciences, offering new perspectives on the work of classical theorists such as Max Weber but also on contemporary scholars that have worked on a variety of themes such as social suffering and theodicy. Second, it will deploy this analytic on select topics and cultural phenomena, including celebrity culture, the welfare state, pandemics, and climate change.

Part I starts with Chapter 2, which investigates the pre-history of modern subjectivity by looking at not only the Hellenic sources of influence (Aeschylus, Sophocles, and Euripides) but also the Abrahamic ones (the Book of Job), understanding them to be intertwined in Western modernity as a result of the influence of Augustine. It then analyzes how these traditions understood the relationship between human beings and the divine, which I argue can be viewed in terms of social scientific debates such as agency and structure. After which, it concludes with a discussion of the significance of the ancient and classical conceptualizations of the will, subjectivity, and agency for contemporary social science in thinking beyond intentionality.

Chapter 3 serves as a transition between the previous chapter, which deals with the Athenian and biblical traditions, and the modern tradition, the subject of the following chapter. This chapter's main purpose is to explicate Aristotle's theory of tragedy, taking stock of one of the most influential definitions of tragedy in public discourse, not only for its own sake but to explain how and why specific aspects of tragedy, namely the tragic hero, catharsis, and the flaw, became so widespread. It discusses each, drawing on interpreters, such as Jacob Bernays, Edmund Burke, and Samuel Weber, and culminates in a reading of Aristotle influenced by Martha Nussbaum, focusing on the fragility of human beings and its significance for thinking about "the individual" in modern social science.

Chapter 4 delves into more recent works of tragedy, assessing the reading of Shakespeare's tragedies as part of the "invention of the human" prevalent in literary theory. Taking this to mean that the tragic heroes of Shakespeare are the bedrock of the modern, psychological individual, the chapter goes onto explore this claim with great scrutiny, recontextualizing it in terms of religious ideas of "self-fashioning," analyzing more contemporary tragic works such as those of Henrik Ibsen and Arthur Miller, with a focus on the social nature of those works.

The following chapter, Chapter 5, marks the transition between Part I, which is more historical and theoretical, and Part II, which analytically explores more contemporary issues. It makes the explicit case that the core of the modern social science can be viewed as always already imbued with a "tragic vision" as it sought to explain the limitations of modernity's promise of progress. In reintroducing the tragic focus of Weber and neo-Weberian theory, this chapter asserts that at the core of social science is the grappling with the fact of suffering. It then moves on to consider the linkages between theodicy and tragic thinking and how that has informed recent scholarship in the social sciences, underscoring the Nietzschean legacy in Weberian thought. It ends with an exploration of how social policy understands suffering, looking at the example of the US state's attempt to address poverty and economic inequality.

Chapter 6 examines celebrity culture, incorporating research from celebrity studies, including the work of Chris Rojek as well as a reassessment and update of the classic work by Daniel Boorstin. It argues that celebrities are today's tragic heroes but with key differences due in part to contemporary media culture.

Using Princess Diana and Kobe Bryant as examples, it analyzes how their respective lives and deaths are mediated as tragic precisely because they are *not* understood as demigods, exhibiting familiarity more than fame.

Chapter 7 focuses what media scholars call "the tragic frame," or how certain events are understood as tragic. It is here that the book investigates the COVID-19 pandemic and climate change, suggesting that these demonstrate the limits of the tragic frame as these are long-term, collective catastrophes that affect the whole of humanity. It argues that an expanded view of tragedy opens up possibilities for thinking about new lines of solidarity. It concludes with a call for a revitalization of the notion of "the commons."

The final, concluding chapter consists of thoughts on how to "do" tragic social science and how it may mean reconceptualizing sociality altogether.

Note

1 For the connection between Mills' work and modernity, see Lemert (2004).

References

Alexander, J., 1995. *Fin De Siecle Social Theory: Relativism, Reduction and the Problem of Reason*. London; New York, NY: Verso Books.

Aronowitz, S., 1990. *The Crisis in Historical Materialism: Class, Politics and Culture in Marxist Theory*. Basingstoke: Macmillan.

Bhattacharya, T., 2017. *Social Reproduction Theory: Remapping Class, Recentering Oppression*. London: Pluto Press.

Bourdieu, P., 1977. *Outline of a Theory of Practice*. Cambridge; MA: Cambridge University Press.

Bourdieu, P., 1984. *Distinction: A Social Critique of the Judgement of Taste*. Cambridge, MA: Harvard University Press.

Bourdieu, P., Bourdieu, P.P., and Passeron, J.-C., 1990. *Reproduction in Education, Society and Culture*. Thousand Oaks, CA: Sage.

Correal, A., Jacobs, A., and Jones, R.C., 2020. 'A Tragedy Is Unfolding': Inside New York's Virus Epicenter. *The New York Times*, 9 Apr.

Critchley, S., 2019. *Tragedy, the Greeks and Us*. London: Profile Trade.

De Landa, M., 2019. *A New Philosophy of Society: Assemblage Theory and Social Complexity*. London: Bloomsbury.

Derrida, J., 1997. *Of Grammatology*. Baltimore, MD: Johns Hopkins University Press.

Dilthey, W., 1989. *Introduction to the Human Sciences*. Princeton, NJ: Princeton University Press.

Eagleton, T., 2020. *Tragedy*. New Haven, CT: Yale University Press.

Elliott, A., 2020. Structuration Theories: Giddens and Bourdieu. In: *Routledge Handbook of Social and Cultural Theory*. London: Routledge.

Felski, R., ed., 2008. *Rethinking Tragedy*. Baltimore, MD: Johns Hopkins University Press.

Giddens, A., 2003. *The Constitution of Society: Outline of the Theory of Structuration*. Berkeley, CA: University of California Press.

Giuffrida, A., 2020. 'Totally awakened': how tragedy has left Italians alert to deadly virus. *The Guardian*, 24 Sep.

Goldin, I., 2021. COVID-19: How Rising Inequalities Unfolded and Why We Cannot Afford to Ignore It. *The Conversation*.

Goldmann, L., 2013. *The hidden God: a study of tragic vision in the Pensées of Pascal and the tragedies of Racine*. London: Routledge.

Howles, T., 2016. Crossed-out God. *Political Theology at the Time of the Anthropocene*.

Kitto, H.D.F., 2011. *Greek tragedy*. London: Routledge.

Latour, B., 1993. *We Have Never Been Modern*. Cambridge, MA: Harvard University Press.

Lemert, C., 2004. *Sociology After the Crisis*. 2nd edition. Boulder, CO: Paradigm Publishers.

Leonard, M., 2012. Tragedy and the Seductions of Philosophy. *The Cambridge Classical Journal*, 58, 145–164.

Lukács, G., 2010. *Soul and Form*. New York, NY: Columbia University Press.

Maffesoli, M., 2008. The Return of the Tragic in Postmodern Societies. In: R. Felski, ed. *Rethinking Tragedy*. Baltimore, MD: Johns Hopkins University Press, 319–336.

Merton, R.K., 1938. Social Structure and Anomie. *American Sociological Review*, 3 (5), 672–682.

Mills, C.W., 2000. *The Sociological Imagination*. Oxford: Oxford University Press.

Morgan, D. and Wilkinson, I., 2001. The Problem of Suffering and the Sociological Task of Theodicy. *European Journal of Social Theory*, 4 (2), 199–214.

Mouzelis, N., 2000. The Subjectivist–Objectivist Divide: Against Transcendence. *Sociology*, 34 (4), 741–762.

Nussbaum, M.C., 2001. *The Fragility of Goodness: Luck and Ethics in Greek Tragedy and Philosophy*. Cambridge: Cambridge University Press.

Seidman, S., 1991. The End of Sociological Theory: The Postmodern Hope. *Sociological Theory*, 9 (2), 131–146.

Simko, C., and Olick, J.K., 2020. Between Trauma and Tragedy. *Social Research: An International Quarterly*, 87 (3), 651–676.

Szondi, P., 2002. *An essay on the tragic*. Palo Alto, CA: Stanford University Press.

Szondi, P. and Hays, M., 1983. Theory of the modern drama, Parts I-II. *Boundary 2*, 191–230.

Taylor, C., 2009. *A Secular Age*. Cambridge, MA: Harvard University Press.

Tompkins, L., 2021. U.S. Surpasses 25 Million Coronavirus Cases, a Staggering Tally. *The New York Times*, 23 Jan.

Wagner, P., 2006. *A History and Theory of the Social Sciences: Not All That Is Solid Melts into Air*. London: Sage.

White, H., 1975. *Metahistory: The Historical Imagination in Nineteenth-Century Europe*. 1st edition. Baltimore, MD: Johns Hopkins University Press.

White, H., 1987. "The Nineteenth-Century" as Chronotope. *Nineteenth Century Contexts*, 11(2), 119–129.

Wilkinson, I. and Kleinman, A., 2016. *A Passion for Society: How We Think about Human Suffering*. Berkeley, CA: University of California Press.

Wright, L., 2020. The Plague Year. *The New Yorker*.

Wrong, D.H., 1961. The Oversocialized Conception of Man in Modern Sociology. *American Sociological Review*, 26 (2), 183–193.

PART I

2
BEYOND INTENTIONALITY

The will, agency, and subjectivity
in ancient and classical tragedy

Introduction

The 20th century is sometimes called the "Freudian century" (Zaretsky, 2011).
Eli Zaretsky argues that this is so because psychoanalysis occupies the flip side of
the coin of modernity:

> Just as men and women did not embark on the transition from agrarian
> society to a market economy for merely instrumental or economic rea-
> sons, so in the twentieth century they did not become consumers in order
> to supply markets. Rather, they separated from traditional familial and
> communal morality, gave up their orientation to self-denial and thrift, and
> entered into the sexualized "dreamworlds" of mass consumption on behalf
> of a new orientation to personal life. Psychoanalysis was the "Calvinism"
> of this reorientation. But whereas Calvinism sanctified mundane labor in
> the family, Freud urged his followers to leave behind their "families"—the
> archaic images of early childhood—not to preach but to develop more
> genuine, that is, more personal relations.
>
> (Zaretsky, 2011: 681)

Psychoanalysis then, according to this telling, is responsible for modernity's
second "transvaluation of values." Whereas Calvinism readied the *verstehens* of
moderns for industrial labor within the context of the family, which Zaretsky
implies is the *first* transvaluation of values, psychoanalysis, he suggests, laid the
groundwork for "mass consumption capitalism." A "form of consciousness" for
a "new historical epoch," psychoanalysis brought with it new terms—better
yet, new *myths*, as Zaretsky writes—with which "a new civilization viewed
itself: youth-oriented, post-liberal, middle-class. Of these, the unconscious,

DOI: 10.4324/9781003110859-3

the Oedipus complex and instincts are the terms that attained mass circulation" (Zaretsky, 2011: 681).

The importance of Oedipus does not merely stop at the level of the figural. Rather, Zaretsky argues, the widespread adoption of Oedipus and its association with Freud represents a larger process—psychoanalysis becoming the "heir to philosophy." In other words, if the story of Oedipus represented the prototypical injunction to "know thyself" to live a good life, then the body of knowledge to address the Delphic challenge was clearly psychoanalysis in the 20th century.

The influence of Freud and Freudianism is not the sole cause for the importance and significance of Attic tragedy and Greek culture more broadly in Western culture and—by reason of colonialism and globalization—the world over. To the contrary, it is more like a symptom. The place of Oedipus, and by implication the place of the history of Greek tragedy, is what allows for something like psychoanalysis to find a footing in the West over the course of the 20th century. While Zaretsky, rightly, puts forth a neo-Weberian argument around the penetration of psychoanalysis into mass culture, rooted in a "substitution" dynamic, he offers a rather quick but not altogether unsubstantial account of what made "philosophy" the dominant orientation of industrial modernity in the first place:

> The heart of the Hellenic influence…was that the middle class or property-owning citizen was a *philosopher*, that is, someone who used reason self-consciously in both public and private life. Critically, the use of reason involved an *inward turn*, away from the sensual and empirical world of appearances and toward the conceptual…The target of the injunction was hubris—in modern terms an exaggerated narcissism or *amour propre*—which prevented rational thought from doing its work.
>
> (Zaretsky, 2011: 682 Emphasis added)

Thus, both philosophy, specifically the Delphic injunction to "know thyself," and psychoanalysis, with its therapeutic ethos, were the twin roots of modern notions of human rationality, both of which involve a turn towards interiority.

The parallels with Weber are obvious. The process of rationalization, which characterized modernity, for Weber, was not only one of external mastery but also that of internal control. Indeed, the "disenchantment of the world" was not only the de-magification of the world under the guise of science and engineering a la Heidegger's "world-picture" of nature as "standing reserve." But, as in the famous example of the streetcar in "Science as a Vocation," Weber also sees mastery and control as, crucially, one that involves a rationalized ethics, which, of course, is contained in his famous interpretation of the "calling":

> And in truth this peculiar idea, so familiar to us today, but in reality so little a matter of course, of one's duty in a calling, is what is most characteristic of the social ethic of capitalistic culture, and is in a sense the

fundamental basis of it. It is an obligation which the individual is supposed to feel and does feel towards the content of his professional activity, no matter in what it consists, in particular no matter whether it appears on the surface as a utilization of his personal powers, or only of his material possessions (as capital).

(Weber, 2005: 61)

In these famous words from *The Protestant Ethic and the Spirit of Capitalism*, Weber understands the calling in modern capitalism as more involved for the individual than in Calvinism in the sense that, in the former, one does actively have to rationalize one's activities towards a particular worldly, end—moneymaking. One cannot simply bank on God's will being done as in the case of salvation within the logic of the Calvinist doctrine of predestination. Instead, one needed to exert control—rational control—over the self. This deliberate instrumentalization of the self that formed the basis of subjectivity in capitalist modernity has a pre-history, one that most certainly precedes Calvin, Luther, and even perhaps Protestantism more generally. Zaretsky says as much when he points out that "the inward turn, away from the sensual and empirical world of appearances" was, in part, due to a "Hellenic influence."

This chapter explores the pre-history of this inward turn that Zaretsky claims as foundational for modern subjectivity by examining the sources of Hellenic influence as well as the Christian ones. In fact, it understands them to be intertwined, examining this connection through Augustine, after which it goes onto discuss ancient Greek texts through the theme of interiority. Drawing on recent classical scholarship, it examines the tragedies of Sophocles, Aeschylus, and Euripides. It then moves on to compare themes present in those Greek texts and the Book of Job, focusing on the relationship between human beings and the divine. After which, it concludes with a discussion of the significance of the ancient and classical conceptualizations of the will, subjectivity, and agency for contemporary social science in thinking beyond intentionality.

The cosmos of interiority

Historians and theologians have pointed to late antiquity and its "recovery" of Greek ideas as informing the rereading of Attic culture in the formation of modernity (Morley, 2009). Augustine, with the widespread reception of his ideas as equating interiority with self and the emphasis on "the soul," is a crucial figure in this regard. Theologian David Tracy, however, suggests that it is *the will* not the soul that is most important, claiming that Augustine is the first philosopher "to elaborate a full-fledge concept of will as central for understanding the self" (Tracy, 2018: 35).

For Tracy, the Augustinian will, like the Freudian unconscious, is a force that pushes us forward for both good and ill. Operating below consciousness, it is, as he writes, "a realm of depth." The will is where "unconscious affects, feelings, emotions, and desires" dwell. These are manifested consciously but only at times—much like desire operates in the psychic apparatus of the id, ego, and superego in the later Freud (Tracy, 2018: 37). The "ultimately Real" in Augustine, as Tracy describes it, is less "[reflected] on the external cosmos than by turning inward into a *tremendum et fascinans* discovery of the abyss of the self, where eventually we find the will in all its conflictual complexity" (Tracy, 2018: 37).

Hence, the Augustinian self does not really know itself. It is both fragile and occluded. This means that the accursed, unavoidable questions of being human, such as "Who am I?", "Is my life or any life worth living?", "How can god exist when there is so much suffering?", "Whence evil?" (Tracy, 2018: 47–48), bubble up in the self during "boundary situations," as Tracy calls them. We experience them as "profound anxiety; a sense of nothing; of absurdity that can suddenly descend on us; our fierce grief at the illness and death of those we love; our confused fear at our own illness, our dying, our encroaching death" (Tracy, 2018: 44). These are all signs of a self defined by sin. In Augustine, sin is not simply an immoral act or thought that results from "a temporary state of moral weakness." It is nothing short of "a state of being" (Tracy, 2018: 48–49).

Tracy draws parallels between a "tragic sensibility" (Tracy, 2018: 47–48), which he labels "Eurpidean," and Augustine, pointing to the latter's focus on the passions and the power of feeling and emotion, affect and mood. For Tracy, there is no one among the ancients "other than Euripides ... more penetrating than Augustine on how our affects and passions can so becloud and take over our minds that we reach the point of impenetrable self-delusion" (Tracy, 2018: 64). For Augustine and Euripides, there is a shared conception of the passions being able to "easily dislocate, even destroy, reason." The passions have power over our "best intentions and most brilliant thoughts." For Augustine, this is so because the passions undermine reason as they bear the mark of "original sin" inherited from the Adamic Fall. The passions demonstrate we are "all marked, in our very origins, with evil." Hence, sin "is not a matter of particular acts of cruelty or violence, specific forms of social pathology, or this or that person who has made a disastrous choice." Instead, it is the acknowledgment that we are not born as blank slates but rather that there is "something deeply, essentially wrong with us" (Greenblatt, 2017).

Even in the most cursory sense, one is able to see where sin and *hamartia* or the tragic flaw overlap. Indeed, Augustine argues that all suffering cannot possibly be caused by individual, human evil. In fact, "sometimes evil just happens," Tracy writes. "Volcano eruptions, floods, tsunamis, earthquakes, the inexplicable suffering and death of infants and children, even ordinary adult illness, death" are "natural" in that they are not caused by the individual sufferers. Hence, the tragic consciousness of the Augustinian self "uncovers sin" by showing the "enormous suffering caused less by personal sin than by mysterious necessity—fate, fortune, chance, providence" (Tracy, 2018: 51). It would be "obscene," Tracy points out, to blame the enormous suffering in human existence—whether a natural disaster like an earthquake or "injustice operative in many social, economic and political structures" on human evil.

If we take Tracy's reading seriously, we can see that, despite not ever referring to "tragedy," there is somewhat of a tragic consciousness detectable in Augustine's concept of the will. There is, for Augustine, a sinful self in need of control in spite of the fact that, in his theological ontology, the world was overseen by a providential God. Augustinian anthropology places a conflicted self, one that is unstable, on edge, and less than perfect, at its core. Despite its capacity for rationality, the self, and its will, is at odds with the world.

Given this, it is surprising that there still remains this idea that Augustine's thought is the archetype for modern Cartesian subjectivity (Hanby, 2003), which establishes, as Charles Taylor describes it, a "clear boundary between mind and world, even mind and body." Sin, in the Augustinian vein, circumvents the sharp distinction between "inner and outer" that characterizes the modern, disenchanted chronotope. It would seem that this would complicate the image of Augustine as the forerunner of Descartes. But Taylor identifies the division between the inner and the outer as precisely what leads scholars to see Augustine in such a way. The establishment of this division is crucial in understanding the formation of the modern, bounded self:

> Whatever has to do with thought, purpose, human meanings, has to be in the mind, rather than in the world. Some chemical can cause hormonal change, and thus alter the psyche. There can be an aphrodisiac, but not a love potion, that is, a chemical that determines the human/moral meaning of the experience it enables. A phial of liquid can cure a specific disease, but there can't be something like the phials brought back from pilgrimage at Canterbury, which contained a miniscule drop of the blood of Thomas à Beckett, and which could cure anything, and even make us better people; that is, the liquid was not the locus of certain specific chemical properties, but of a generalized beneficence.
>
> (Taylor, 2009: 37)

In such a disenchanted world, melancholy is felt as a result of "body chemistry" or hunger, or a "hormone malfunction," that is, as some *internal* mechanism within the modern bounded, buffered self. The earlier, enchanted self is a porous one. Taylor describes it in the first person thusly:

> As a bounded self I can see the boundary as a buffer, such that the things beyond don't need to "get to me," to use the contemporary expression. That's the sense to my use of the term "buffered" … This self can see itself as invulnerable, as master of the meanings of things for it…[T]he porous self is vulnerable: to spirits, demons, cosmic forces. And along with this go certain fears that can grip it in certain circumstances. The buffered self has been taken out of the world of this kind of fear.
>
> (Taylor, 2009: 38)

This new sense of self, as Taylor explains, came out of a shift in the relationship between the interior and the exterior in the constitution of a new conception of "world," which he refers to as "cosmos."

The cosmos is not "a world of spirits and powers," with selves vulnerable and porous to them. But rather it is full of those with "confidence in [their] own powers of moral ordering" (Taylor, 2009: 27). The disappearance of this world saw the rise of a new one, one whereby "the locus of thoughts, feelings, spiritual elan is what we call minds." In this cosmos, Taylor explains, the only minds are those of humans. These minds are bounded in the sense that "thoughts, feelings, etc.," are understood to exist "within" these minds (Taylor, 2009: 29). The mind is therefore a "space constituted by the possibility of introspective self-awareness." In other words, the mind is capable of "radical reflexivity" (Taylor, 2009: 30).

Taylor identifies key impacts of this new world of interiority, the most significant of which is on "personal agency." In an enchanted world, there is no distinction between the interior and the exterior, between "personal agency and impersonal force" (Taylor, 2009: 32). Examples are plentiful in this regard. "There is a whole gamut of forces," Taylor writes, "ranging from…super-agents like Satan himself…down to minor demons, like spirits of the wood….ending in magic potions." The enchanted world is characterized by "an absence of certain boundaries which seem to us essential" (Taylor, 2009: 33), from the perspective of modernity. In such a world, meaning is found in the object or a non-human agent, "independently of us." In fact, this object/non-human agent can, by communicating with us, "bring us into a field of its forces." For instance, an evil spirit does not simply impose itself on us, thus resulting in some subsequent change internally. "The malevolence," Taylor writes, "is more invasive than this. It can sap our very will to resist, our will to survive. It can penetrate us as living, willing beings, with our own purposes and intent." He concludes, "We can't restrict its action to the 'external' realm" (Taylor, 2009: 36):

> By definition for the porous self, the source of its most powerful and important emotions are outside the "mind": or better put, the very notion that there is a clear boundary, allowing us to define an inner base area grounded in which we can disengage from the rest, has no sense.
>
> (Taylor, 2009: 38)

And thus boundaries between mind and world are porous in an enchanted world. Cosmic forces breach such boundaries and "can act within." They are not "personalized creatures like us." To understand them, Taylor suggests, "we need a quite different model" of ontology. It must take into account, for instance, the moral influence of a substance like black bile or even the way in which an object can "possess" a person. In sum, the fuzziness between self and other must be placed at the core of thinking about the process that Weber refers to as "disenchantment," under which he brought together the processes of secularization and modernization (Taylor, 2009: 39).

Interestingly, Taylor zeroes in on the Greeks as an important transitional point between the boundaryless, porous world of enchantment to the ordered, universe of disenchanted modernity. Specifically, he points to Aristotle, who, in his estimation, was the key figure in bringing forward the idea of an apex and a Center God. Aristotle represents a view of the cosmos as ordered, that is, limited and bounded. After all, "the principle of order in the cosmos was closely related to, often identical with, that which gave shape to our lives" (Taylor, 2009: 60). While not utterly rationalized like the modern "world-picture," the Greek cosmos had a hierarchy; there were lower and higher levels of being, the apex of the latter being the Ideas or God, or both together, that is, "Ideas as the thoughts of the creator." As a result, modern culture is an heir to the Greeks in this regard. He goes so far as to say that Biblical religion, by the fact of its entry into "Greco-Roman, later Arab, worlds" also formed within the cosmos idea. Hence, "we come to see ourselves as situated in a defined history, which unfolds within a bounded setting." It is only this sort of view of the self and the world that makes it possible for "the whole sweep of cosmic-divine history can be rendered in the stained glass of a large cathedral" (Taylor, 2009: 60).

While his way of rendering the story of disenchantment provides an appreciation for the relationship between world-conception and self-conception, Taylor unusually limits "Greek thought" to the pre-Socratics. Indeed, this may also be why he uses Aristotle as the basis for understanding Greek thought more generally, as well as his use of the latter's term "cosmos" as a precursor to a rational universe. But this has the effect (intended or not) of dismissing what comes right before the pre-Socratics, namely the tragedians.

The specter of Aristotelian tragic ontology

This tendency in Taylor is not all that surprising as many scholars interpret Aristotelian ontology and metaphysics without engaging tragedy (Husain, 2001). More specifically, Aristotle's *Poetics* is understood as simply an application of his metaphysics onto tragic drama. As Jean-Pierre Vernant and Pierre Vidal-Naquet note, after Aristotle, tragedy takes on the status of something like "a science" such as Euclidean geometry or "an intellectual discipline" such as philosophy (Vernant and Vidal-Naquet, 1990: 241). But when tragic ontology is taken seriously on its own terms as do contemporary classicists like Vernant and Vidal-Naquet along with Martha Nussbaum and Ruth Padel, it does not exactly reflect Taylor's caricature.

Nussbaum explicitly defends Aristotle by providing a different reading, recontextualizing his definition of tragedy as a transitional point between Plato and the modern view of tragedy, arguing that Aristotle did have "a high regard for tragedy" (Nussbaum, 2001: 378). She explains "the general anthropocentrism of his ethics and his rejection of the Platonic external God's-eye standpoint leads him turn for moral improvement, not to representations of divine non-limited beings but to stories of good human activity" (Nussbaum, 2001: 378). For

Nussbaum then, contrary to Vernant and Vidal-Naquet, Aristotle actually attributes certain values to emotions and feelings, "both as parts of virtuous character and as sources of information about right actions," which leads him to reconsider certain texts that "Plato had banished on account of their representation of and appeal to the emotions." The thrust of Nussbaum's argument consists of viewing Aristotle's theory of tragedy as having some appreciation of emotionality in addition to what most scholars of Greek tragedy hold to be true of Aristotle's *Poetics* in particular: the importance of plot, that is, "the arrangement of the events" (Nussbaum, 2001: 378). But in Nussbaum's interpretation, for Aristotle, it is in tragedy's plot that a "representation not of human beings but of action and a course of life" can be found. Hence, in Nussbaum's rendering, Aristotle is focused less so on "characteristic" and more on action (more on this in the following chapter).

According to Aristotle,

> ...the world does not simply provide the agent with instrumental means to an activity that can be identified and specified apart from the external; it provides a constituent part of the good activity itself. There is no loving action without someone to receive and return it; there is no being a good citizen without a city that accepts your claims to membership. In these cases, hexis and praxis, character and activity, are so intimately connected that it would not even be possible to represent the appropriate character-states without representing action and communication—and, therefore, vulnerability. This means that interference from the world leaves no self-sufficient kernel of the person safely intact.
>
> (Nussbaum, 2001: 381)

Here Nussbaum identifies the complexity of action in the context of the tragic world. In effect, there is no agent as understood in a modern context since the agent as described above cannot act instrumentally. The decision-making process as commonly espoused in contemporary psychology is a strictly *cognitive* activity of drawing on some sort of knowledge or belief to decide on a course of action; it assumes a central, interior core of the agent's being—the psyche. However, in Aristotle's *Poetics*, as Nussbaum makes clear, the causal chain between character and action is reversed.

This blurred distinction between interiority and exteriority signals, in Ruth Padel's words, the Greek imagination's divinization of "all kinds of things, activities and relationships between people." The same can even be said of "different moments of relationships, different stages of life, different states of body and feeling" (Padel, 1994: 3). What this means is that for fifth-century Greeks, gods were in bodies, minds, homes and cities. They were, as Padel notes, "like electricity" (Padel, 1994: 3). If this is the case, that bodies, minds, homes, and cities are all full of divine energy, then what a "body" is, what a "mind" is, and ultimately what a "self" is is challenged. To put a finer point on it, what distinguishes a body from a mind from a home from a city is not all that clear.

To illustrate this point, Padel pursues an analysis of tragic psychology, expounding on the concept of "innards."

> [A]ll this equipment of feeling and thinking. The poets treat these words fluidly as organs, vessels, liquid, breath. But I am not suggesting these tragedians "blurred" distinctions we make between mind and body, or that these words were ambiguous, or that the psychological "overlapped" the physical in Greek thought. These critical metaphors of blur and overlap would imply that the Greeks perceived two different things to blur, two meanings to slip between. If the distinctions and meanings are ours, not theirs, then there were no two things for them to blur or to be ambiguous about. It is useful to project semantic fields of our own words, like heart, soul, mind or spirit, or to talk in terms of slippage.
>
> (Padel, 1994: 39)

In tragedy, there were, of course, persons. However, in tragic drama, what was important was a person's "splanchma" or guts. This, she is quick to note, has "practically nothing to do with the head." More specifically, "splanchma" refers to "the general collection of heart, liver, lungs, gallbladder and attendant blood vessels." Other words that come to mind are entrails, bowels, feeling, mood, temper and mind (Padel, 1994: 13).

A contemporary audience may see this list of terms as hardly having to do with one another. But in tragedy the word "phren" is used to refer to where feeling and thinking take place. While it is often understood as "mind" or the location of thought (hence the connection to the deplorable science of "phrenology"), "phren" is vulnerable. "The emotional and intellectual activity whose center they are often wounds them," Padel writes. Phren is more often than not "acted on than active." Someone's "phrenes" can be "struck and gashed by fear" or by the gods." This can lead to a person being "paralyzed, incapable of action or judgement" (Padel, 1994: 22). Put simply, "physical inner organs" are linked to "psychological agency." Emotional and intellectual activity are inseparable from one another (Padel, 1994: 39). We can think of "two-way imaginative traffic between our body and its activities on the one hand and the objects in the external world on the other"(Padel, 1994: 51). This is no better illustrated than in tragedy where our bodies are indeed "porous" not only to suffering but also interference. "The heaviest danger," Padel writes, "is from things outside coming in" (Padel, 1994: 59). She likens this to contemporary medical language. Thus, "emotional suffering, like perception or disease, is due to intrusion" (Padel, 1994: 63).

In Aeschylus' *Agamemnon*, the chorus describes Agamemnon's motivation for sacrificing Iphigenia as both active (in that he considered the alternatives, "reversed his mind," and thus became a sacrificer of his own daughter) but also as passive, with external forces akin to "a wind" ascribed as the "the causation of his act" (Gill, 1986: 263). This wind is not just any wind but specifically "adverse winds" sent by Artemis that "[blow] with the blasts of fortune that fell upon him." Likewise, his decision to kill his daughter is ascribed to "base-counseling wretched infatuation," which makes men "bold." As Gill notes, "infatuation" is *parakopa,* which is literally "something that knocks the mind sideways." It is a synonym, he notes, for *ate,* the term for "mental delusion" and "blindness." Gill writes:

> The idea that there can be something in a person that is not "him" but some intrusive force process at work in him (while still somehow leaving him as the responsible agent) is a recurrent one in the [Oresteia] trilogy. Elsewhere too people describe themselves (and are described by others) as both acting and acted on, as people, but also as "embodiments" of an avenger (*alastor* or *erinus* (fury) that works through them, while still leaving the act somehow "theirs," and their responsibility.
>
> (Gill, 1986: 263)

This explains the phrase, "he slipped his neck through the strap of compulsion's yoke." Gill even demonstrates this tendency in Euripides, whose plays are viewed as "humanizing" the gods. In *Hippolytus, Heracles* and *Bacchae,* Gill writes, "figures are presented, at key moments, as acting under the influence of a god (and hence acting madly or irrationally); and yet the acts are still treated as theirs, and the people are not wholly exonerated." Clytemnestra, after she murders Agamemnon, says, "You claim that the act is mine; but do not say I am the wife of Agamemnon. Appearing in the shape of a dead man's wife, the ancient spirit (*alastor*) that takes vengeance for the misdeed of the cruel feaster Atreus has now rendered this full-grown as payment to the young, a crowning sacrifice." As Gill notes, her words amount not only to a defense but also "highlight the fanaticism that can make a person identify herself with a spirit of vengeance (*alastor*), even while she recognizes that this spirit causes hideous deaths in successive generations, and is, by the same logic, likely to lead to her own" (Gill, 1986: 266). Gill shows this in *Medea* as well, quoting the monologue that precedes the murder of her children, whereby the titular character is angry that she has been "mastered" by that *thumos[spiritedness]* (Gill, 1986: 268).

In tragedy, for the most part, external and internal causalities shift against each other. As Padel concludes, in the fifth century, the dominant influence is not the inner world but the outer (Padel, 1994: 57). Gill frames this as the distinction between the active and the passive as well as between the psychological and supernatural. In either case, as Sewall writes, tragedy emerges from a world that "antedates the conceptions of philosophy, the consolations of later religions and whatever constructions the human mind has devised to persuade itself that its universe is secure" (Sewall, 1959: 5). In other words, tragedy *precedes* the modern, Western self—the agent, that is, "the performer of deliberate actions…which exhibit stable qualities we can assess" (Gill, 1986: 271), according to Padel and Gill. In other words, tragedy is full of human beings that do not yet hold what Vernant and Vidal-Naquet call "the will."

The will

The category of the will, in the psychological history of the West, can be said to "begin" in Greek tragedy's "anxious questioning concerning the relation of the agent to his actions"(Vernant and Vidal-Naquet, 1990: 46). Greek tragedy, they suggest, asks:

> To what extent is man[sic] really the source of his actions? Even while he deliberates concerning them deep within himself, taking the initiative and responsibility for them, does not their true origin lie somewhere outside him? Does not their significance remain opaque to the one who commits them, since actions acquire their reality not through the intentions of the agent but through the general order of the world over which the gods preside?
>
> (Vernant and Vidal-Naquet, 1990: 46)

In contemporary Western societies, thanks in no small part to Augustine, the will is equated with the predominant conceptualization of a person *as* agent. The will is what allows us to view selves as sources of action. Thus, the concept of will assumes the following:

1. that there are actions (and even a string of actions) that can be perceived as "purely human and sufficiently interconnected and circumscribed within space and time," all of which "constitute a unified line of behavior"
2. the individual is recognized as an agent
3. notions of personal merit and culpability take on importance
4. the beginnings of analysis of various levels of intentions, on the one hand, and the deeds accomplished by the act.

(Vernant and Vidal-Naquet, 1990: 54)

Selves can thus be "held responsible before others and to which it furthermore feels inwardly committed" (Vernant and Vidal-Naquet, 1990: 49). Selves with wills reflect what Vernant and Vidal-Naquet identify as "the modern insistence on the uniqueness and originality of the individual person." They rightly note that this perspective on the integrity of the individual stems from an expectation of continuity of the subject. They describe it thusly:

> ...the permanence of the agent who is responsible today for what he did yesterday and whose awareness of his own internal existence and coherence is all the stronger in that the sequence of his actions forms a chain, ... [constituting] a single, continuous career.
>
> (Vernant and Vidal-Naquet, 1990: 49)

This presupposes that a person is "oriented toward action," and thus "the human subject is assumed to be the origin and efficient cause of all the actions that stem from him." The agent of will then understands himself as "a kind of center of decision, holding a power that springs neither from the emotions nor from pure intelligence." To make decisions and act "as he wills" is as natural for this modern, buffered model of person as it is to "have arms and legs" (Vernant and Vidal-Naquet, 1990: 49).

But for Vernant and Vidal-Naquet, Greek tragedies hardly exhibit such a dynamic, neatly interlocking will and action within an individual. The will is not a "datum of human nature" but rather a "complex construction whose history appears to be as difficult, multiple and incomplete"(Vernant and Vidal-Naquet, 1990: 50). In Aeschylus' plays, for instance, the tragic heroes are always faced with the need to act and thus on the threshold of action. They are faced with an *aporia*, a crossroads on which their entire fate depends (Vernant and Vidal-Naquet, 1990: 51). This decision is, they write, "without choice." Their responsibility is "divorced from intention" (Vernant and Vidal-Naquet, 1990: 55). This is clear in the trajectory of Orestes in the *Oresteia*. He is compelled to kill his mother Clytemnestra to avenge her murder of his father Agamemnon. He is even advised to do so by Apollo. The Chorus also weighs in. In the moment where he must do the deed, he hesitates and can only do so upon urging and a reminder of his duty.

The tragic hero, or the agent, can be said to be without "choice," understood in the sense of deliberate action completely internal to the subject because the "tragic decision" (and all that stands behind it) is attributable to whatever is occurring inside of the hero—or agent—and also the acts of *daimon* or divine power. Therefore, the origin of action lies within and without (Vernant and Vidal-Naquet, 1990: 77). So, it would be difficult to say that the agent is "either sufficient cause and reason for his action." It would be more accurate to say, "it is his action, recoiling upon him as the gods have, in their sovereignty, ordered, that reveals him to himself, showing him the true nature of what he is and what he does" (Vernant and Vidal-Naquet, 1990: 80). In the works of Aeschylus, Sophocles and Euripides, Vernant and Vidal-Naquet argue, the agent's actions sit in "a temporal order over which he has no control and to which he must submit passively, his actions elude him; they are beyond his understanding" (Vernant and Vidal-Naquet, 1990: 82). For them, tragedy demonstrates the "weakness inherent in action" as well as an "internal inadequacy of the agent." The gods are working behind human beings' backs. So, even when "exercising choice" by making a decision, the agent, or the hero, "almost always does the opposite of what he thinks he is doing" (Vernant and Vidal-Naquet, 1990: 83).

The notion of the will in ancient Greek thought marks a moment in the psychological history of the West. It is during this period that the categories of action and agent are being debated but had not "acquired enough consistency and autonomy to make the subject the center of the decision from which his actions were believed to emanate" (Vernant and Vidal-Naquet, 1990: 82). In the last analysis, in their estimation, tragedy shows the relative "inconsistency of the Greek category of the agent" and its lack of internal organization (Vernant and Vidal-Naquet, 1990: 83). As the concepts of "innards" and "the will" show, while there is a sense of self, it is clearly "porous," to recapitulate Taylor. But it would be wrong to assume that "ancient" only refers to ancient Greece. While Aeschylus' productions were being staged for the Dionysia, the annual Festival of Dionysus, where new plays would be staged, the author of Book of Job was writing, according to the best estimations provided by scholars. The Book of Job is, arguably, the other major ancient text from which Western culture has drawn to ask questions about "ultimate justice and human destiny."

The suffering of job

Many modern scholars suggest that the Book of Job was written sometime between the seventh and second centuries with most believing that the story of a pious sufferer had existed long before the book in the form of a folktale (Roper, 2005: 757). There is some contention as to the origin of this folktale—with some believing that it has Arab origins and others believing it can be traced to Edom (Roper, 2005: 761). Others are convinced that the story traces to ancient Egypt. Yet, most scholars today agree that the author of the Book of Job is of Israelite origin (Roper, 2005: 762) and that the work responds to the Hebrew "wisdom tradition" (Roper, 2005: 763). Like Greek tragedy, wisdom literature was rooted in the question of divine retribution. The theology of the wisdom tradition assumes that "God's actions could be explained completely in terms of a specific theological system." In other words, "everything that happened to people in this world could likewise be explained in terms of a certain set of rules such as the dogma of retribution" (Roper 2005: 765).

According to Roper, the author of the Book of Job was *questioning* this notion of divine retribution and speculates that the author likely "experienced that righteous people could suffer just as much (or even more) than the ungodly" (Roper, 2005: 764). This inkling is supported by those who believe that it was written during the period of Babylonian exile or even immediately after, and thus the suffering of Job is believed to be representative of the suffering of Jews during the exilic period.

Like its Greek counterparts, the Book of Job consists of a story made up of inexplicable suffering, doubt, and divine intervention. But most importantly, the story of suffering is meant to give insight into the human experience. Suffering, then, like for Aeschylus, Euripides, and Sophocles, is represented in the work to "yield knowledge." Job is undoubtedly, like Oedipus, a "towering tragic figure of antiquity." But this is not exactly for the same reasons as his Theban counterpart. While today, in the wake of revisionist theological efforts, especially among liberation theologians, Job represents dissent, he, in the traditional and even the contemporary popular understanding today, embodied extreme faith and piety. Despite the trials and tribulations undergone as a result of what one could easily characterize as a "bet" between God and Satan, Job never rebukes God.

In addition, biblical tragedy offers a slightly different relationship between the divine and the human being than in the Greek tradition. In the latter, not much love is lost in the transaction of humans with the gods. The gods were, for the most part, always "fallible, imperfect, finite and above all, laws unto themselves." Rebelling against them would be pointless as well as catastrophic but it would not lead to a spiritual dilemma of any kind. After all, they are just like us humans in many ways. But Jehovah is believed to be "righteous, just and loving—a being to whom one could appeal in the name of all these virtues" (Sewall, 1959: 11). Thus, the disappointment in the divine is always greater in some respect, for the Abrahamic monotheist when reading about the suffering of Job.

Contemporary critical commentators have pointed out that the uniqueness of the Book of Job is the centrality of speech. Unlike in the Theban plays, there is no plotted physical action on the part of Job, his friends, Satan or God. For example, at no point does Job try to "get back" at God. Instead, his disillusionment and suffering are expressed in *words* (Sewall, 1959: 13). For the author of the Book of Job, "ideas [and] inner realities" function like actions in the Greek works (Sewall, 1959: 13). Job's tragedy is driven therefore more by "character" and "incident" rather than major actions. The drama in the Book of Job is an interior one. "Job's disillusionment," writes Sewall, "was deeply personal and a cosmic breach of faith" (Sewall, 1959: 11). Who could blame Job for feeling injured when he became all but a pawn in a game between God and Satan?

Yet, Job's refusal to reject God, the liberation theologian Gustavo Gutierrez argues, is what cements the injustice of his suffering (Gutierrez, 1987: 4). For Gutierrez, the main theme of the Book of Job is not "precisely suffering" but rather how to *speak* to God in the face of suffering (Gutierrez, 1987: 13). This distinction may seem unnecessarily academic. What is the purpose of distinguishing between speaking of suffering and suffering *tout court*? For Gutierrez, this has great import for the clarification of theodicy. If there is a way for Job to speak *back* to God, it is because the suffering endured is implicitly unjust. If the suffering inflicted upon Job is unjust, how can there be a God that is all-knowing if he not only allows suffering but inflicts it? Thus, when Job "rebels" by speaking back to God, he does so as "a rebellious believer" (Gutierrez, 1987: 13).

What Job speaks out against is not suffering in general. Rather, as many other leftish interpreters have pointed out, it is specifically the doctrine of retribution. Gutierrez associates retribution with what he calls "traditional doctrine" (Gutierrez 1987: 19), which, in the Book of Job, is embodied by Eliphaz. As any reader of the Book of Job knows fairly quickly that of the three "friends," who visit Job, Eliphaz is the least comforting. He constantly reminds Job of his sins. Meanwhile, Job's other friends are more sympathetic. Bildad reasserts the mystery of divine omnipotence, and Zophar maintains the importance of surrender. More to the point, he implies that Job *must* have done something to warrant God's wrath. To counter this, Gutierrez points out, would be for a human to all but claim that he is "more righteous than God" (Gutierrez, 1987: 22). The potential for blasphemy in Job's indignation is what instigates Eliphaz to ask Job to repent.

According to Gutierrez, Eliphaz represents the "prevailing doctrine at the period when the author of the Book of Job was writing." It is rooted in a rather simplistic, but solid, theology that God is all-powerful and all-knowing (Gutierrez, 1987: 22). He is just. There is no suffering that is unfounded or unexplained. The doctrine of retribution is "convenient" and "soothing" as there are no unaccounted-for examples of human suffering. But Job cannot admit guilt, nor can he blaspheme God. Placed between this rock and hard place, he examines himself and concludes that he did not do anything to deserve the level of punishment, which includes the loss of his children, his possessions, and his health. By not admitting guilt, Job is waging, in short, a protest against his suffering; it is a way of saying that the punishment is not simply disproportionate but unjust (Gutierrez, 1987: 24). Hence, Gutierrez concludes, Job's speaking out against, but not denouncing, God amounts to a critique of a certain kind of theological reasoning that dominated during the time that the Book of Job was written.

Job exercises a "theology of contemplation" as opposed to a theology of retribution (Gutierrez, 1987: 97). "Contemplation" is "beyond justice" in that it bucks the causality of retribution, which sees justice as simply a mathematical equation. There never is a resolution that Job comes to, which then frees him from suffering. His suffering ends because God allows it to. "The Book of Job does not claim to have found a rational or definitive explanation of suffering;" Gutierrez writes, "the poet is quite aware that the subject is a complex one" (Gutierrez, 1987: 93).

The political philosopher Antonio Negri draws from this reading to suggest that Job's suffering stands in for the exploitation of the worker in a capitalist mode of production. For the autonomous Marxist Negri, the Book of Job serves as an allegory of the extraction of surplus value from workers by capital. The injustice suffered by Job is comparable to that of labor in contemporary capitalism. More specifically, for Negri, Job's suffering does not so much undermine the logic of retribution but rather acts as "a symptom of the impossibility of measure and the exhaustion of the mechanisms of equivalence" (Negri, 2009: xi). And it is the "culture of measure" that is at the core of capitalist ideology.

"Measure" for Negri is undoubtedly "retribution" for Gutierrez. Measure, based on the false idea of equal exchange (for instance, the assumption that one is paid fairly for one's labor-time), buttresses an Eliphazian theory of justice, "which rests on a calculus that equates crimes with punishments and virtues with rewards" (Negri, 2009: ix). According to this logic, there must be some kind of sin that Job had committed for him to be inflicted with so much pain and suffering.

As Negri reminds us, however, pain—and Job's suffering specifically—is "incommensurable" (Negri, 2009: xix). It is, to the contrary, "immense." Pain escapes linguistic capture; it exceeds representation. It not only resists language, as Scarry famously put it, "but actively destroys it" (Scarry, 1996: 4). Pain's resistance to language "is not simply one of its incidental or accidental attributes but is essential what it is" (Scarry, 1996: 5). Despite the discoveries of recent scientific research, most famously the "gate-control theory of pain" that informs something like the McGill Questionnaire, there are still more questions than answers on what pain even is. Even medicine in this way "depends on physician's acuity with which he or she can hear the fragmentary language of pain, coax it into clarity and interpret it" (Scarry, 1996: 6–7).

The language that we do use for pain is a "verbal strategy" utilized "under the pressure of the desire to eliminate pain." But to represent pain in this manner is merely "analogical" (Scarry, 1996: 17). It is not stable but simply a way to have certainty. As Scarry writes:

> The deeply problematic character of this language, its inherent instability, arises precisely because it permits a break in the identification of the referent and thus a misidentification of the thing to which the attributes belong. While the advantage of the sign is its proximity to the body, its disadvantage is the ease with which it can be spatially separated from the body.
>
> (Scarry, 1996: 17)

For these reasons, Negri describes Job's conceptualization of justice as one that acknowledges pain and suffering as "beyond human understanding." The Book of Job is a "provocation *against* the seduction of reason" (Negri, 2009: 8 Emphasis added). The pain of Job is so immense that it "cannot be numbered" (Negri, 2009: 8). Thus, Job stands before God not trying to reason with him but rather indignantly, even angrily.

In fact, Negri reads Job's rebellion based on the simple fact that the primary affect of Job with regard to God's power is pain, not fear. Fear would maintain a vertical relation between Job and God, according to Negri. Pain, on the other hand, is horizontal, placing Job on the same level as God (Negri, 2009: 14). To problematize the relationship of humans to God, demonstrating that God is standing "silent" in the face of his suffering, Job engages in a form of rebellion (Negri, 2009: 13).

The "rebellion" in the Book of Job is not really an action. Job does not *do* anything physically. But he does in the sense that he speaks. Speech, especially speaking back to God, is, as Gutierrez writes, "his facing up to God" (Gutierrez, 1987: 102). By expressing his suffering, Job commits a "speech-act" that appeals to absolute justice, demonstrating the arbitrariness of his suffering (Negri, 2009: 22). The act of speaking out—again, not against God but rather against his suffering—functions as a critique of the "retributive model" of justice (Negri, 2009: 36). There is no reason for his pain. The conclusion that Job reaches is that God's logic cannot be known to humanity. To attempt to understand it, as his friends and other interlocutors in the Book of Job try to do, is to try to measure the immeasurable. Yet remarkably, for Job, it was not incumbent on humans to accept this state of affairs.

Beyond intentionality

Talal Asad recognizes the power of the Abrahamic tradition and the ancient tragedies in their respective capacity to provide alternative, non-triumphalist versions of agency (Asad, 2000: 29). In his trenchant critique of the recent resurgence in agency in the social sciences, Asad notes that there is an "essentialized human subject" that sits at the heart of the recent agency resurgence. By privileging agency over structure, recent social scientific research has tried to attack the top-down nature of statistical reasoning alongside the determinism of the notion of historical forces in order to preserve or "save" the individual. It celebrates the capacity of human beings to empower themselves and make history (Ortner, 2005).

But this coin of agency also has a flipside. Agency, when defined as "a completed personal action from within an indefinite network of causality by attributing an actor responsibility to power" (Asad, 2000: 34), approximates a legalistic framework, whereby "a world of apparent accidents is rendered into a world of essentials by attributing to a person moral/legal responsibility on whose basis guilt and innocence (and therefore punishment or exoneration) are determined." This understanding of the agent-as-individual is ineluctably individualist. It emphasizes, and even celebrates, voluntarism and conscious intention but also attributes singular causes to specific individuals (Asad, 2000: 30). To be an agent is to be responsible "for something." But there are instances in contemporary life where agents do "not coincide with an individual biological body and the consciousness that is said to go with" it. For instance, corporations carry liability under the law. In 2010, the United States Supreme Court, in Citizens United v. Federal Election Commission, ruled that corporations are able to donate an unlimited amount to political campaigns as a matter of protecting the freedom of speech contained in the First Amendment of the U.S. Constitution. Part of the justification was that corporations were indeed persons, which means that companies could hold property, enter contracts, and to sue and be sued just like a human being. Corporations, in this instance, are agents but lack subjectivity. Likewise with agents, there are instances whereby subjectivity and responsibility are uncoupled. For instance, my intention does not factor into assessing responsibility when someone gets injured on my property accidentally.

Intention, still, is seen as central to agency in the social sciences. It remains *the* chief indicator of agency. According to Asad, this amounts to a kind of metaphysics. The conscious agent-subject is inherently oriented toward increasing self-empowerment. At the most general level, this is due to the tendency to romanticize resistance and the adherence to an uncomplicated, definitional attachment of freedom to the human subject. The human subject, in this view, should give into her own desires and interest. Her agency is defined by a normative orientation of the subject to "take control of her own life," including her body and mind. As Asad notes, there is an implicit definition of power that sees it as "external and repressive to the agent." It is understood as "subjecting" her but the agent, as an "active subject," not only has the desire "to oppose power but the responsibility to get more powerful" (Asad, 2000: 32). The agent is understood to have what Vidal-Naquet and Vernant call "will."

Notwithstanding the rising interest in agency as a means of "historicizing social structures by according responsibility for progressive change to consciousness actors," Asad sees the lack of attention to the body as a site for agency in the social sciences (Asad, 2000: 30). In particular, the body is seen as unproblematically subservient to the will, intention, or consciousness of the human subject. But in fact, the body is not simply owned by a mind, as he notes, drawing not only on Islamic theology but also on the Greek tragic tradition. In those traditions, the body can act as both agent and victim, defying the dichotomy between being the author of the story and becoming its passive object. Pain in these traditions is often itself a kind of action. This is certainly so in *Oedipus Rex*.

Asad argues that the tragedy of Oedipus depicts disempowerment that is "neither voluntary nor involuntary" (Asad, 2000: 36). For Oedipus, the responsibility he bears is not to a single authority—no court or even a human or superhuman entity (Asad, 2000: 37). He in fact never suggests that he did not cause the death of a man at the crossroads. He does, however, take umbrage with patricide, which, as Asad argues, is "a different act." Oedipus, one could argue, tried his hardest to avoid such an act. Is Oedipus responsible for patricide per se? For Asad, Oedipus clearly sees that he is the owner of an act—and is thus an agent. At the same time, however, the act "turned out not to be his own." He was an "unwitting instrument" of the gods. His intention was irrelevant. He was up against his destiny.

Asad maintains that Oedipus' story cannot be interpreted through the concept of responsibility (Asad, 2000: 38). He did not knowingly murder Laius. His moral action must be assessed through criteria other than intention. It is *habitus* which Asad settles on, as it is sensitive to the idea that one's action has ethical significance but without necessarily attributing certain effects to them in a simplified, casual manner. "Habitus," Asad writes, "is not something one accepts or rejects, it is part of what one essentially is and must do. (The ethics of necessity encompasses tragedy.)" (Asad, 2000: 38). The habitus, that is, an "embodied moral sensibility," of Oedipus exists in accordance with his experience and situation (Asad, 2000: 40). It is lived "as a necessary condition" of his form of life. Thus, Oedipus is left with nothing but "impossible choices" (Asad, 2000: 40). Is there room, Asad, ultimately asks, to think about agency in this somewhat constrained manner?

Conclusion

It is my contention that if we are to do so, we necessarily must draw on the lessons of ancient and classical tragic thinking as it pertains to contemporary conceptions of interiority and exteriority for it impacts how we understand the actor in the social sciences. One way to do so is to view the world in a reenchanted, that is, classical/ancient manner. It is to recognize that, as William Connolly says, "humans are not the only actors in it":

> The world flows over with diverse "energies" and "forces" that impinge on human life in multiple ways and that sometimes react to human impingements on them in unpredictable and uncanny ways. If a human actor is one who makes a difference in the world without quite knowing what it is doing, then germs, volcanoes, crocodiles, and whirlwinds have some of the characteristics of actors too; the term actor now gathers within it a plurality of variable dimensions, blurring or ambiguating the familiar divisions of nature/culture, humans/machines, will/cause, and creator/creature. Moreover, even within human life, "the will," "the soul," and "the subject" can now be seen to be insufficient or uncertain sources of behavior: The self contains pools of "energy" and "impulse" that flow through and over these officially defined centers of agency. When one emphasizes the metaphorical status of terms such as energy and impulse in characterizing "drives" within and without the human animal, the corollary metaphorical standing of will and subject begins to shine through more brightly. The Greek idea of demon is no more problematic than the Christian idea of will: It is just that the latter stands at the center of modern conceptions of intrinsic moral order and, therefore, needs to be problematized more actively today for ethical reasons.
>
> (Connolly 2002: 11)

As Connolly notes, there is certainly a degree of continuity between the Christian ideas of will and Greek ideas of *daimon*. His reasoning for problematizing Christian ideas is its more immediate impact on modern ideas of morality. In listing various divisions of the modern chronotope, he is calling for a new *language* of social science, one that denaturalizes the fixed relations assumed at the heart of modern notions of subjectivity. But, as the following chapter will further explore, it is not simply Christianity that has impacted the modern conception of the actor. It is also the influence of a specific reading of Aristotle focused on the figure of the hero as well as its impact on conceptions of the "modern individual."

References

Asad, T., 2000. Agency and Pain: An Exploration. *Culture and Religion*, 1 (1), 29–60.

Connolly, W.E., 2002. *The Augustinian Imperative: A Reflection on the Politics of Morality.* Revised edition. Lanham, MD: Rowman & Littlefield Publishers.

Gill, C., 1986. The Question of Character and Personality in Greek Tragedy. *Poetics Today*, 7 (2), 251–273.

Greenblatt, S., 2017. How St. Augustine Invented Sex. *The New Yorker*, June.

Gutierrez, G., 1987. *On Job: God-Talk and the Suffering of the Innocent.* Maryknoll, NY: Orbis Books.

Hanby, M., 2003. *Augustine and Modernity.* London: Routledge.

Husain, M., 2001. *Ontology and the Art of Tragedy.* Albany, NY: SUNY Press.

Morley, N., 2009. *Antiquity and Modernity.* Hoboken, NJ: John Wiley & Sons.

Negri, A., 2009. *The Labor of Job: The Biblical Text as a Parable of Human Labor.* Durham, NC: Duke University Press Books.

Nussbaum, M.C., 2001. *The Fragility of Goodness: Luck and Ethics in Greek Tragedy and Philosophy.* 2nd edition. Cambridge: Cambridge University Press.

Ortner, S.B., 2005. Subjectivity and Cultural Critique. *Anthropological Theory*, 5 (1), 31–52.

Padel, R., 1994. *In and Out of the Mind: Greek Images of the Tragic Self.* Princeton, NJ: Princeton University Press.

Roper, L.A., 2005. The Social Context of the Book of Job. *Verbum et Ecclesia*, 26 (3), 756–772.

Scarry, E., 1996. *The Body in Pain: The Making and Unmaking of the World.* New York, NY: Oxford University Press.

Sewall, R.B., 1959. *The Vision of Tragedy.* New Haven, CT: Yale University Press.

Taylor, C., 2009. *A Secular Age.* Cambridge, MA: Harvard University Press.

Tracy, D., 2018. Augustine Our Contemporary: The Overdetermined, Incomprehensible Self. *In*: W. Otten and S. Schreiner, eds. *Augustine Our Contemporary: Examining the Self in Past and Present.* Notre Dame, IN: University of Notre Dame Press, 27–74.

Vernant, J.-P., and Vidal-Naquet, P., 1990. *Myth and Tragedy in Ancient Greece.* Princeton, NJ: Princeton University Press.

Weber, M., 2005. *The Protestant Ethic and the Spirit of Capitalism.* Abingdon, Oxon; New York, NY: Routledge.

Zaretsky, E., 2011. Why the Freudian Century: Reflections on the Statue of Athena. *American Imago*, 68 (4), 679–688.

3

THE TRAGIC INDIVIDUAL

Catharsis, the hero, and the flaw in Aristotle and beyond

Introduction

It is more than likely that most people encounter the concept of tragedy through the thought of Aristotle. For Aristotle, a tragedy requires six elements: plot, character, thought, diction, melody, and spectacle (Reeves, 1952: 186). In the main, most students learn about the importance of the first element. Plot maintains its status as a key to Aristotle's theory of tragedy, in part, because of what the philosopher, who wrote the *Poetics* after the death of Euripides, describes as the main purpose of tragedy, which is to evoke the emotions of pity and fear.

The mechanism of emotional evocation in Aristotle, we are taught, relies on some form of identification with a character, indeed, the *main* character or the hero, on the part of the spectator. Identification with the hero is ensured by what Aristotle calls "mimesis" or imitation. Imitation, in this context, is not exactly mimicry. For Aristotle, tragedy is supposed to imitate *action*, which, he clarifies as "being serious and also, as having magnitude, complete in itself." Moreover, it is not slavishly bound to its "real-life" referent. Action can take place in "a dramatic, not in a narrative form" (Reeves, 1952: 185). In other words, tragedy approaches reality not sequentially but emotionally. Action within a tragic work functions to fulfill its ultimate, emotional end: the catharsis of pity and fear. Tragedy, it turns out, actually does not aspire to capture reality perfectly.

Catharsis—translated as "purification" or "purgation"—can only occur if the action is deliberate, according to Aristotle. The tragic hero must have a recognizable, that is relatable, psychology that motivates him to the action. This means that the emotions of the tragic hero are not "irrational but human." The staging of emotion, either by dialogue or through plot, must then express the fact that emotions inevitably affect our judgments and how we act in the world. Hence,

DOI: 10.4324/9781003110859-4

catharsis is not so much predicated on relating to what the hero does but rather on how the hero feels.

Yet, while the action itself is not unsurprising, tragedy, at the same time, also does not rely on shock value. There is a logic behind tragic action. Had everyone known everything, each would see the inevitability of the eventual outcome. So, it is not a result of deficient thinking or a lack of rationality that the tragic hero meets his or her demise. The "tragic flaw" is not a matter of character, which many interpretations maintain to this day. It is, to put it simply, a mistake. For Aristotle, it is the mistake that allows for pity and fear to be aroused in the audience. Indeed, it is the change of fortune—the reversal—that even allows for the audience to recognize a shift in state—from ignorance to knowledge—in themselves but also the hero. There must be some sort of "causal chain." In Aristotle's formulation, catharsis is facilitated by the simultaneity of the reversal of fortune and the recognition of what lay behind it.

A key sticking point in the scholarship has been about what Aristotle meant by "hero." When looking at the text, we can see that the hero is not someone who is of "noble background" as some commentators have interpreted it. Aristotle describes the hero as "a good man." The hero need not be "pre-eminently virtuous and just." He does not need to be prosperous but simply "honest or upright." (More on this in Chapter 4.) Likewise, the hero need not be someone who suffers from pride or hubris. Walter Kaufmann notes that pride is not ever mentioned in the *Poetics*. The outsized focus he claims, comes from a Christianized reading of tragedy, which maps tragedy onto the Adamic fall. Pride, Kauffman asserts, is not the same as sin (Kaufmann, 1980: 15). But this is only the case if "sin" is defined as acting badly. In fact, one could argue that pride is very much *like* sin in that it is the ontological mark of being human, as discussed in the previous chapter in relation to Augustine. As Critchley describes *hamartia*, it is "not ... a tragic flaw but ... a basic experience of human fallibility and ontological limitedness" (Critchley, 2019: 190).

The presentation of such limitations of human agency and autonomy more specifically, according to Eagleton, has an instrumental function—"political homeopathy." It ensures that "controlled doses of certain emotions (pity and fear), which might otherwise prove disruptive" to the polis or society, are released (Eagleton, 2020: 5). This regulation is ensured only by the pre-existence of a social bond, of which pity is the most significant affect as it draws open an openness to otherness (Eagleton, 2009: 154). But this method of identification must be facilitated through entertainment, that is, through a "mixture of the sublime and beauty" (Eagleton, 2009: 153). Likewise, says Critchley, tragedy "does not seek to persuade its audience of audience or educate them." Instead, he argues, the yielding of affects is the goal rather than the inflammation of passions." These characters, while completely unlike us, are still worthy of experiencing "fellow feeling for their suffering." However, this is not accomplished through mimetic accuracy but rather through a dramatic reenactment that produces pleasure. Catharsis then, for Critchley as well as for Eagleton, is not so much a purgation but rather "a safe environment in which emotions are raised and then relieved" (Critchley, 2019: 190). Rather than purgation, a term that has come to the fore in recent scholarship on tragedy is "pruning" (Keesey, 1978: 196). Whereas "purgation" or "purification" assumes some sort of cure via elimination, "pruning" asserts an ongoing process—space for growth (Keesey, 1978: 200). To purge these emotions for the sake of a return to order—what often was described as an innate human "rage"—is what most theories of catharsis emphasized.

In the face of these discussions around the history, function, and form, contemporary understanding of "tragedy" still very much remain within an Aristotelian framework. *The New York Times* columnist David Brooks goes so far as to state that, "One tragedy of our day is that our culture hasn't fully realized how much Aristotle was correct" (Brooks, 2021). But there is plenty of evidence to suggest that Aristotle is not forgotten in the least. Former U.K. Prime Minister Boris Johnson is described as a "classical Greek hero" in the headline of one outlet, with the subtitle reading: "'The change from good fortune to bad,' said Aristotle, 'in the life of some eminent men' is the subject of every tragedy" (Fernandez-Armesto, 2021). Aristotle's name is even mentioned in a critical piece on the American television series *Succession*, which dramatizes the corporate and familial politics of a Rupert Murdoch-like figure and his children. There, the writer argues that the show can be viewed as "a Greek tragedy" pointing to "two elements Aristotle noted," including "the startling realization (Anagnorisis) and change in the reversal of fortune (peripeteia)." She continues, "tragedies come with the promise of catharsis—a feeling marked by pity (at the characters) and fear (that one may be condemned to a similar fate because of shared values)."

The meaning and function of catharsis

One of the most influential discussions of catharsis has been by Jacob Bernays, the German philologist and relative of Sigmund Freud. Reflecting his training as a classical philologist, Bernays' work on catharsis can be characterized as semantic in the sense that he is attempting to search for the "true meaning" of catharsis. Particularly, he is fixated on perspectives that asserted a definition of catharsis as purification. For Bernays, "purification" gives a false impression that there is a "higher purpose" that catharsis serves, be it moral, pedagogical or aesthetic.

What Bernays insists on is "the medical meaning" of the term. Catharsis, in his reading of Aristotle, is physiological (Porter, 2015: 16). He demonstrates this through an expansive reading of catharsis, not limiting himself to the *Poetics* when searching for Aristotle's usage of the term. Throughout the oeuvre, Bernays finds that Aristotle discusses catharsis as "lifting or alleviation of illness brought about by means of medical relief." By this, he means catharsis is a

...designation transferred from the somatic to the mental for the type of treatment given to an oppressed person that does not seek to transform or suppress the element oppressing him, but rather to arouse and drive it into the open, and thereby to bring about the relief of the oppressed person.

(Bernays, 2004: 329)

This *physical* understanding of catharsis is then more of a "violent discharge," closer to an "orgiastic reaction," to vomiting and evacuation (Porter, 2015: 16). Discharge, for Bernays, as Porter clarifies, is neither purgation nor the quieting of emotions as these—again falsely—attribute a regulatory dynamic to the process. It is decidedly not, as Porter puts it, "the elimination of undesirable quantities of affect." Rather it is a "form of excitation and release of inner states, both physical and psychological" (Porter, 2015: 21). There is no telos of permanent elimination. Discharge is temporary and repeatable. It is not a one-and-done event. Hence, it is no surprise that Porter describes catharsis in the language of ecstasy (*ekstasis*), in the sense of being temporarily "thrown out of [a] normal state of equilibrium ... being affected from without ... to eventually return to [oneself]." This return, which Porter dubs "assuagement," is what can be experienced as pleasure. But, as he is quick to note, pleasure for Bernays is not uncomplicated. In this context, it comes at the cost of pain in that the experience of *ekstasis*—to be out of oneself—is painful as it "disturbs me within" but it also is pleasurable "in that it opens my world to a richer world beyond" (Porter, 2015: 23).

Unlike other, more pedagogic or civic readings of catharsis, say in Critchley and Eagleton, Bernays' foregrounds this connection between the ecstatic and hedonic elements, in particular, that of the person watching's "return" to "the primordial condition of experience tout court." In turn, Bernays has a very specific sort of "tragic subject," one which is "directly capable of an expanded sensation—that is, capable, of participating in the ecstatic nature of the 'primary pathos'" (Porter, 2015: 28). Catharsis therefore aims to enlarge, even "universalize" the self in two ways. First, it places the self outside of itself; secondly, it facilitates an identification with humanity-at-large (Porter, 2015: 30). This latter universalization—identification—is achieved through pity, seeing one's position in relation to the laws of the universe and its "incomprehensible power." Within the self, not fear but trembling (or shuddering: *Schauder*) and shock are experienced (Porter, 2015: 31). Thus, tragedy "leaves one with a *feeling* not with an understanding or cognition;" it does not necessarily "clarify" or "educate.'" Porter describes Bernays' catharsis as a "life-affirming hedonism" that acknowledges that "for all its terrors and oppressiveness is at the same time a source of unrivalled and unadulterated pleasure" (Porter, 2015: 32 Emphasis added).

This aligns with Kaufmann's insistence that Aristotle's definition of tragedy is largely emotional (Kaufmann, 1980: 52). For him, the idea that the central theme of Greek tragedy is "pride" before the fall is "very wrong" and a projection of

Christian values "where they have no place." Pride is *not* sin, he argues, but "an essential ingredient of heroism" (Kaufmann, 1980: 15). In fact, hubris, he claims, is mentioned sparingly in Aristotle (Kaufmann, 1980: 15).

Perhaps the most prominent example of a "Christianized" reading is Kenneth Burke, who points out that "pity" is translated as "mercy" in the New Testament, "where it designates the Lord's attitude" (Burke, 1959: 344). To feel pity is to also be "merciful," which in turn could even be to be Lordly. Here, the "lowly man," as Burke puts it, "can be exalted." By seeing the fate of the lowly, tragic hero as "pitiful," we, as the audience, experience a magnanimity. Instead of kissing our teeth, we approach the actions on stage with a kind of solemn recognition, with a corresponding "half-recognized, vaguely shame-faced suggestion of relief at the thought that the same calamity has not befallen us" (Burke, 1959: 347). Again, hamartia here is not so much "tragic flaw" but simply an "error." Or, as Glassberg puts it, it is "missing the mark" (Glassberg, 2017: 201). (Interestingly, Burke notes in a footnote that it is "sin" in the New Testament but offers up the explanation that, because it is a "mere flaw in character," it is indeed "a remarkably efficient way of engaging an audience.") The fact that tragic hamartia is understood as an error, the hero/sufferer becomes "in some notable way like ourselves." It avoids making the hero either too bad or too good. The error is a misstep in action, a misperception of a situation not a state of being (Glassberg, 2017: 201).

While Burke goes so far as to move away from understanding *harmatia* as a character flaw, he retains the concept of the stable ego, in spite of his drawing on the ideas of Freud, in particular his use of the language of the body in understanding catharsis. For Burke, Freud's value in the discussion of catharsis is limited to the deployment of the language of the body and also the significance of the family and intimate relationships. Like Wrong, he does not extend his conceptual drawing on psychoanalysis to the problematization of the ego as such, which Sam Weber argues is precisely what drew Freud to tragedy in the first place. Although hamartia is not viewed as inherent in a self, Burke does not argue this from the position of rejecting the concept of the tragic hero as such.

But Freud's account is rather different. As Weber notes, while he also offers up a "theatrical" account of the Ego, Freud rejects the idea that the conflict is "of its own making, [or] even attributable to it" (Weber, 2000: 30). To argue as much would be moot because of course the desires or drives of the ego contribute to the conflict situation. Tragic pretensions, as Weber characterizes Freud's thinking, "are only part of a more general burlesque role that the Ego plays." The ego is, as Freud calls it, a "slapstick clown," performing "to create the appearance of being in control." In doing so, it props up the "basic axiom of Western modernity: the autonomous, active subject" (Weber, 2000: 31).

On this count, Weber argues that there is a homology between the tragedy of Aristotle's *Poetics* and Freud. In the *Poetics,* Aristotle argues that the power of tragedy is related to the pleasure afforded to recognition, that is, in learning. Like many of the commentators already discussed above, Weber finds that Aristotle's definition of tragedy homes in on, "above all, the representation upon the stage of an action that is complete, unified, and therefore meaningful." It is only such a meaningful representation of action that Aristotle suggests can count as "mythos" or plot (Weber, 2000: 33).

Part and parcel of this focus on action, or praxis, argues Aristotle, is the requirement of what Weber specifies as *actants* or *actings* not actors. As Weber explains:

> The reason the noun, "acting" is so bizarre, particularly when it is used in the plural, is that it suggests a multiplicity of elements that themselves seem more like ongoing processes than like stable entities. The notion of "actor" is still morphologically individual and hence identifiable with the subject of a single, self-same action or set of actions. And indeed, *prattontes* can refer as easily to the characters represented on stage, as to the persons representing, the actors. But actants or even more, actings, need not refer to a person or thing at all. Persons are doubtless involved, but qua individuals they need not be the principle of whatever unity may be attributed to the representation.
>
> (Weber, 2000: 34)

In remarkable similarity to the use of the term in actor-network theory, Weber argues that Aristotle's use of the term *prattontes* demonstrates that his conception of tragedy is not in line with "that which has become familiar to us over the past four hundred years is precisely Aristotle's refusal to place character at the center or fundament of tragedy" (Weber, 2000: 34). Weber correctly quotes Aristotle, "a tragedy cannot exist without a plot, but it can without characters" (Weber, 2000: 34). Oddly, when read closely, Weber argues, Aristotle "marks an irreducible distance to the dominant tendency of 'Western' theatre in the modern period, a tendency that Artaud was to attack bitterly as 'psychologistic'" (Weber, 2000: 35). In other words, the ego emerges from the narrative or plot, according to Aristotle's *Poetics* (Weber, 2000: 41). Even so, this does not mean that there is not a sense of interiority. In fact, Aristotle's reading of *Oedipus Tyrannus* attributes the "error" of Oedipus to what is *within* Oedipus but not *to* Oedipus. (This is remarkably similar to the Asad's analysis of Oedipus in the previous chapter.) Indeed, the actant does not come from the outside but is rather "born if not bred" (Weber, 2000: 37). It is this that allows Weber to declare that "in the *Poetics*," we are never "very far from Freud and psychoanalysis" (Weber, 2000: 37). The action provides insight into the actant, which may or may not involve individual consciousness. Thus, when viewing a tragedy, such as *Oedipus Tyrannus*, the viewer's experience is that of the Uncanny, "when the self reveals as the return of the other it has never fully ceased to be" (Weber, 2000: 47). Following Kierkegaard, we could argue that the assertion of the "psychologistic" reading of Aristotle is a "decisive marker of modernity," and that the historical animating force of tragedy is the "*nexus* of relationships that bind in an objective way" (Surin, 2005: 120 Emphasis added).

The hero as victim

While Freud certainly noted the family in the psychoanalytic toolkit early on, it was his younger colleague/disciple Otto Rank, who coined the term "family romance." In *The Myth of the Birth of the Hero*, Rank analyzes hero myths from across cultures and historical epochs but drills down on what he believes to be structurally parallel across nearly all of them. In a striking prefiguration of Levi-Strauss' structural study of myth, Rank suggests that hero myths bear the following features across cultures:

> The hero is the child of most distinguished parents; usually the son of a king. His origin is preceded by difficulties, such as continence, or prolonged barrenness, or secret intercourse of the parents, due to external prohibition or obstacles. During the pregnancy, or antedating the same, there is a prophecy, in the form of a dream or oracle, cautioning against his birth, and usually threatening danger to the father, or his representative. As a rule, he [i.e., the son] is surrendered to the water, in a box. He is then saved by animals, or by lowly people (shepherds), and is suckled by a female animal, or by a humble woman. After he has grown up, he finds his distinguished parents, in a highly versatile fashion; takes his revenge on his father, on the one hand, and is acknowledged, on the other, and finally he achieves rank and honors.
>
> (Rank, 2004: 47)

Rank's description of what makes a hero is indeed a "mytheme" by another name. For him, the hero's journey tells a common story, where the individual struggles to be free in the face of parental authority. It is, while painful, undoubtedly a necessary developmental achievement (Rank, 2004: 49). As he explains, this is why there is usually a period of "exposure" in hero myths. It usually "represents birth in difficult circumstances." It is the fact of being born, that fact of being itself, that "appears as the first magnificent feat (task), during which many perish, but which the hero survives, despite all difficulties" (Rank, 2004: 71). Rank even offers up examples, which includes the flood in the book of Genesis. "Whereas in the hero myth the father is warned of his dangerous son in a dream," Rank writes, "here the brave son is warned by the father himself of his destructive plans" (Rank, 2004: 80). And thus the hero's heroism is the maintaining of his life in spite of the forces working against him (as in the case of Oedipus). As Rank puts it, "the most human trait is and remains…birth, which mythology, precisely for this reason, often portrays as supernatural" (Rank, 2004: 83). It is the experience of birth and the fact of existence that most people identify with. The hero's heroism is not so much a triumph in terms of deed or accomplishment. Likewise, there is almost no emphasis on the overcoming of adversity itself or resolution, which runs counter to many formal perspectives on tragedy. The separation from parental authority, that is, "the individual struggle for independence and personal will expression," is what characterizes the hero (Seif, 1984: 373).

The identification of the audience with the hero is dependent on the fact that "the hero represents the natural need for every person to realize himself as a separate, autonomous being." This drive for personal mastery and self-determination, "the essential human drama," is what is symbolized in the hero myth (Seif, 1984: 376). Rank later on describes this process as the formation of the will, "the essence of the hero." The hero, as we all do, "must express his will in spite of the great pain implicit in the separation" (Seif, 1984: 377). Oedipus, in Rank's reading, "represents the tragic side of individual willing and separation, the wrenching price of personal freedom which is finally the apprehension of inevitable death" (Seif, 1984: 379).

Ernest Becker, the social theorist most clearly working in the tradition of Rank, draws on him when he formulates his definition of heroism, not so much as an assertion of a will-to-live, but in its inverse—as "death-transcendence." In doing so, he sharpens Rank's focus, zooming in on heroism as a means of fighting "extinction," especially "extinction with insignificance" (Becker, 1997: 4). According to Becker, culture itself is a symbolic system that allows for "artificial self-transcendence" (Becker, 1997: 4). In a sense, Becker's definition is much like Durkheim, in that culture is "sacred," allowing for the "perpetuation of its members" (Becker, 1997: 4). Unlike Durkheim, however, Becker deems society as "[providing] codes for...self aggrandizement." Interestingly enough, he understands "importance" or "significance" as simply "durability" (Becker, 1997: 13), drawing explicitly on Rank's conceptualization of "will."

To stand out as a hero is "to transcend the limitations of the human condition and achieve victory over impotence and finitude" (Becker, 1997: 31). Far less than a feat or accomplishment, the focus of culture in terms of death-transcendence is to offer "self-esteem" (Becker, 1997: 37). This, of course, is not to say that heroic acts, or attempts at cosmic greatness are not included in hero myths. But, for the most part, the basic role and function of the hero in history are simple. He "gambles with his very life and successfully defies death."

The hero stands as the basic symbol of culture, which, through it, guarantees a group's self-perpetuation. And thus, it is the group that an individual can "immerse himself so completely" so as to be "conferred" immortality. "The symbolic engineering of culture," Becker argues, serves as "an antidote to terror by giving them a new and durable life beyond that of the body" (Becker, 1997: 92). Hero worship is thus, for the group, "a vicarious catharsis of our own fears, fears that are deeply hidden" (Becker, 1997: 109). According to Rank, this is rooted in the process of transference. Heroism is the "transference to a powerful other" and it takes care of the "overwhelming-ness of the universe" (Becker,

1997: 127). However, Becker is quick to note, there is, undoubtedly, "a tragic aspect of human heroics." It is the scapegoating that inevitably occurs because there is no hero system that can actually ensure victory over evil and death (Becker, 1997: 124).

And it is at this point regarding the scapegoat where Becker connects immortality, the hero and evil. For the most part, social institutions are able to provide a channel for the human being's "hunger for righteous self-expansion and perpetuation" (Becker, 1997: 135) effectively "without excessive repression and within legal safeguards" for individual freedoms. This, in some way, is the conservative version of the Freudian argument regarding repression and sublimation. However, as Freud himself notes, in his most energistic moment, the repression of desire can result in its uncontrolled breech. On the flipside, as Becker posits, individuals would do anything "society wanted in order to earn it" (Becker, 1997: 134). This is because there is, in human beings, an innate desire, "a driving impetus" to "merge with a larger whole." There must be "something to dedicate his existence to."

The paradox, which of course Rank and Freud before him identified, is that the need to self-perpetuate, when it occurs through transference onto the heroic myth of the group, is what propels the destruction of humanity. This is because humans "will do anything for heroic belonging to a victorious cause" (Becker, 1997: 142). Humans "need transference in order to be able to stand life":

> Man [sic] immunizes himself against terror by controlling his fascination, by localizing it and developing working responses toward the sources of it. The result is that he becomes a reflex of small terrors and small fascinations in place of overwhelming ones. It is a forced and necessary barter: the exchange of unfreedom for life. From this point of view history is the career of a frightened animal who has to deaden himself against life in order to live. And it is this very deadening that takes such a toll of others' lives.
>
> (Becker, 1997: 148)

After all, the collective, the group, the society behind any given set of institutions, usually operates through a cosmic system of heroism. It is out of this impotence to guarantee absolute meaning in life, and significance in the cosmos, the human being's "urge to self-transcendence, his devotion to a cause, has made more butchery than private aggressiveness in history, and that the devastating group hatred is fed by the love of its members, their willingness even to die in its name" (Becker, 1997: 139). From this point of view, the truly tragic aspect of human existence is that humans "make fantasies about evil, see it in the wrong places, and destroy themselves and others by uselessly thrashing about" (Becker, 1997: 150). Or, as he more succinctly puts it, we "cause evil by wanting heroically to triumph over it." We fail to understand that "no one is invulnerable no matter how much of the blood of others is spilled to try to demonstrate it."

Given this, we can say that tragic drama is the ritual staging of a mimetic representation of the attempt to relieve such evil. True to its etymology ("tragos" or goat), tragedy, to the best of our knowledge, evolved from the actual sacrifice of an animal in ancient times. Like religion, as Rene Girard argues, tragedy's core function is to maintain social order and communal bonds. By regularly relieving the community's built-up tension (for the theorist of mimetic desire Girard, this was of course characterized by envy), the ritual prevents the Hobbesian state of nature. When viewed in this way, ritual sacrifice is what preserves civility, that is, prevents violence (Gans, 2000: 57).

In the context of the performance of tragic drama in ancient Greece, the function, according to a certain school of classicists, is much the same. But of course, there is a key difference as the relationship to the "victim" is rather different. Tragic catharsis in the dramatic context requires a form of identification with the protagonist—the hero. In the context of ritual sacrifice, there must be something more than spectatorial identification with the victim (Mulvey, 1988). There must be some degree of "involvement, active or passive, in the sacrificial act itself" (Gans, 2000: 54). Yet, in tragic drama, the suffering hero stands in for victims of the tragedies of everyday life. We feel pity for the protagonist, who should be known, more aptly, as a "hero-victim" (Gans, 2000: 54). But one would not be wrong to say that the audience could easily feel pity for the goat (putting aside for a moment the fact in ritual there was most likely not a separation between audience and stage). Yet, what ancient Greek tragic drama does is to narrativize, that is frame, the ritual formally by representing it while retaining the function. Put differently, it maintains the form and replaces the content.

And with the delinking of content and form, tragic narrative actually subverts aspects of the tragic itself. It immanently critiques the basis of the genre of tragedy. By the fact of its representation in the form of a staged performance, tragic narrative reveals the "arbitrary choice of the victim." It is, therefore, at once myth and "antimyth," in the words of Eric Gans. The victim for the most part does not make decisions rashly or without thought. In fact, as the Greek tradition reminds us, the hero-victim has no choice but to act in such a way. ("Choice" is hardly the right word.) And indeed, within the plot, there is not much that the hero–victim can do, since, as members of the audience, we know that the denouement is blood, or "at least the sweat and tears, of the scapegoat-protagonist" (Gans, 2000: 59). Yet, we militate against the form, specifically its cruelty. In identifying with the hero, we cannot help but "hope," which Gans characterizes as "vain but real," that the protagonist pulls through. In doing so, we rebel against tragedy's arbitrariness while "accepting its necessity" (Gans, 2000: 65). It is this "maximal tension between form and content," from the perspective of the audience, as Gans puts it, that expresses the "the appetite for immortality" (Gans, 2000: 65).

On fragility

The understanding of the tragic hero as a suffering hero is what properly contextualizes Aristotle's formal definition of tragedy, according to Nussbaum, who has reinterpreted his tragic theory through the lens of fragility (Ruprecht, 1989: 591). For Nussbaum, Aristotle's theory of tragedy rests less on the plot and the hero, as many commentators would have it, but more on the impact of fortune and luck *on* the hero.

As readers of her work will be aware, Nussbaum's concerns have been wide-ranging but in the realm of political theory and political economy, her "capabilities approach" has garnered much attention (Alexander, 2016; Nussbaum, 2001a, 2013). What is less remarked upon is the connection between her political theory and her earlier work on tragedy. Even at that early stage, Nussbaum suggests that the normative argument of Aristotle's theory of tragedy can be captured in a single takeaway: "We need to be born with adequate capacities, to live in fostering natural and social circumstances, to stay clear of abrupt catastrophe, to develop confirming associations with other human beings" (Nussbaum, 2001b: 1). Tragedy begs the following questions:

> To what extent can we distinguish between what is up to the world and what is up to us, when assessing a human life? To what extent must we insist on finding these distinctions, if we are to go on praising as we praise? And how can we improve this situation, making progress by placing the most important things, things such as personal achievement, politics and love, under our control?
>
> (Nussbaum, 2001b; 2)

It is clear then that Nussbaum's Aristotle is an ethical Aristotle, and for her, the proper reading of Aristotle's tragic theory is to think it through what in the previous chapter I called "constrained" models of agency after Talal Asad. This is clear when examining a widely discussed rhetorical image from *The Fragility of Goodness*. It is that of the agent and the plant. As Nussbaum puts it, in first person, "I must constantly choose among competing and apparently incommensurable goods and that circumstances may force me to a position in which I cannot help being false to something or doing some wrong." In some cases, an "event that simply happens to me may, without my consent, alter my life" (Nussbaum, 2001b: 5). Like a plant, the agent is subject to "everyday facts." Whether the agent survives or thrives has much to do with "external contingency" (Nussbaum, 2001b: 7) much in the way of a plant. An agent must also be tended to. Otherwise, it is really a matter of "luck," and what the world outside of the agent brings to and interacts with the "ungovernable parts of the human being's internal makeup," including its appetites, feelings and emotions. "We are dependent upon the world and upon other people; as often as not, they both fail us" (Ruprecht, 1989: 591).

According to Nussbaum, Greek tragedy demonstrates good people "being ruined" as a result of things that just happen to them. But it also shows that good people do bad things. These bad things do not originate from their innate ethical character but rather because of "circumstances." In these instances, there is some sort of constraint on the hero-victim—whether it is physical or a form of intractable ignorance. This can take the form of a tragic flaw, which "takes in a variety of important goings-wrong that do not result from settled badness" (Nussbaum, 2001b: 382). Hence, hamartia is also a constraint and can be considered a part of *tuche*. Tuche not only refers to forces from without but also from within. It can "[work] through the agent's system of beliefs in others...through the internal ungoverned tuche of the passions" (Nussbaum, 2001b: 382). As one critic of Nussbaum writes, "fragility is...both inside us and outside us, an essential component of our being-together, yet also a brute fact, an impersonal element of the world in which we live" (Ruprecht, 1989: 595).

It is hamartia that evokes a certain kind of emotional response from the spectator, which is pity. Aristotle's identification of pity, Nussbaum asserts, is also a kind of anthropocentric ethic as it is "distinct from moral censure or blame" (Nussbaum, 2001b: 383). It can only come out of a "belief that the person did not deserve the suffering." If we were to see the suffering as somehow "brought on by the agent's own bad choices," we would not pity (Nussbaum, 2001b: 383):

> The central tragic emotion depends on some controversial beliefs about the situation of human goodness in the world: that luck is seriously powerful, that it is possible for a good person to suffer serious and undeserved harm, that this possibility extends to human beings generally.
> (Nussbaum, 2001b: 384–385)

In Nussbaum's telling, Aristotle understands pity as dependent on a form of identification based on fear. "What we pity when it happens to another," she writes, is precisely something "we fear... it might happen to ourselves." This view of pity assumes "the perception of one's own vulnerability, one's similarity to the sufferer, then pity and fear will almost always occur together." Fear, in Aristotle, is connected to the expectation of future harm or pain (Nussbaum, 2001b: 387). To even feel fear is to express the capacity to identify with the hero-victim. Therefore, as Nussbaum reminds us, the hero "cannot be too perfectly good," since it is the "intermediate" status of its personage that is important to the audience's pity and fear. "Thus Oedipus' shortness of temper," Nussbaum notes, "is not the cause of his decline; but it is one thing about Oedipus that makes him a character with whom we can identify" (Nussbaum, 2001b: 387). This is not really a tragic flaw. And it is here that we can see the crux of Aristotle's theory of tragedy, and its value proposition regarding the heightening of human self-understanding. It is by moving the audience to respond to these emotions that tragedy occasions the "recognition or acknowledgement of the worldly conditions upon our aspirations to goodness" (Nussbaum, 2001b: 390).

This recognition is what provides catharsis, the famed notion that Nussbaum insists does not mean "intellectual clarification" but simply "clarification." While seemingly a semantic difference, Nussbaum's reading of Aristotle presumes a more "generous view of the ways in which we come to know ourselves." Behind this is the reclamation of emotion and the assertion of emotional responses as potentially giving us "access to a truer and deeper level of ourselves, to values and commitments that have been concealed beneath defensive ambition or rationalization" (Nussbaum, 2001b: 390). And it is on these points—not only about "the mechanisms of clarification" but also about "what, in the good person, clarification is" (Nussbaum, 2001b: 391)—that Aristotle, in Nussbaum's estimation, differs most drastically from Plato. In reading the tragic hero in such a way, Aristotle maintains the basic principle of tragedy as Nussbaum sees it: "the vulnerability of human lives to fortune, the mutability of our circumstances and our passions, the existence of conflicts among our commitments" (Nussbaum, 2001b: 13).

Conclusion

Seeing tragedy, and specifically, the tragic hero in this way provides a chief lesson. As David Roochnick describes it:

> Tragedy discloses the limits of human reason, of virtue, of heroism, of love. It reveals what occurs at the juncture, often the collision, of human striving with the boundaries of efficacy.
>
> (Roochnik, 1988: 285)

What would it mean to transpose the idea of the limit to social science?

One significant challenge would be that of agent responsibility. As Charlotte Witt notes, "Aristotle's theory of agent responsibility renders the relationship between the characters in a tragedy and what they have done problematic at least for those plays where *hamartia* plays a central role in the plot" (Witt, 2005: 70). For instance, what if, as in the case of Oedipus, the hero-victim unknowingly tries to help his city-state by answering the riddle that seems to be plaguing it, "he is committing the actions that will eventually lead to his own downfall." As Witt notes, "Although the fact that Oedipus acted unknowingly removes what he did from the realm of voluntary action, it does not follow that he did not cause his own downfall" (Witt, 2005: 73). But there must be some way of discussing this with greater nuance. And thus, Witt suggests an analytic distinction between two kinds of agent responsibility: accountability and culpability (Witt, 2005: 71).

Accountability refers to the action as a private matter. In large part, it is being accountable to oneself. It is being responsible for one's actions and their consequences—unintended or not. Culpability on the other hand is public, even legalistic. It is the model of agent responsibility that is suited to "rewards and punishments, and praise and blame" (Witt, 2005: 71). Likewise, Witt offers up two kinds of voluntary actions: errors (*hamartia*) and misfortunes (*atuxema*). But both analytic distinctions are rooted in what Witt calls "conditions." In order to measure the degree of agent responsibility, there are two conditions—causal and epistemic—that a voluntary action must satisfy. The former, causal, can be understood as demonstrated by hamartia, whereas the latter, epistemic, is represented by atuxema. Oedipus unknowingly kills his own father. While he does cause his own downfall, he lacked the knowledge of his own identity (Witt, 2005: 73). Thus, according to Witt, hamartia only

> ...satisfies the causal but not the epistemic condition for voluntary action. The error is an error of fact and circumstance, and not a flaw in character. Indeed, in Aristotle's view, the audience response to the agent's reversal of fortune depends in large part on the fact that the agent is good; like us (so we can identify) but a bit better.
>
> (Witt, 2005: 79)

What happens to the hero must not be something beyond the realm of possibility for the audience. As Nussbaum puts it, there must be a "judgement of similar possibilities." Pity, Nussbaum quotes Aristotle, concerns misfortunes that a person might expect to suffer:

> Pity does indeed involve empathetic identification as one component: for in estimating the seriousness of the suffering, it seems important, if not sufficient, to attempt to take its measure as the person herself measures it. But even then, in the temporary act of identification, one is always aware of one's own separateness from the sufferer—it is for another, and not oneself, that one feels; and one is aware both of the bad lot of the sufferer and of the fact that it is, right now, not one's own.
>
> (Nussbaum, 2001b: 35)

The crucial point is that the spectator has "possibilities and vulnerabilities to those of the sufferer." There is "some sort of community between myself and the other." This "commonness" as Nussbaum puts it is the heart of agency in Aristotelian poetics (Nussbaum, 2001b: 36). The hero is a "worthy person, whose distress does not stem from his own deliberate badness" (Nussbaum, 2001b: 37).

In Nussbaum's neo-Aristotelian view as well as in psychoanalytic theory, and in Rank specifically, the hero's heroism consists of simply living and being subject to luck and fortune. The agent—in this case the "hero"—is also undoubtedly a plant. Unlike that of mythology, the hero of tragic drama is relatable, and thus to be identified with, rather than cultishly worshipped; we humans are heroes as well as the victims. We all err because we are all subject to *tuche*.

References

Alexander, J.M., 2016. *Capabilities and Social Justice: The Political Philosophy of Amartya Sen and Martha Nussbaum*. London: Routledge.

Becker, E., 1997. *The Denial of Death*. New York, NY: Free Press.

Bernays, J., 2004. On Catharsis: From Fundamentals of Aristotle's Lost Essay on the 'Effect of Tragedy' (1857). *American Imago*, 61 (3), 319–341.

Brooks, D., 2021. The Awesome Importance of Imagination. *The New York Times*, 12 Nov.

Burke, K., 1959. On Catharsis, or Resolution. *The Kenyon Review*, 21 (3), 337–375.

Critchley, S., 2019. *Tragedy, the Greeks, and Us*. New York, NY: Pantheon.

Eagleton, T., 2009. *Sweet Violence: The Idea of the Tragic*. Malden, MA: Blackwell.

Eagleton, T., 2020. *Tragedy*. New Haven, CT: Yale University Press.

Fernandez-Armesto, F., 2021. Boris Johnson Is a Classical Greek Hero: The Audience Is Waiting for Him to Fall. *The Telegraph*, 18 Dec.

Gans, E., 2000. Form Against Content: René Girard's Theory of Tragedy. *Revista Portuguesa de Filosofia*, 56 (1/2), 53–65.

Glassberg, R., 2017. Uses of Hamartia, Flaw, and Irony in Oedipus Tyrannus and King Lear. *Philosophy and Literature*, 41 (1), 201–206.

Kaufmann, W., 1980. *From Shakespeare to Existentialism*. Princeton, NJ: Princeton University Press.

Keesey, D., 1978. On Some Recent Interpretations of Catharsis. *The Classical World*, 72 (4), 193–205.

Mulvey, L., 1988. Visual Pleasure and Narrative Cinema. In: C. Penley, ed. *Feminism and Film Theory*. New York, NY; London: Routledge; BFI, 57–68.

Nussbaum, M.C., 2001a. *Women and Human Development: The Capabilities Approach*. Cambridge: Cambridge University Press.

Nussbaum, M.C., 2001b. *The Fragility of Goodness: Luck and Ethics in Greek Tragedy and Philosophy*. 2nd edition. Cambridge: Cambridge University Press.

Nussbaum, M.C., 2013. *Creating Capabilities: The Human Development Approach*. Cambridge, MA: Harvard University Press.

Porter, J.I., 2015. Jacob Bernays and the Catharsis of Modernity. In: J. Billings and M. Leonard, eds. *Tragedy and the Idea of Modernity*. Oxford: Oxford University Press, 15–41.

Rank, O., 2004. *The Myth of the Birth of the Hero: A Psychological Exploration of Myth*. Expanded&updated edition. Baltimore, MD: Johns Hopkins University Press.

Reeves, C.H., 1952. The Aristotelian Concept of the Tragic Hero. *The American Journal of Philology*, 73 (2), 172–188.

Roochnik, D.L., 1988. The Tragic Philosopher: A Critique of Martha Nussbaum. *Ancient Philosophy*, 8 (2), 285–295.

Ruprecht, L.A., 1989. Nussbaum on Tragedy and the Modern Ethos. *Soundings: An Interdisciplinary Journal*, 72 (4), 589–605.

Seif, N.G., 1984. Otto Rank: On the Nature of the Hero. *American Imago*, 41 (4), 373–384.

Surin, K., 2005. Theology and Marxism: The Tragic and Tragi-Comic. *Literature and Theology*, 19 (2), 112–131.

Weber, S., 2000. Psychoanalysis and Theatricality. *Parallax*, 6 (3), 29–48.

Witt, C., 2005. Tragic Error and Agent Responsibility. *Philosophic Exchange*, 35(1), 69–86.

4

MODERN TRAGEDY AND ITS SUBJECTS

Shakespeare, Freud, and post-Christian metaphysics

Introduction

Many commentators characterize Shakespeare's work as the literary inauguration of modernity. By this, they usually mean to refer to the phenomenon of individualism. The famous phrase of Harold Bloom's is that Shakespeare "invented the human." This of course is a much stronger claim, rhetorically at least, than the suggestion that Shakespeare's work helped found the idea of the modern. But in actual fact, these arguments are linked.

Bloom's claim is perhaps the most well-known and highly circulated. For Bloom, Shakespeare's work represents the birth of a certain kind of human and the universalism of the inner self. "What Shakespeare invents," he writes, "are ways of representing human changes, alterations not only caused by flaws and by decay but effected by the will as well, and by the will's temporal vulnerabilities" (Bloom, 1999: 2). This way of representing changes to the will has become somewhat of a "secular Scripture." Only the Bible, Bloom notes, has a "circumference" like that of Shakespeare. Shakespeare's works, he states, are "simply the fixed center of the Western canon" (Bloom, 1999: 3). At the core of this is "the idea of the Western character, of the self as a moral agent," which Shakespeare, in line with Homer, Plato, Sophocles, the Bible, and Augustine, articulates what we would call "personality." This, Bloom asserts, is the reason for his "perpetual pervasiveness" (Bloom, 1999: 4).

Like many Shakespeare critics before and after, Bloom puts forth the figure of Hamlet as a model of this kind of individual. The self, in *Hamlet*, is "an abyss." Hamlet is caught between "clashing realizations." We can relate to Hamlet because "being mortal, we too cofound knowledge with knowledge" (Bloom, 1999: 7). Bloom goes so far as to claim that "Shakespeare is the original psychologist, Freud the belated rhetorician" (Bloom, 1999: 174). What Bloom points out in Shakespeare's plays is the "representation of human nature" oriented around

DOI: 10.4324/9781003110859-5

human action, especially "the way such action frequently was antithetical to human words" (Bloom, 1999: 722) due to passion and desire (Bloom, 1999: 733). For Bloom, the dissonance between desire, words, and actions in Shakespeare's representation of the human that is so powerfully modern.

Yet Bloom's argument has far more in common with the comments of Kaufmann, who describes Freud as something of a "Great Emancipator." Psychoanalytic theory's articulation of the tragic failings of human beings affords a view of "criminals" and "madmen" as not "devils in disguise." The basic lesson of Freud, from this perspective, is that "the great are no different from the small." Or perhaps more radically, no one is great (Kaufmann, 1960: 469).

But this, according to Kaufmann, is infused with a Nietzschean "reversal" or "transvaluation of values." Not only does Freud suggest that no one is great but that human beings are great *in their failure.*" This "tragic virtue" is exemplified in both *Hamlet* and *King Lear* (Kaufmann, 1960: 470). In giving these two examples, Kaufmann connects the tragic orientation of Shakespeare and Freud in a more specific way than Bloom by suggesting that they overlap in their admiration of "nobility," defined not in the stratified sense of cast or class or worldly success but rather as "dignity," a theme that comes up in the modern tragedies of Ibsen and Miller.

In spite of this pairing of Shakespeare and Freud, however, Kaufmann's final analysis of Shakespeare's plays is that they are "not primarily psychological" (Kaufmann, 1980: 33). He says this too about Aeschylus and Sophocles, whose works he claims, are more strongly "*anti*-psychological" (Kaufmann, 1980: 34 Emphasis added). By this, Kaufmann is suggesting that the ancient Greek tragedies and those of Shakespeare, while different in so many ways, still share a common feature of being "supra-psychological" (Kaufmann, 1980: 37). The religious dimension of the plays of Aeschylus and Sophocles betrays a "cosmic significance" of the plays' characters and actions. Likewise, the presence of the chorus most often has a pedagogic effect, defining Athenian citizenship, producing and reproducing "the ideology of civic community" (Hall, 1997: 95) by expressing the citizenry's "fears, hopes, questions, and judgments the feelings of the spectators who make up the civic community" (Vernant and Vidal-Naquet, 1990: 34). In *Othello*, for instance, Iago's motivations are psychological but have to do with the *social* roots of his *ressentiment.* Othello's race, status, and military rank—all social things—drive Iago's vengeance. Shakespeare's plays do not contain an obvious inevitability like that of the Greeks and also provide a "wealth of psychological detail…restricted to the hero." This could be read either as a consequence of Shakespeare's modernity or a symptom of it. Nevertheless, his plays "mark the end" of a "unified world" of gods and other superhuman forces. They show the individual thrown into a world much like ours, "on the verge of disintegration" (Kaufmann, 1980: 41).

But the milieu of Greek tragedy was not exactly as Kaufmann describes. There was a shift from the pre-Sophoclean Homeric society of "given and predetermined place" of human beings in society to that of the fifth century BCE, which included a recasting of social roles regarding duty and work. It is a muddying up of the "clear understanding of what function a person performs and what actions are required to fulfill that function." According to Malcolm Woodfield, this period is characterized by the acceptance of the divorce between oneself and one's actions. "One is not adequately expressed in one's actions...we have hidden depths" (Woodfield, 1990: 198):

> The emergence of Greek tragedy coincides with the flourishing of the Athenian city-state and is a part of the social, political and legal structure of the "polis." As part of this process, the individual emerges as responsible, as an agent subject to law.
>
> (Woodfield, 1990: 198)

While in my view, the emergence of the individual as subject-to-law is questionable given the work of Vidal-Naquet and Vernant, the larger point that "this process of democratization and its new concepts of individual rights and responsibilities" in the formation of the polis "has important parallels in the transition of Shakespeare's society from a Christian feudal to a secular, capitalist culture and economy" stands.

Woodfield rightly points out that Greek tragedy explored a specific form of individual, that is, the citizen of the polis, and in particular the conflicts within them arising from the renewed secularity of tragic drama. Myths no longer carried onto-cosmological weight but were now "source material" for what was clearly a staged production, that is, a representation. When viewed from this secular framework, the hero of the old myth was no longer a model but a challenge to the bedrock institutions of the polis.

It is on this basis that Woodfield claims that the hero is "the paradigmatic figure of modernity," responsible for, yet incapable of resolving, the dilemmas facing him. The hero in Greek tragedy is not sufficiently autonomous to be self-sufficient. He lacks *metis*, whose model traditionally has been Odysseus (Woodfield, 1990: 200). Oedipus, to the contrary, practices not so much an "intelligence," which is sometimes how *metis* is translated, but, to the contrary, enacts something like a "conscious improvisation as a means of survival" (Woodfield, 1990: 202). The modern, tragic hero's habitus is, as Woodfield tellingly puts it, to "self-fashion" (Woodfield, 1990: 202).

The description of the modern hero as needing to "self-fashion" is to recapitulate the language used by Stephen Greenblatt, one of the most influential scholars of the Renaissance, and Shakespeare in particular. In the early modern period, according to Greenblatt, a major "change took place in the intellectual, social, psychological and aesthetic structures that govern the generation of identities" (Greenblatt, 2005: 1). Specifically, "selves" that could be fashioned had emerged.

A self, Greenblatt writes, is constituted by "a sense of personal order, a characteristic mode of address to the world, a structure of bounded desires." It comprises "elements of deliberate shaping in the formation and expression of identity." In the 16th century, he argues, there was "a new stress on the executive power of the will and also a sustained and assault upon the will."

In other words, within this dialectic, there was an "increased awareness of self-consciousness about the fashioning of human identity as a manipulable, artful process" (Greenblatt, 2005: 2).

The idea of fashioning, that is, to impose upon a person or physical form, comes from Christian, more specifically Augustinian, notions of modeling oneself after Christ. This seems like a rather straightforward ethic. The idea is to construct a "distinctive personality, a characteristic address to the world, a consistent mode of perceiving and behavior" (Greenblatt, 2005: 2) in the shape of Jesus Christ. Yet, as Greenblatt notes, it can, in fact, be anxiety-inducing. We need to be more like Christ but how? The question of "What would Jesus Do?" results in an uncertainty much like the one described by Weber's reading of the Calvinist *certitudo salutis*. While one is theoretically "predestined" to be saved or not, one nevertheless adheres to Christian values just to be sure (Weber, 2005). To imitate Christ, that is, to fashion oneself in the image of Christ is to comport oneself in a specific way as it pertains to manners and demeanor. It can even extend to what today would be called performativity, which Greenblatt characterizes as "a deceptive adherence to outward ceremony" (Greenblatt, 2005: 3).

This turning of the self to a "cultural artifact" can be said to be "the beginnings of self-representation" (Greenblatt, 2005: 3). But this self-representation of the Renaissance period can hardly be understood as "pure, unfettered subjectivity" (Greenblatt, 2005: 256). To the contrary, Greenblatt argues, "self-fashioning is in effect the Renaissance version of…control mechanisms, the cultural system of meanings that creates specific individuals by governing the passage from abstract potential to concrete historical embodiment" (Greenblatt, 2005: 4). Yet there is a considerable degree to which these selves are able to "transform given materials into one's own scenario." Greenblatt rather helpfully calls this "improvisation," giving detail to the process of self-representation. Fashioning the self, he argues, depends on "the ability and willingness to play a role, to transform oneself, if only for a brief period and with mental reservations to another." The phrase Greenblatt uses is "the divorce between the tongue and heart" (Greenblatt, 2005: 227) in the self. The Renaissance, according to Greenblatt, gives rise to a certain "mode of behavior" rooted in "above all a sense that one is not forever fixed in a single, divinely sanctioned identity" (Greenblatt, 2005: 235) yet is "remarkably unfree" (Greenblatt, 2005: 256) that we can see in the characters across Shakespeare's tragic oeuvre.

Some critics even claim that Shakespearean subjectivity is "the governing model for subjectivity in literature *after* Shakespeare" (Fineman, 1984: 299 Emphasis added). As mentioned earlier, *Hamlet* is identified by one scholar as "the birth of romantic individualism" (van Oort, 2006: 319). This is for reasons that have not only to do with intellectual history, in particular, the effect of German Romanticism's inauguration of *Hamlet* as a quintessentially "modern work" but also because of the potentialities of juxtaposing Oedipus and Hamlet (van Oort, 2006: 320). Oedipus, in its Romantic articulation, is a hero. He suffers for things he did unknowingly. He is "totally ignorant." Hamlet, however, has a different relationship to suffering. He "internalizes" representations of what his uncle has done (killing his father and marrying his mother). For Oedipus, as the classical hero, the torment comes from without *and* within. He is banished and also injures himself for transgressions that are social. For Hamlet, the modern hero, the suffering only comes from within. He is haunted by the death of his father and fantasizes "scenes by which he attempts to relieve himself of his ethical duty to revenge" (van Oort, 2006: 323).

For many scholars, it is Christianity that accounts for such a shift from the classical hero, who arguably falls victim to misfortune and superhuman forces and thus acts unknowingly, to the modern protagonist that "gets in his own head," as the contemporary phrase goes. Specifically, they point to a Christian "moral sentiment," not Christianity writ large. Karl Jaspers thought that "a Christian is bound to misunderstand" Shakespeare because "he shows man as he really is" (Jaspers, 1953: 39). Shakespeare's work, one could argue, is "naturalistic" in the sense that the tragedies are no longer driven by conflict "between the individual and the overpowering." As Robert Hall describes it, "the element of mystery and ineffability and wonder implicit in the Presocratic view of physis underlying the mythic structure of the Aeschylean-Sophoclean tragedy" falls away. This mythic structure that animates the interior and exterior is replaced by the simple "unfolding action" (Hall, 1960: 106). After all, the universe in Shakespeare as Jaspers puts it is made up of "purely secular stage" (Jaspers, 1953: 30). The role of Christianity in the history of tragedy is as a bridge in the kind of self that it posits, a position consistent with that of Greenblatt and Tracy, but with a specific difference. For Greenblatt, self-fashioning emerges not from Christian theology per se but a Christian *ethic* of comportment. Thus, the tragic heroes of Shakespeare's tragedies can be said to embody a *post*-Christian self.

Shakespeare's secular universe of the self

A "universe without absolutes" is not an entirely wrong description of the Renaissance. As Jonathan Dollimore makes clear, God was "in trouble" then and Shakespeare most certainly reflected the tenuous situation of Christian ethics during the Elizabethan period. "Obeying the old rules," as Franco Moretti puts it, "which are the only ones [the tragic hero] knows, the world can only fall apart" (Dollimore, 2003: liii). But what *exactly* accounts for the old rules no longer working for the self? For Dollimore, it was a crisis in "the Elizabethan world picture," the set of metaphysical groundings, or chronotope, as well as the social order that is believed to be a divinely designed that would allow the self to operate in the world. In the Renaissance, this metaphysics was synonymous with the Christian God.

To suggest that God in this period was in trouble is to suggest that this larger "metaphysical scheme of things" was undergoing a transformation. This, as Dollimore asserts, includes "man." The reason for this is that "in

Christianity," as he writes, "identity is metaphysically constituted." Identity is "[derived] from and is dependent upon, divine and natural law." Human beings are "an effect of God" in the sense that they are part of "creation," understood as "in accordance to a certain plan." This extends beyond the human realm to nature.

Dollimore chooses to call this "providentalist" to underscore the fact that contained in the work of Shakespeare are early traces of a deconstruction of God. It must be said that the point here is not to suggest that the "death of God" theology of the 1960s was prefigured in the Renaissance resulting in a widespread anti-clerical movement. Instead, what he, and his fellow *literary* (as distinct from the anthropological) cultural materialists (Milner, 2002), point out was a general trend toward the secular in the form of a de-metaphysicalization that specifically resulted in the "decentering" of what Foucault calls "the figure of Man" (Foucault, 1992).

For Dollimore, "to deconstruct God is to decenter man" due to the fact that this relationship between the universal and particular is specific to Western metaphysics. In Shakespeare's works themselves, there is "instability in the constituting structure of necessity" or fate. And it is this instability of fate, a seeming oxymoron, that gets fed back into a subject constituted by the very unstable nature of necessity—and vice versa. "In plainer terms," Dollimore argues, "in subverting the idea of a divinely ordered universe, these [works] also subverted its corollary: the unified human subject supposedly positioned at the center of the universe" (Dollimore, 2003: lx). Elizabethan tragedy challenged this "amalgam of religious belief, aesthetic idealism and ideological myth" by "disclosing" it as a "misrepresentation," and "seizing on and exposing its contradictions and inconsistencies and offering alternative ways of understanding social and political processes."

In Shakespeare, this is accomplished via a mode of portraying characters that approximate the Foucaultian notion of the individual as an "effect of power," rather than the Christian essentialism that was commonplace prior to the 17th century in England (Dollimore, 2003: 154). The "soul" as the indivisible "unit" of essential identity, can be found in the thought of Augustine and Aquinas. For Augustine, "man" [sic] was constituted by sin whereas for Aquinas, man is rational, able to obtain a knowledge of the world governed by "natural law, itself grounded in God's eternal law" (Dollimore, 2003: 161). Rationality, according to a Christian essentialist logic, gave evidence to human being's divinity. It was the proof that linked creation to its creator. Yet, when examining Sheakespeare's tragedies, there are hardly any characters that embody such a rationality. There is, as Dollimore describes it, an "absence of character consistency." The heroes of his tragic works do not demonstrate any sort of "spiritual or psychological unity" (Dollimore, 2003: 176). They are "remarkably unfree, the ideological product of the relations of power in a particular society" (Dollimore, 2003: 181).

Take, for instance, the example of Brutus in *Julius Caesar*. As William Cain notes, the dominant reading of Shakespeare singles out Caesar's best friend as providing adept representations of the inner life of characters. Frequently, critics point to Brutus as "the first tragic hero with any significant interior life to appear in English drama." While he is believed to be a key figure in Shakespeare's artistic development, most of the critical attention has centered on his soliloquys. It is in the soliloquy, in which one is speaking to oneself, where "interiority, inwardness, inner life, consciousness" can be located. For Cain, this is an incomplete view. Inner life in Shakespeare's plays is made up of omission and evasion. The characters are *not* like us, as Cain suggests. They do not "think like us." Brutus is not "a person, a human being with an interior life akin to our own" (Cain, 2017: 41). When looking at Brutus' soliloquy in Act 2, Scene 1, when he is visited by Cassius and the other conspirators, Brutus is not making a decision to kill Caesar then and there. In fact, he has already made the decision even before delivering the soliloquy as his oath to Rome is his top priority. It is, as Cain rightly points out, a *post-facto* rationalization (Cain, 2017: 42). After all, he does begin with "He must die. Now, as for me, I don't have any personal reason to remove him, except for the general welfare of Rome."

For Cain, this is what adds credence to the argument that Shakespearean renditions of subjectivity are more effects than causes. It is precisely that Brutus' soliloquy does not adhere to a rationalist view of inner life that is transparent and self-evident. Instead, what makes it so powerful is because "we do what Brutus does," as he puts it:

> ...the decision precedes the argument; the decision is not the result of any thinking we have done but rather antedates it. We might try to conceive of this lack or absence as a part of interior life, as a feature of inwardness. More to the point, we do not know how our decision, our choice, transpires or where it comes from. This is what Shakespeare is intimating, a form of showing by not showing.
>
> (Cain, 2017: 42)

Not knowing our decisions or choices, and indeed the sources from which they emerge, is arguably the bedrock of Freud's theory of consciousness. Like Brutus, the individual, according to Freud, does not "decide" but rather "succumbs to" a choice. The reality of tragic characters not deciding or choosing to do anything but rather having a choice "happen," extends to other works, including *Hamlet*. And, thus, unsurprisingly Cain maintains that Hamlet's soliloquys do not provide insight into what he is thinking. We know what he is saying but "not what he is thinking." There is no disclosure of interiority but rather "the exclusion of the reader and spectator from it, and…from it of Hamlet himself" (Cain, 2017: 42). The language and the organization of the action all work to "forestall knowledge of Hamlet's interior life" (Cain, 2017: 45). For the Shakespearean tragic hero,

> ...something happened, and at that moment it was a surprise, not explicable, without thought on his part. He has changed, or at least his perspective

on life has shifted. No thought or self-willed action made this come about. The most precise form for the matter is to say that it somehow happened.

(Cain, 2017: 46)

This presents a rather ambivalent relationship to Christian understandings of selfhood—both in the way that Dollimore frames Christianity through providentialism and the way that Greenblatt sees "self-fashioning" as post-Christian ideology. On the one hand, the very command of the self to alter him- or herself emerges out of the Augustinian imperative to be more like Christ. Yet, this would, one assumes, require some degree of self-knowledge—a way of identifying what to alter and how. Adhering to this would assume semblance of self-sovereignty, that a stable self can scrutinize itself, as if it were a "cultural artifact" in order to figure out what to change and how to do so. This is an idea that is somewhat foreign to Christianity as the self is never ultimately his own within, for instance, a providentialist theology. To believe as much could be considered a form of blasphemy. Somehow, Shakespeare's tragedies retain the truth of both tendencies, embodying what Raymond Williams would call a "post-Christian metaphysic."

The post-Christian metaphysic

The post-Christian metaphysic is Williams' way of discussing what he calls "secularization" of the tragic, which began in the Renaissance and culminated in modern, liberal society. The secularization of the form equates to "the emptying of content behind a retention of terms" (Williams, 2013). Whereas in the neo-classical period, say, around the 17th century, tragedy focuses on the historical, during the Renaissance, however, tragedy emphasized on more recent themes, namely "the falls of famous men" (Williams, 2013: 25). The exalted rank of these heroes operates as a means of broadening its representative quality and as a means of identification. As Williams sees it, their stature is necessary to demonstrate that no one was "exempt from the turns of Fortune" (Williams, 2013: 26). There is nothing about one's nobility that somehow immunizes him from tragedy. It is, in the work of Shakespeare, a "matter of behavior, rather than either a metaphysical condition or metaphysical fault."

Williams argues that this is reflective of the emphasis on human dignity, across social strata that begins in the modern period. This coincides with "the progressive internalization of tragic cause" in the works of Shakespeare, among others during this time. If the cause of tragedy is brought about not by one's place in the world but by one's own, very human, decisions, then any spectator—regardless of social background—too can experience it. Even someone so high up can fall so low by erring, on his own. In making the hero more relatable by democratizing suffering, the dignity of every human being's capacity to suffer and to relate to suffering is maintained by both admiration and commiseration with a noble tragic hero.

The moral question, of the nature and therefore the effect of a tragic action, becomes a question in abstracted human nature: that is to say, not an inquiry into a specific response which must then necessarily include the action to which the response is made, but an attempt to find reasons for an assumed general form of behavior.

(Williams, 2013: 27)

For Williams, neo-classical tragedy was simply an aristocratic recapitulation of Greek tragedy. Elizabethan tragedy, to the contrary, was unique in its inheritance of order with previous forms but with "elements of a new humanism" (Williams, 2013: 30). It is this progressive injection of what Williams identifies as humanism, which, from this perspective, is the proxy or symptom of "secularization":

What has mainly to be shown, if the historical development of the idea of tragedy is to be fully understood, is the very complicated process of secularization. In one sense all drama after the Renaissance is secular, and the only fully religious tragedy we have is Greek. Yet the decisive factor is probably not this immediate context, in institutions, but the wider context, in beliefs. Elizabethan drama is thoroughly secular in its immediate practice, but undoubtedly retains a Christian consciousness.

(Williams, 2013: 30)

A key point in the "secularization of tragedy" thesis is that it refers to both the "loosening of Christian belief" as well as the rereading of the Greek form. More specifically, Williams points to a certain relationship between these two tendencies. Over the course of the 19th and 20th centuries, he notes, the move away from Christian belief has meant the contemporaneous "systematization" of Greek tragic philosophy—namely, the ideas of Fate, Necessity, and the nature of the gods (Williams, 2013: 17). For example, one major innovation of the medieval period was the relegating of Fortune to a space "outside any general and common human destiny." The radical dualism of the human being and the world meant that the human individual stood apart from it, marking a departure from the Greek idea of tragedy wherein individuals were only individuals as "a member of a group or kind rather than a separable and unique being" (Williams, 2013: 20).

Evidence of this "unique being" can be found as early as in neo-classicism, where there was a growing emphasis on rational morality. This is perhaps clearest in Racine and Corneille, whose works Francis Fergusson describes as "the drama of reason, for it bears a relation to Rationalism, from Descartes to Kant, similar to that of Sophoclean drama to the philosophy of Aristotle" (Fergusson, 1948: 188). In linking tragic action to something *within* the human being, there was a decidedly human rationale for suffering, rather than some kind of external, supernatural force (Williams, 2013: 31). Later on, in the 19th and 20th centuries, a new emphasis on moral rationality brought forth the possibility of redemption.

After all, if tragedy ensues as a result of a decision solely within the control of the individual ego, then, there would be, logically, the possibility of fixing the situation. This slight shift is quite significant as it means that "change was possible," even "when error had been demonstrated" (Williams, 2013: 31). A new, "poetic justice" is inaugurated with the ethic of "the bad will suffer and the good will be happy." Tragedy in this vein becomes less about misfortune and more about individual missteps; suffering was the logical result of human error and thus, happiness, was "a consequence of virtue." Tragic heroes, therefore, are capable of recognizing and changing. The spectators are meant to be able to do the same (Williams, 2013: 31). For Williams, this expresses a particularly *Christian* understanding of suffering, which views it as an outgrowth of evil, for which the only answer is repentance. The proper response to suffering is redemption. To phrase it differently, suffering becomes a step toward redemption.

This is especially evident in "liberal tragedy," of which the work of Ibsen is most exemplary. A man stands at the center of such a tragedy, "at once aspiring and being defeated." The tension, even conflict, between this individual and the forces that destroy him is explored via the language of psychology (Williams, 1963: 54). The work of Ibsen among others finds the "tragic flaw" within the psyche of characters rather than in their actions. The foregrounding of *personal* destiny is an inheritance from the Renaissance. In both Marlowe and Shakespeare, there is the active shaping of a familiar structure: "an individual man, from his own aspirations, from his own nature, sets out an action that leads him to tragedy" (Williams, 1963: 55).

Williams bluntly assesses this as "a rejection" or even "an evident loss...of the human connection at anything more than a private level." This anti-social tragedy that focuses on the individual hero, he calls, rather ironically, "humanitarian." The basis for this description is simple. In the 18th century, tragedy embodied emergent middle-classness and emphasized pity, keeping within the Aristotelian framework. Pity was the affective mechanism for sympathy, a mark of this growing "humanitarianism." As Williams goes on to explain, humanitarianism "expresses sympathy and pity between private persons but tacitly excludes any positive conception of society, and thence any clear view of order or justice" (Williams, 1963: 58). In this process of embourgeoisement, tragedy undergoes a permanent shift away from the enchanted world of Greek tragedy to the individualized, alienated "heroic tragedy" (Williams, 1963: 58), with the classical categories such as rank turning into class. For Williams, this transformation meant "a new definition of tragedy." Rank was associated with order and connection; class was the basis of separation "within an amorphous society." The modern tragic hero faces woe and distress privately (Williams, 1963: 58). He was increasingly "buffered," to use Taylor's language.

Yet, the sources of distress are social. The hero butts up against the conventions of a false society (Williams, 1963: 60). This is certainly the case in the work of Ibsen, where the hero usually interprets the world in oppositional terms, "full of lies and compromises and dead positions." But the struggle against it is fraught and frustrating as the "tragic recognition" is usually the acknowledgment that he "belongs to this world and has its destructive inheritance himself" (Williams, 1963: 62). There is then a movement in liberal tragedy, from the hero as "individual liberator" waging a fight against society, to the self that becomes "self-enclosed, guilty, [and] isolated." He, over the course of the work, is recast as is "his own victim" (Williams, 1963: 64). And thus, the "lesson" offered to the spectators of this sort of tragedy is not tragic resignation but rather to "die fighting" (Williams, 1963: 63).

For a Marxist critic such as Williams, the issue with this form of tragedy is obvious. This sort of play is simply not "social enough," putting forth a private ethic rooted in pity and sympathy (Williams, 1963: 59):

> All we can say, perhaps, reflecting on Ibsen's tragedy, is that the deadlock reached there, the heroic deadlock in which men die still struggling to climb, was indeed necessary. There is no way out, there is only an inevitable tragic consciousness, while desire is seen as essentially individual.
>
> (Williams, 1963: 64)

Liberal tragedy then is a step removed from Greek tragedy in several senses. For one, Greek tragic action was not rooted in individuals nor in individual psychology. Rather, it is, "rooted in history, and not a human history alone." Williams continues:

> Its thrust comes, not from the personality of an individual but from a man's inheritance and relationships, within a world that ultimately transcends him. What we see is a general action specified, not an individual action generalized. What we learn is not character but the mutability of the world.
>
> (Williams, 1963: 54–55)

Moreover, the hero is a hero not by the sheer fact of being a self struggling against society but rather due to "inheritance, kinship and duty." These "social aspects" of the hero were, of course, contained within a personality. In Elizabethan tragedy and beyond, there is a "personality within and beyond the similarly defining status" (Williams, 1963: 57). But the liberal tragedy of Ibsen, suffering is dramatized as not only a part of the natural order but as a "vital and energizing part" (Williams, 2013: 44). Even in the increasingly secular moral universe of Shakespeare and the completely Godless plays of Ibsen, there is this spiritual remnant, a post-Christian metaphysic, especially in the modern hero who is both savior and victim—destroyed by society but also able to save it (Williams, 2013: 44). The hero is the exemplary "tragic protagonist," of which Jesus is the prime example (Eagleton, 2018).

According to Williams, what has happened over the course of the 20th century in authors like Ibsen and Miller is that this post-Christian "interpretation" has proliferated to the point of hegemony. It has "been imposed as an absolute meaning, and as identical with all tragedy" (Williams, 1963: 57). The isolation of the tragic hero facing death alone is a reading that undermines the reality of a world beyond the hero. There is no such thing in a post-Christian metaphysic. Tragedy is only "what happens to the hero" rather than "what happens *through* the hero" (Williams, 1963, 55 Emphasis added). The world as such is psychological. It is a triumph of the therapeutic, to use Rieff's phrasing (Rieff, 1987).

This gradual individualization and secularization influence what is understood as tragedy. As Williams points out, an event is only ever a tragedy when it can be connected to a larger body of facts. When it cannot, it is a mere accident. An accident has no general meaning. This indicates a larger separation between ethical control and human agency from our understanding of social and human life (Williams, 2013: 48–49). In other words, the whole meaning of "accident" has shifted. "Fate or Providence had been beyond man's understanding," Williams reminds us, "so that what he saw as accident was in fact design, or was a specifically limited kind of event outside this design" (Williams, 2013: 51). Today, this "design" is embodied in social institutions. Social orders are the vessel of metaphysics. The great Americanism, "It is what it is," speaks to this.

The new metaphysics is largely capitalism. The dramatist that most powerfully captures the experience of this new metaphysics is Arthur Miller. For Williams, Miller is the "most important agent of [the] break-out" of social thinking in modern tragedies (Williams, 1959: 140). Extending Ibsen's stylings, Miller breaks through the "social realism" tradition toward "social expressionism." Countering the argument that the lack of tragedy in the modern era had to do with the "paucity of heroes among us" or that moderns no longer have blood flowing through their "organs of belief" as a result of the skepticism imbued by science, Miller's work expands the notion of the hero to include "the common man." This is because modern life wounds all of us. It takes away the dignity of all human beings. As was for Kaufman, all tragic heroes, from Orestes, Medea, Hamlet, and Macbeth, are struggling for the same thing, which is to secure a "sense of personal dignity," according to Miller. This attempt to gain a "rightful position" in society is what underlies tragedy. To insist upon a hero's rank is simply to "cling" onto "the *outward* forms of tragedy."

Hence, the character of Willy Loman, among other Miller protagonists, is indignant, to the point of "compulsion," as he puts it. This compulsion is not a "tragic flaw" befitting of noble characters like kings. "Nor is it necessarily a weakness," Miller writes. It is "really nothing—and need be nothing." Miller finds virtue in this flaw. The fact that there is, within the common man, an "inherent unwillingness to remain passive in the face of what he conceives to be a challenge to his dignity, his image of his rightful status." As Miller says, "most of us are in that category." The Salesman is among those of us that "act against the scheme of things that degrades them." Loman's fear is that of displacement, "being torn away from our chosen image of what and who we are in this world." He likens this process to the totally examining what is supposedly an "unchangeable" environment. In scrutinizing this "stable cosmos surrounding us," the common man confronts the additional "terror and fear" underpinning existence. But this too is virtuous for Miller as it is an attempt to reveal a "wrong or an evil in his environment." Thus, tragedy "enlightens" the audience by pointing "the heroic finger at the enemy" of freedom, thereby "exalt[ing]" this "thrust for freedom."

The relative lack of tragedy in the modern era then is partly attributed to the predominance of two views of life—the purely psychiatric and the purely sociological. While these views seem to be "oppositional," in fact, they represent a similar tendency. Both render action impossible. "If all our miseries, our indignities, are born and bred within our minds," or "if society alone is responsible for the cramping of our lives," then, in the first instance, there would be nothing for the human being to do as everything would be hard wired, bearing no responsibility. Likewise, in the latter, the common man would be "so pure and faultless." In both, the common man's condition is utterly explained. There is no struggle; there is only pathos. When there is only pathos, Miller argues, "a character has fought a battle he could not have possibly won." While Miller believes that tragedies are revered because "in them, and in them alone, lies the belief—optimistic, if you will, in the perfectibility of man," his characters hardly ever seem to overcome this condition.

The name of this condition is alienation. "For this is a man," Williams says of Willy Loman of *Death of a Salesman*, "who from selling things has passed to selling himself, and has become, in effect, a commodity which like other commodities will at a certain point be economically discarded" (Williams, 1959: 145). It is in the figure of the Salesman that the key to social drama, which includes social realism and social expressionism, can be the full embodiment of Miller's credo that "every personal aspect of personal life is radically affected by the quality of the general life, yet the general life is seen at its most important in completely personal terms" be seen. The inseparability of the individual from society and vice versa in Miller's work, "in which neither is the individual seen as a unit nor the society as an aggregate," is best encapsulated in *Death of a Salesman*. It is here that alienation is embodied both in social action and in personality. Loman is alienated from "ordinary social responsibility" (Williams, 2013: 143). And thus, in evaluating him, Miller puts it, it is not difficult to see how:

> He is not a partner in society, but an incorporated member, so to speak, and you cannot sue personally the officers of a corporation. I hasten to make clear that I am not merely speaking of a literal corporation but the concept of a man's becoming a function of production or distribution to the point where his personality becomes divorced from the actions it propels.
>
> (Miller, 2015: 19)

And it is precisely on this point, regarding the status of the individual and its "divorced" relationship between the personality and action, that Williams sees hints of the "Greek idea of tragedy" in Miller. His tragedies involve individuals in the "first historical" sense. Loman is "a member of a group or kind rather than a separable and unique being" (Williams, 2013: 20). While Miller offers this vision of the social individual, his work stops short of what Williams calls "social tragedy." In social tragedy, humans are destroyed by "power and famine." It is an entire "civilization…destroying itself" (Williams, 2013: 121). Miller's works still exist within the framework of "personal tragedy." Hence, in spite of his admiration, Williams couches the work of Miller within modernist "tragic humanism." *The Death of a Salesmen* undoubtedly demonstrates that "tragedy lies in the common condition," which for Miller is capitalism. The suffering is collective, but the revolt is individual (Williams, 2013: 176).

Conclusion

In contemporary times, Williams suggests that seeing "no ethical content or human agency" in social phenomena such as capitalism, war, hunger or poverty is a grave admission of the "strange and particular bankruptcy" (Williams, 2013: 49) of tragedy. Instead of seeing tragedy "where suffering is felt" (Williams, 2013: 47), we see suffering as an inevitable byproduct of the social order. In this regard, he is not too far removed from the "death of tragedy" thesis as purported by George Steiner. While there is no doubt that they differ in almost every other way, in politics especially, both Williams and Steiner conceptualize the relationship between religion (specifically, Christianity) and tragedy as incongruous.

Christianity, writes Steiner, made total tragedy "implausible." One could understand that this claim in several ways. The first is that salvation precludes the possibility of tragedy. The "fall" of Adam is simply a prehistory to the birth and death of Christ. Adam's "original sin" is in this sense simply the first step in the arc toward "man's mastery" (Steiner, 2004: 13). There is no tragedy in Christianity because there is redemption. But this is only a partial analysis. For Steiner, the crisis of modern tragedy is not simply due to its Christian heritage. Indeed, the post-Christian metaphysic points to a larger issue of collective mythology. What is missing then is a collective mythology that "[centers] the imaginative habits and practice," that is, the "inner landscape" of the masses. There is not a set of "primal memories and historical experience" that constitute a "great myth." Mythology when it reaches a saturation point can be "articulated as language itself" (Steiner, 1963: 323).

According to this view, the conditions for mythology, however, are no longer. The world is disenchanted. We do not ask the question of why because there is no why (Steiner, 2004: 12). Like Weber's streetcar, all things *can* be explained. Such a world is truly secular, even "atheist" (Steiner, 2004: 6). Tragedy's decline, then, is "concomitant" with democratization and the "eclipse of imperative destiny in...power relations" (Steiner, 2004: 9). Thus, tragedy hinges on a rearrangement of the hero's position in a particular chronotope.

When suffering occurs in such a world, the possibility of some sort of "melioration" and even "therapy" is conceivable. The very fact of being able to think of a "redress" to social issues means that we are no longer in the realm of tragedy but in melodrama, Steiner argues (Steiner, 2004: 7):

> In tragedy, there are no temporal remedies. The point cannot be stressed too often. Tragedy speaks not of secular dilemmas which may be resolved

by rational communication, but of the unaltering bias towards in humanity and destruction in the drift of the world.

(Steiner, 1963: 291)

From Steiner's perspective, this world is not "tragic" because the suffering is attributable. Its root cause can be found—in humanity, within ourselves:

> Each day we sup our fill of horrors—in the newspaper, on the television screen, or the radio—and thus we grow insensible to fresh outrage. This numbness has a crucial bearing on the possibility of tragic style. That which began in the romantic period, the inrush of current political and historical emotions on daily life, has become a dominant fact of our own experience. Compared with the realities of war and oppression that surround us, the gravest imaginings of the poets are diminished to a scale of private or artificial terror.
>
> (Steiner, 1963: 315)

There is no true "estrangement from life" in the sense of a "fall from grace." Today, there is simply displeasure, alienation, and unease (Steiner, 2004: 4). Therefore, there can be no authentic tragedy.

It is not exactly clear whether Steiner is arguing *prima facie* that humanism has ended tragedy or that it simply claims to have done so. There is certainly a difference, for the humanism of the Enlightenment does amount to a kind of myth. As nearly the entirety of structuralist social theory has pointed out, it is one thing to claim that secularization has occurred as a result of modern rationalization processes, and it is another to claim that humanism has "replaced" it, so to speak.

Jean-Luc Nancy in "After Tragedy" hints toward tragedy's "sloppy" usage in a wide range of phenomena. Concentration camps, September 11, Rwanda, Nigeria, child hunger, and human trafficking are all described in such a way. This is because, today, the "inherent sense of the word escapes us." And thus, he floats the idea that the history of modernity is "also the history of the various interpretations of tragedy itself, but as both an enrichment (no matter how contradictory) and a permanent return to a lost and uninterpretable secret" (Nancy, 2014: 170). One could very well tell the story of modernity as the story of dealing with the end of tragedy. But, for Nancy, tragedy *already* spells the "after" or the "end" of religion, specifically the religion of sacrifice and worship. As Nancy writes:

> Leaving worship, tragedy exited religion. Leaving religion signifies leaving a regime of social culture in which there is communication with the gods. This regime assumes the presence of gods and the possibility of establishing connections with them. Worship consists in implementing those connections.
>
> (Nancy, 2014: 170)

The story of modernity is not simply the story of the end of tragedy, but it is about humanity dealing with the end of religion.

References

Bloom, H., 1999. *Shakespeare: The Invention of the Human.* New York, NY: Riverhead Books.

Cain, W.E., 2017. Rethinking Shakespeare. *Philosophy and Literature*, 41 (1), 40–59.

Dollimore, J., 2003. *Radical Tragedy: Religion, Ideology and Power in the Drama of Shakespeare and His Contemporaries.* 3rd edition. Durham, NC: Duke University Press Books.

Eagleton, T., 2018. Tragedy and Liberalism. *Modern Theology*, 34 (2), 252–257.

Fergusson, F., 1948. Action as Rational: Racine's Bérénice. *The Hudson Review*, 1 (2), 188–203.

Fineman, J., 1984. Shakespeare's 'Perjur'd Eye'. *Representations*, (7), 59–86.

Foucault, M., 1992. *The Order of Things: An Archeology of the Human Sciences.* London: Routledge.

Greenblatt, S., 2005. *Renaissance Self-Fashioning: From More to Shakespeare.* Chicago, IL: University of Chicago Press.

Hall, E., 1997. The Sociology of Athenian Tragedy. *In*: P.E. Easterling, ed. *The Cambridge Companion to Greek Tragedy.* Cambridge: Cambridge University Press, 93–126.

Hall, R.W., 1960. Being and Tragedy. *Chicago Review*, 14 (3), 99–106.

Jaspers, K., 1953. *Tragedy Is Not Enough.* 1st edition. London: Victor Gollancz.

Kaufmann, W., 1960. Freud and the Tragic Virtues. *The American Scholar*, 29 (4), 469–481.

Kaufmann, W., 1980. *From Shakespeare to Existentialism.* Princeton, NJ: Princeton University Press.

Miller, A., 2015. *Miller Plays: 1: All My Sons; Death of a Salesman; The Crucible; A Memory of Two Mondays; A View from the Bridge.* London: Bloomsbury Publishing.

Milner, A.J., 2002. *Re-Imagining Cultural Studies: The Promise of Cultural Materialism.* 1st edition. Thousand Oaks, CA: SAGE Publications Ltd.

Nancy, J.-L., 2014. After Tragedy. *In*: L. Cull and A. Lagaay, eds. *Encounters in Performance Philosophy.* London: Palgrave Macmillan UK, 278–289.

Rieff, P., 1987. *The Triumph of the Therapeutic: Uses of Faith After Freud.* Chicago, IL: University of Chicago Press.

Steiner, G., 1963. *Death of Tragedy.* London: Faber & Faber Limited.

Steiner, G., 2004. 'Tragedy,' Reconsidered. *New Literary History*, 35 (1), 1–15.

van Oort, R., 2006. Shakespeare and the Idea of the Modern. *New Literary History*, 37 (2), 319–339.

Vernant, J.-P., and Vidal-Naquet, P., 1990. *Myth and Tragedy in Ancient Greece.* Princeton, NJ: Princeton University Press.

Weber, M., 2005. *The Protestant Ethic and the Spirit of Capitalism.* Abingdon, Oxon; New York, NY: Routledge.

Williams, R., 1959. The Realism of Arthur Miller. *Critical Quarterly*, 1 (2), 140–149.

Williams, R., 1963. From Hero to Victim. *New Left Review*, 1 (20), 54–68.

Williams, R., 2013. *Modern Tragedy.* New York, NY: Random House.

Woodfield, M.J., 1990. Tragedy and Modernity in Sophocles, Shakespeare and Hardy. *Literature and Theology*, 4 (2), 194–218.

PART II

5

THE THEODICY OF SUFFERING

Abjection under capitalism

Introduction

While Steiner asks whether tragedy could even exist in modernity as a result of the waning of religion, Jonathan Dollimore actually notes that tragedy fulfilled the role of religion, serving as a form of theodicy, in a secularizing age. Tragedy played an important role as it offered "some account of why there was suffering in the world, plucking an intimate meaning from what seemed like senseless destruction." All the while, as Dollimore declares, "tragedy was everything that modernity was not," noting that it was "elitist rather than democratic, spiritual rather than scientific, absolute rather than contingent, cosmic rather than earthly, universal rather than culturally specific, a matter of destiny rather than self-determination" (Dollimore, 2003: xi).

Dollimore's argument, clearly, is a rather different one than Steiner's. For Steiner, tragedy could not exist in modernity whereas Dollimore suggests that tragedy could only exist in it because it was modernity's negative. At first glance, this difference could appear to be purely academic, but I would submit its significance for considering the import of tragic thinking in the social sciences, especially because of the latter's emergence and formation under the conditions of modernity. If, commentators like Steiner are right, modernity and tragedy are *not* compatible, it would therefore mean that modern social theory's early definition as *tragic* by Max Weber was fundamentally misguided. But as contemporary scholars that have adopted the Weberian perspective demonstrate, Weber's work rightly begins from the problem of suffering, or, as many have taken pains to point out, *social* suffering. This, for them, is the legacy of theodicy on Weber's thinking (Kleinman et al., 1997).

In reintroducing the tragic focus of Weber, this chapter asserts that at the core of social science is the grappling with the fact of suffering and in turn questioning the very basis of modernity and its chronotope. It begins with an excavation of Weberian

DOI: 10.4324/9781003110859-7

and neo-Weberian social theory and the way in which contemporary interpreters utilize "theodicy" in discussing capitalism. It then moves on to consider the linkages between theodicy and tragic thinking and how that has informed recent scholarship in the social sciences, underscoring the Nietzschean legacy in Weber. In detailing recent theoretical developments in social theory, medical anthropology and urban sociology, the chapter emphasizes the significance of this line of social-scientific tragic thinking as it pertains to the notion of "structure," drawing on the example of poverty and gender in the context of state-based welfare.

Theodicy before and after Weber

To argue that theodicy is an influential framework for Weber is not radical. Indeed, much of the contemporary work on "social suffering" points out that Weber, instead of attempting to reconcile the problem of evil and suffering within the context of monotheistic belief, tried to address the promise of modernity and the Enlightenment within the realities of social life that include adversity, inequality, and human suffering, all of which go against modernist ideals and the dream of Progress.

The theodicy of old, as first named by Leibniz in the 17th century, in the words of Kenneth Surin, "reconciles the existence of an omnipotent, omniscient and morally perfect God with the existence of evil" (Surin, 1983: 225). But since at least the medieval period and, most certainly since the Enlightenment, the possibility (and even necessity) of formulating a theodicy has been waning. With the innovations of Newton in the 17th century, the world was understood to be mechanical. While this appears to be a giant step towards secular modernity, with the driving mechanism being something *other* than God, there is still, in this view, a precise order that is posited to be latent in the natural world itself. As many scholars have pointed out, there exists a great deal of intellectual continuity between modernity and its more religious pre-history (Barbour, 1997; Gillespie, 2009; Koyre, 2012). There is, as Surin notes, still the acknowledgment of evil, in the sense of pain, suffering, and death. But crucially, after the Enlightenment, the idea of evil becomes "abstract" and "depersonalized" (Surin, 1983: 230). Evil can no longer be addressed as a "problem." Theodicy is only possible when there is something that cannot be understood. Without a "divine order" that is mysterious, theodicy does not exist. It is, if anything, "anthropodicy" (Surin, 1983: 228).

The point then is to differentiate Weber's argument from that of traditional theodicy, which "defends" belief and attempts to seek justification for the unanswerable problem of evil. According to these scholars, Weber's project is something else, which is to point out how secular, modern worldviews do not cope so easily with suffering perceived as unjust and undeserved. As Weber writes:

> The age old problem of theodicy consists of the very question of how it is that a power which is said to be at once omnipotent and kind could have

created such an irrational world of undeserved suffering, unpunished injustice, and hopeless stupidity.

(Weber, 2009: 122)

Theodicy is then a matter of justifying the world as it is. But in a *secular* world without an identifiable creator and guarantor of truth nor a singular omnipotent force, one could ask whether there are secular forms of theodicy at all.

Robert Schaefer seems to think not, stating that the term "theodicy" is not right at all since Weber is not referring to the justification of the secular modern order (Schaefer, 2021: 84). In fact, there is, as I will shortly discuss, a tragic element to Weber's diagnosis of the spiritual hollowness of modernity. Some say that Weber's work is better described as "cosmodicy" as it seeks to justify "the actual state of the world in light of the utopian notions of an ideal world" (Schaefer, 2021: 83). The "ideal world," in this case, is that of modernity and the Enlightenment values that underpin its project. For Schaefer, Weber's critique of modernity is tragic precisely because he points out how short it falls from delivering on its ideals. But in addition to the actual fact of modernity's inability to fulfill the promises of the Enlightenment, cosmodicy also speaks to the lack of explanation for its failures. Hence, "cosmodicy" reveals two different problems.

According to Iain Wilkinson and Arthur Kleinman, Weber's sociological conception of the problem of suffering defines theodicy as a "crisis of moral meaning" (Wilkinson and Kleinman, 2016: 113). This is especially important for the work of Weber as he suggests that the process of rationalization and disenchantment is both the cause and effect of a lack of sufficient meaning (Wilkinson and Kleinman, 2016: 114). By this, Weber makes a distinction between the secular theodicy of modernity—or "cosmodicy"—with that of religious theodicy. In the case of the latter, there was a clear solution offered by Christianity, especially in its post-Augustinian mode, whereby suffering and evil are privatized as "sin" (Morgan and Wilkinson, 2001: 201). As Weber puts it:

> The primeval attitude towards suffering has been thrown into relief most drastically during the religious festivities of the community, especially in the treatment of those haunted by disease or other cases of obstinate misfortune. Men, permanently suffering, mourning, diseased or otherwise unfortunate, were, according to the nature of their suffering, believed either to be possessed by a demon or burdened with the wrath of a god whom they had insulted.
>
> (Weber, 2009, 271)

And thus, "sin" was something to be combatted by individual believers, who were responsible for avoiding temptation "by assuming more effective control over their conduct in the everyday world" (Morgan and Wilkinson, 2001: 202).

Suffering was attributable not to any external entity or supernatural force but solely to the soul, which, according to the doctrine of "original sin," was onto-logically disposed to sin and thus suffer. This is the so-called "Adamic inher-itance" mentioned in previous chapters. By viewing suffering as "a symptom of odiousness in the eyes of the gods and a sign of secret guilt," religion explained not only the misfortune that befalls some but also the good fortune that comes to others (Weber, 2009: 270). Suffering and evil, in this case, were not without meaning as it was meant to demonstrate the vast separation between God and humanity. Of course, in Christian theology, it is this distance between the divine and the human that would be the necessary precondition for redemption via the Son of God, Christ. But "theodicy" is not limited to Christianity. Weber frames it thusly:

> One can explain suffering and injustice by referring to individual sin com-mitted in a former life (the migration of souls), to the guilt of ancestors, which is avenged down to the third and fourth generation, or the most principled—to the wickedness of all creatures per se. As compensatory promises, one can refer to hopes of the individual for a better life in the future in this world (transmigration of souls) or to hopes for the successors (Messianic realm), or to a better life in the hereafter (paradise).
>
> (Weber, 2009: 272)

The need for an "ethical interpretation" of the "meaning" of the differential distribution of fortune increases with disenchantment and rationalization in modernity. In a disenchanted world centered on the "rationalist belief in the power of reason to resolve every problem it poses for itself," there could not be an unexplained instance of suffering (Morgan and Wilkinson, 2001: 202). Suffering meant not that there was an error in the values and principles of modernity but rather a mistake in implementation. There was "human error" in the sense of a misapplication of reason but reason itself was not ever under the microscope. The same can be said of science, technology, capitalism, and democracy. Yet, "indi-vidually 'undeserved' woe," as Weber writes, was all too frequent. "Bad" men do succeed (Weber, 2009: 272). And thus, in the case of secular theodicy, while there is also an attempt at the elimination of the meaninglessness of suffering, it remained ultimately unsuccessful. The question, is "unequal distribution of wealth in society deserved?" remains unanswered (Fuller, 2011: 95).

Theodicy and tragedy

Crucially, Weber frames this open question of suffering in tragic terms:

> The irrationality of "fate" and, under certain conditions, the idea of a vague and deterministically conceived "destiny" (the Homeric *Moira*) has stood above and behind the divinities and demons who were conceived

of as passionate and strong heroes, measuring out assistance and hostility, glory and booty, or death to the human heroes.

(Weber, 2009: 283)

Scholars suggest that Weber's tragic framing with the deployment of the language of fate and destiny with regard to the question of secular theodicy has been influenced to some degree by Nietzsche. There are some who think that Nietzschean thought was pervasive in the intellectual culture of the time. Thus, its impact on Weber would be unremarkable. However, according to Wilkinson and Kleinman, the senselessness of suffering and its potential contribution to nihilism in Weber's thought bears the direct influence of Nietzsche (Wilkinson and Kleinman, 2016: 116). The dissatisfaction with the experience of modernity and the vulnerability resulting from disenchantment—that is, "the radical loss of selfhood, moral purpose, and social meaning" (Wilkinson and Kleinman, 2016: 117)—is clearly drawn from Nietzsche's proclamation that we are all destined to perish. Weber, like Nietzsche, attempts to explain—albeit sociologically—nihilism and warn against it. Like that of his predecessor, Weber's critique stems from the potential "cognitive and emotional distress" that comes from the massive cultural change that accompanied bureaucratization and rationalization (Wilkinson and Kleinman, 2016: 118). In fact, "the more highly rationalized an order, the greater the tension" (Wilkinson and Kleinman, 2016: 120) caused by the existence of suffering as it was "supposed to have [been] monitored, regulated and controlled by processes of rationalization." Suffering itself appears "irrational." The "sickness," as Nietzsche puts it, or "irrationality" resulting from rationality is captured Weber's famed characterization of moderns as "sensualists without spirit" and "sensualists without heart."

In addition to the conceptual parallels in their respective oeuvres, there is also textual evidence where Weber deliberately deploys Nietzschean terms:

The theodicy of suffering can be colored by resentment. But the need of compensation for the insufficiency of one's fate in this world has not, as a rule, had resentment as a basic and decisive color. Certainly, the need for vengeance has had a special affinity with the belief that the unjust are well off in this world only because hell is reserved for them later. Eternal bliss is reserved for the pious; occasional sins, which, after all, the pious also commit, ought therefore to be expiated in this world. Yet one can readily be convinced that even this way of thinking, which occasionally appears, is not always determined by resentment, and that it is by no means always the product of socially oppressed strata. We shall see that there have been only a few examples of religion to which resentment contributed essential features. Among these examples only one is a fully developed case. All that can be said is that resentment could be. and often and everywhere has been, significant as one factor, among others, in influencing the religiously determined rationalism of socially disadvantaged strata. It has gained such

significance, in highly diverse and often minute degrees, in accordance
with the nature of the promises held out by different religions.

(Weber, 2009: 276)

In his assessment of the influence of Nietzsche on Weber, Bryan Turner homes in
on what he calls "the resentment theme" (Turner, 2011: 75). Weber, he suggests,
"transported" the concept of resentment to map it on to the analysis of politics
and power. Specifically, the Nietzschean influence on Weber is made up of a
certain view of world without a transcendent value system that provides scripts
for action and meaning. Thus, with the collapse of natural law and the secularization of Western Christianity, social life would consist of "endless struggle"
(Turner, 2011: 80) as human existence would lack a "final vocabulary" for action
(Turner, 2011: 76). More to the point, social life without God nor a singular set
of moral codes and associated meanings would necessarily breed resentment as
there would be no final legitimacy for the extant suffering experienced by some
and the good fortune available to others. What we see then is the formation of
the theory of *ressentiment* in Nietzsche is actually rooted in what Weber would
later dub "disenchantment." For Turner, nihilism is synonymous with disenchantment as rationalization would necessarily breed *ressentiment* (Turner, 2011:
79). We could go so far as to say that nihilism was a symptom of being in a disenchanted world.

Nietzsche puts a finer point on his argument regarding *ressentiment* and nihilism by demonstrating the "disappearance of the heroic individual" that achieves
self-mastery. Whereas in the ancient world, the heroic individual could be cul-
tivated through warfare, "in the standardized and rationalized world of modern capitalism," there was hardly any opportunity for its development (Turner,
2011: 80). Yet, against simple nihilism, Nietzsche argued—albeit in a completely
misguided manner—for a renaissance of the heroic individual by reorienting
the values of modernity away from the "slave morality" of Christianity, which
would ultimately result in "unhealthy" individuals, full of *ressentiment* (Turner,
2011: 81).

Weber's sociology, like Nietzsche's philosophy, begins from the idea that
the more acclimated to living in bureaucratic-rational systems, the greater
the chances of being "morally unsettled and emotionally disturbed by events
and experiences that painfully expose us to the 'irrationality of the world'"
(Wilkinson and Kleinman, 2016: 120). Both point to what Iain Wilkinson
identifies as the "cultural poverty of a secular society" (Wilkinson, 2001: 428).
Whereas at one point people could very well explain their own suffering and that
of others through religious cosmology and thus be able to "read moral, social
and Providential meaning into their most negative experiences of the world,"
secular culture leaves them "unable to satisfy the human needs of for account of
our dignity as creatures." In fact, as Wilkinson argues rather forcefully, it strips
human beings from treating the experience of pain and suffering with the requi-
site outrage it deserves. When the social order is defined by technical rationality,

there is no meaning behind affliction, as it can only be explained as "glitch" in the context of the "modern presumption that every question can be solved in principle by rational calculation." It potentially "leads to a profoundly irrational way of life, precisely because the ultimate and most sublime values have retreated from public life."

It is for this reason that David Morgan argues that late modernity is confronted by an "inverse" problem of theodicy. Whereas theodicy's challenge is to explain or reconcile pain and misfortune with the "moral expectations of the world," the challenge of "secular theodicy" is quite different. Pain and suffering are "dissociated from ethical and political contexts and the quest for meaning." In other words, suffering and pain are too frequently encountered for moderns to be troubled by them. The exposure to suffering "in the guise of injustice, affliction, deprivation and pain" does not necessarily lead to a "need for 'other-worldly' (magical, ecstatic, and religious) meanings for experiences that cannot be purposively explained" (Morgan, 2002: 307). In Morgan's estimation, then, the modern world "presents an historically unprecedented problem of theodicy" because there is almost no hope for resolution or even the "possibility of a 'meaningful' interpretation of suffering and pain" (Morgan, 2002: 312):

> The belief that all problems will eventually yield to the ingenuity of science has displaced the irrational and tragic with an epic vision of the technical perfectibility of the secular world. Things "that should not happen" are attributed to unforeseen anomalies within expert systems of risk and surveillance that now monitor almost every aspect of human life from the heartbeat of a foetus, to carbon emissions and violations of human rights.
>
> (Morgan, 2002: 319)

For Weber, the "fate of our times" was that we precisely lacked fate and the security it provides. The "demand for an ethically meaningful conception of the world" could not be met by "the impersonal and instrumental systems of rationality." In either case, we can follow Wilkinson, who speaks of the denial of cultural resources that allow for "individual experiences of pain and misery" to gain public recognition and "endow them with a proper social meaning." Both religion and tragedy are symbolic forms that give "sufficient meaning to the experience of acute pain." But in secular culture, with an absence of such forms, there is an increase in personal distress of those who suffer.

The tragic suffering of the secular body

The question of bodily suffering has been the subject of intense discussion by a group of scholars in medical anthropology and has contributed to what has been identified under the heading of "social suffering." Influenced by Weber and other theorists, these scholars have called for a social scientific turn towards suffering in order to forge a new discourse, "to disturb our collective consciousness and stir it into practical action that moves beyond pity," as Lawrence Langer puts it (Langer, 1997: 47).

For Talal Asad, the therapeutic function of religion is rooted in a certain view of the body. There is in liberal modernity, he argues, a "secular body" (Asad, 2011: 657), which is "finite" and has a certain relationship to pain. For the secular body, pain is seen as a problem, a malfunction (Asad, 2011: 658). Pain accompanies the secular body until death. And once the secular body dies, there is nothing beyond. The end is final and there is nothing else. This idea of bodily finitude is at the heart of what he calls "epistemological secularism" (Asad, 2011: 662). Epistemological secularism, Asad writes, "assumes a particular mode of life and a polity in which some norms of health (social, theological, and corporeal) are to be promoted and other norms discouraged." In this sense, epistemological secularism is a form of biopolitics wherein keeping the body alive and functioning becomes a priority for the state (Asad, 2011: 664). Hence, bodily suffering is always already "social suffering." It is an "assemblage of human problems that have their origins and consequences in the devastating injuries that social force can conflict on human experience."

Social suffering, as a perspective, is a way of understanding "what political, economic and institutional power" can do to people. It is a way of accounting for the health conditions that atrocity gives rise to. It is a means of linking, for example, poverty, health, and death. It is, ultimately, a way of viewing health as a *social* indicator (Kleinman et al., 1997: ix Emphasis added). When framed in this manner, human problems cannot be so easily individualized as psychological or medical. In effect, what social suffering points to is the "close linkage of personal problems with societal problems," revealing "the interpersonal grounds of suffering." For these scholars, the concept of "social suffering" works to move away from the Western preoccupation with the individual experience of pain, which, they note, comes from a certain metaphysics whereby pain is understood to be "incommunicable." Pain is individual because it is understood to be so personal that it cannot be expressed through language. From the perspective of social suffering, however, an individual's ability to have certainty or not around their pain "simply seems a less interesting, less important question to ask than that of how such suffering is produced in societies and how acknowledgement of pain, as a cultural process, is given or withheld" (Kleinman et al., 1997: xiii). For these scholars, pain is produced *through* the social order, which includes language. As Kleinman and Kleinman note, collective modes of experience "shape individual perceptions and expressions." These "visible patterns of how to undergo troubles" are learned. The medical sociologists Glaser and Strauss, after Talcott Parsons, outline something called "sick role," where being sick is not simply a condition but a cluster of social norms to which we are expected to adhere as patients. In a more radical sense, it is being subject to authority. Cultural representations of suffering are "authorized by a moral community and its institutions." They also "elaborate different modes of suffering" (Kleinman et al., 1997: 2). And thus to state that suffering "exceeds" language is to "essentialize" it (Kleinman and Kleinman, 1996: 2). Langer even argues that to describe the Holocaust as "inconceivable…[prompts] us to build bunkers of inner security to shield us from their assault" (Langer, 1997: 53).

However, Das reminds us that pain and suffering do not simply threaten meaning-making in the social order but are at times "actively created and distributed by the social order itself" (Das, 1997: 564). There are instances in which pain and suffering can sometimes be the price of belonging. This is the case in many "rites of passage" across cultures. The body of the initiated "internalizes" the laws of society through pain, which then legitimizes society itself. But in addition to this integrative example, there is the exclusionary one, which is far more recognizable today. As Marx demonstrated clearly, the social order produces suffering in the form of exploited, alienated labor. It cannot simply be explained away as one of the "continencies of life" since it is absolutely at the core of the mode of production.

We can say that Weber, in the wake of Marx, tried to understand the "social psychology" of the experience of modern capitalism. He grabbed the term "theodicy" to describe "meaning-making in the face of history's inevitable tragedies," as Arthur Kleinman puts it (Kleinman et al., 1997: 317). For Kleinman, the term for a similar project for our times is "sociodicy," which, instead of seeing pain and suffering as something to be solved and thus justify the divine order in the face of its theological inconsistencies, aims to critically evaluate meaning-making "as a political tool that reworks experience so that it confirms to the demands of power" (Kleinman et al., 1997: 317). This is especially important, Kleinman notes, for societies like the United States where suffering is regarded as "something no one need feel, that one can and should avoid…as something to which society should respond primarily with the high technology that defines our age" (Kleinman et al., 1997: 323). Yet, these societies produce so much suffering and pain all the while being a "disenchanted garden in which meaningful life is replaced by mere routine, mechanical discipline and technical efficiency." Didier Fassin goes so far as say this *is* the "world that Nietzsche criticized as simply cultural nihilism" (Fassin, 2013: 85).

Yet, as Morgan and Wilkinson point out, sociodicies today operate in not only a disenchanted garden but also an unmanicured one. There is all manner of untrimmed growth. By this, I mean to refer to the fact that sociodicies today cannot presume the status of a stable system of meaning. The secular today hardly has the status of "sacred canopy" (Berger, 1990). More than ever, while there is no doubt that "technical efficiency" is hegemonic, there is clear evidence of incredulity towards some aspects of modern rationality. One only needs to see the swirl of conspiracy theories that have emerged in the wake of the COVID-19 pandemic and the global vaccination effort to see how "science" has not exactly served as a salve for nihilism. It is rather interesting to know that the slogan of the counter-conspiracy movement in the English-speaking world has been the quasi-religious motto: "Believe the science" (Douthat, 2020). For the conspiracy theorists and their adherents, what Weber understood as the "imperative of consistency" seems to not apply.

The shirking of consistency as a baseline epistemological standard is not limited to anti-vaxxers, QAnon conspiracists, and their ilk. In fact, as Morgan and Wilkinson point out, there is plenty of tolerance for inconsistency on display among those of us who remain culturally attached to the notion of progress in spite of "things that should never happen" occurring more frequently than ever. The effects of climate change, the ever-increasing gap between the rich and the poor, the desperation of migrants fleeing political violence and poverty are not unknown to many of us. And yet, the dissonance or disorder does not, for most people in the global North, turn into an incoherent conception of the world (Morgan and Wilkinson, 2001: 208). The challenge of sociodicy today is that there is a widespread "awareness of others' neglect and discrimination, or intention to kill and maim." Therefore, it cannot simply "rationalize suffering" but must rise to the level of "self-conscious critique," showing the "disparity between the millennial aspects of modernity and the reality in which we live" (Morgan and Wilkinson, 2001: 208).

Social misery and social policy

One of the most earnest efforts in the social sciences in this regard has been Pierre Bourdieu's *The Weight of the World*. Written in collaboration with a team of colleagues, it is made up mostly of stories of what they call "social misery" experienced by French people across the social spectrum. This includes farmers whose way of life was rapidly changing as a result of changing economic well as young people of North African background, whose "negative symbolic capital"—their names, accents, and places of residence—placed them at supreme disadvantage in terms of academic success (Bourdieu, 2000: 185). For Bourdieu et al, the decision to give voice to those who suffer was a concerted one. Their aim was to attend to the "complex and multi-layered representation of articulating the same realities but in terms of that are different and sometimes irreconcilable" (Bourdieu, 2000: 3). Crucially, this was done via transcription. Most of the text is filled with people "explaining their situation in their own words" (Wilkinson, 2012: 187). These individuals "stumble over their words and frequently lapse into silence." By keeping all of this in the final version of the text, Bourdieu and his colleagues highlight how elusive social suffering is vis-à-vis "formal analysis." As this sort of suffering "inheres within a welter of daily experience," it becomes difficult to pin down analytically. In incorporating the everyday language of the interviewees, *The Weight of the World*, at least from the perspective of the authors, stays truer to how larger social forces "constitute people's distress" (Wilkinson, 2012: 187).

There are significant overlaps with this approach and that of medical anthropology. Both demonstrate a similar sensitivity towards individual moral experiences of the world rooted in a principle of social science *not* reproducing the "technocratic ideology" that reduces human misery into forms of objective measurement (Wilkinson, 2004: 113). For the anthropologists, there is a focus on highlighting the problem of language and representation in terms of relaying the experience of human suffering. And thus, ethnography becomes important as a methodological way of addressing this concern, so that social science can go beyond "the bio-mechanics of pain, the sheer numbers of people killed in conflict zones or a calculated level of disability, scarcity and want" (Wilkinson, 2004: 114). Bourdieu's concern is more so about how the "symbolic violence" of modernist social science vocabularies could potentially silence the "genuine voice of suffering people" by the sheer fact of "[translating]...their experience into the language of science and technical expertise" (Wilkinson, 2006: 3).

According to Wilkinson, the major lesson for social science of both approaches to "social suffering" can be summarized as "bearing witness." According to him, viewing pain as "social suffering" recognizes the intractable fact that pain usually "defies meaning." By offering "silent recognition" of the plight of the sufferer, social science "honors" their human dignity. In this view, the task of social science vis-à-vis social suffering is to understand its own "intellectual limitations and moral failures" (Wilkinson, 2004: 118). By this, a social science fully cognizant of its limits is one that respects the limits of language to explain and express the pain of suffering. For Wilkinson, there is value in the "ongoing failure" of language as it "may produce a greater empathy for what suffering does to people" (Wilkinson, 2004: 119). Hence, the call is for social science to simply "bear witness" to pain and suffering and not "attempt to render the cultural grammar of suffering accountable to the rationality of scientific analysis" (Wilkinson, 2004: 119).

"Bearing witness" is but one lesson of "social suffering." In fact, the "social misery" approach, which includes not only Bourdieu himself but associated scholars such as Phillipe Bourgois and Loic Wacquant, aims to investigate material inequality in its impact on "people's lived experience of domination and repression," which includes feelings of humiliation, anger, despair, resentment that accompany poverty, class or race (Frost and Hoggett, 2008: 439). Liz Frost and Paul Hoggett read this as a challenge not only to the post-liberal state's means of dealing with the well-being of its citizens but also how it conceptualizes citizens *as* subjects. As they explain, usually, social policy does so by crafting ways of distributing goods, services, and resources without considering the "lived experience of domination and exclusion and the feelings" (Frost and Hoggett, 2008: 441). It uses "material poverty as the sole measure of all suffering" and it "keeps us from seeing and understanding a whole side of the suffering characteristic of the social order" (Frost and Hoggett, 2008: 441). Put simply, this means that social policy addresses the citizen in a particular ontological fashion, that is, as the liberal subject of the Enlightenment—autonomous, coherent, and able to exercise rationality and agency. Hence, through a battery of "incentives," the state attempts to create net outcomes for the population by steering behavior by assuming adherence to a baseline economic rationality (Lindbeck, 1996).

In the 1990s, under the Clinton Administration, the United States implemented reforms in welfare provisions for the poor by introducing something called "workfare." Sticking closely to his campaign promise of "ending welfare as we know it," President Clinton "reformed" programs such as the Aid to Dependent Children Act (which later became the Aid to Families with Dependent Children Act in the 1960s), which provided financial assistance to mothers raising children (Semuels, 2016). In the 1980s, 40 percent of those enrolled in the program were black women. As a result of mounting conservative backlash, exemplified in the writings of political scientist Charles Murray, but also in public culture with the racist media trope of the "welfare queen," public opinion of welfare was that it caused poor adults who could work to not work, which, in turn, would result in dependency, with some people embracing it as "a way of life," encouraging people to have children out of wedlock and discourage marriage (Matthews, 2016).

While most scholars agreed that the first was probably true (this is the case even among left-leaning scholars who were in support of a jobs guarantee rather than cash payments), many, if not most, people were convinced of the second, which then extended to the third, as the concern that people (specifically black women) "cheated the system" boiled into a moral panic of sorts. With public opinion as it was, the compromise that the Clinton administration reached with Congress was a far cry from the campaign promise of "every welfare recipient would get a subsidized job if needed, along with child care and transportation assistance and everything else they might need to thrive in the workforce." In fact, the welfare reform act put a limit of two years on cash benefits, after which participants would have to work. If they could not, a government job would be provided. Furthermore, it would only apply to people who were 23 and under. By the time it was passed in 1996, the Personal Responsibility and Work Opportunity Act included a new version of the Aid to Families with Dependent Children program rebadged as the Temporary Assistance for Needy Families program, effectively ending welfare as an entitlement with heavy restrictions on who could receive aid and also for how long. Moreover, states would receive "block grants," and would have control over how assistance programs were administered.

Critics have shown the failures of "welfare reform" of the 1990. Some suggest that it has even deepened poverty. Briefly, what I wish to draw attention to here, however, is not only the legislation itself but the discourse around work and entitlements in that era and how it informs social policy. The ideal liberal subject of the American welfare state was the white housewife with children. The earliest forms of welfare, such as the Aid to Dependent Children (ADC) program, which started in the 1930s, were meant to help single mothers—but only those deemed deserving. This meant that divorced mothers and those with children born outside of marriage were more than likely excluded. It also left out racial minorities. By 1960, after the racial discrimination clause had been eliminated, the program was 40 percent black. Nearly two-thirds of the program was made up of divorcées and unwed mothers. As the purpose of this program was to keep women in the home, ensuring the "cult of true womanhood," the fact that so many black women, many of whom were expected to work, as maids, nannies, and agricultural workers, were in a position where they would *not* be working if they were recipients, added to the ensuing anti-welfare backlash among conservatives.

A major point of umbrage among critics of welfare reform was that these programs actually discouraged work due to its phaseout rate. Each dollar earned in a job would translate to one less dollar in benefits. As one economist is quoted as saying, "Students come in thinking welfare recipients are lazy, and then you talk them through the basics of the economics and describe the incentives of the program, and people were like, 'Of course, why would you work in this program?'" Ethnographic accounts of recipients supported this as well. Instead of opting for low-wage work, which would "leave them no better off than they were with welfare, that it might leave them worse off if they lost their job and were forced to reapply for welfare, and that the jobs they could realistically get would not prepare them for better, higher-paying work in the future." Despite this, because of how small these payments were, there were welfare recipients, who still needed to find other sources of income. In one study, "about 64 percent of their income came from AFDC, food stamps, and other safety net programs." The rest came from informal and underground work and from friends and family members. As David Theo Goldberg notes, this reality is imbued with meanings tied to racist exclusions going back to the Enlightenment (Goldberg, 1993). The belief that black Americans were unable to exercise proper, "rational" economic behavior animated much of the discourse and policy of welfare reform. By making work "unattractive," the welfare system would contribute to poverty, the thinking went. In flipping this, and thus making welfare relatively unattractive, the government could do away with poverty by overturning this incentive structure. Yet, as the sociologist William Julius Wilson found in his work, welfare recipients actually wanted to be working (Wilson, 1997).

The logical fallacy of solving poverty by getting rid of the safety net designed to mitigate it can be explained by social policy's tendency to understand social problems in a—yes, materialist, economistic fashion—but by the assumption of the existence of a liberal subject that exercises "choice" within the logic of cost–benefit analysis. The value of the "social suffering" perspective is its differing ontology—that of the *post*-liberal subject. The post-liberal subject is a psychosocial subject, one that not only possesses rationality but also an unconscious. It is social in the sense that it is relationality *not* autonomy that characterizes it. For the post-liberal subject, "reason, passion and embodiment are integrally related not in opposition" (Frost and Hoggett, 2008: 440). This is the viewpoint adopted by the stress and coping model, which "looks at incidence of personal stress in relation to indicators such as social class, ethnicity and so on as well as individual capacity to 'cope' (to exercise some form of first order agency and/or control) in the face of such stresses." The Clinton administration hardly considered the stresses of being poor and the experience of abjection, that is, "being done to" (Frost and Hoggett, 2008: 441). While contemporary critics point to exacerbation of "deep poverty" as a result of these reforms, what has not been mentioned as often is the associated emotional effects, especially shame, of the new system that jettisoned direct cash payments to families in favor of vouchers and food stamps. One of the key components of welfare reform is the burden for those receiving food stamps to verify their income. Misreporting this could result in criminal charges. Additionally, without cash to pay for expenses like rent or fuel, families were forced into desperate measures such as selling plasma to make quick cash when work was hard to come by. Others were reported to "sell their food stamps for cash—a rare practice generally, but common among the extremely poor."

Thus, in addition to the fact "that the share of households with less than $2 per day, per person, shot up from 1996 to 2011" by 153 percent, there is the "hurt and loss accompanying the abjection that is a consequence" of welfare reform in the United States. As Frost and Hoggett write:

> Because the exercise of "power over" others appears natural and legitimate, the hurt that produces shame and humiliation and the losses that lead to grief become detached from the social relations which generate them. The suffering that then results becomes individualized and internalized—built into subjectivity. Secondary damage is experienced when the defenses an individual deploys to cope with hurt and loss have destructive consequences for self and others and therefore further separates the person from their sense of relatedness/belonging to the group.
>
> (Frost and Hoggett, 2008: 446)

This is referred to as "double suffering." As the experience of social suffering exceeds the capacity to deal with it due to the dearth of symbolic resources to make sense of them, these populations face powerful social forces as "objects" rather than "agents" (Frost and Hoggett, 2008: 449). This has the potential to be incorporated into subjectivity itself.

Double suffering as abjection

This concern with the subjective effects of poverty can be seen in critical perspectives of the welfare state, especially from scholars and activists that have been pushing for "full employment." These scholars, from at least as far back as the U.S. civil rights movement in the 1950s and 1960s, were not pushing solutions to poverty such as guaranteed income, which recently has garnered public attention in the United States via the political discourse of "universal basic income" (Standing, 2017). Instead, figures like Bayard Rustin and Coretta Scott King, articulated the importance of dignity that comes with work, especially in a society like the United States where work is moralized and attached to personal worth. In 1964, Rustin called for a redefinition of work to include dignity, which necessarily means that the "public sector must come in and play a larger role" (Stein, 2014).

These scholars and activists identify not only the material effects of poverty but also its potential to result in the experience of the abject, which Julia Kristeva equates to marginalization. The abject bears the "weight of meaninglessness… which crushes" the subject. It is what pushes one to the "edge of nonexistence and hallucination." Not unlike the Lacanian notion of The Real, the abject is difficult to acknowledge as it can undo the subject. The example that Kristeva draws on is the corpse. The physical and material aspects of a corpse are far less shocking than, as she argues, the traumatic reminder of our own materiality. It is for this reason that the abject is jettisoned, loathed, and radically excluded. Drawing on Mary Douglas' conceptualization of "dirt," Kristeva suggests that the abject is what threatens the order of things (Douglas, 2002).

As a psychoanalytic theorist, Kristeva's understands abjection to do the work of preservation of what she calls a "pre-objectal relationship," understood in the Lacanian sense. For Lacan, the subject emerges, as a separate but integral identity, as a result of its objectification through the mirror. As an infant sees its *imago* reflected back, it realizes that it is indeed a "stable" and "singular" (that is, unattached) being. It is not simply a complex of limbs and appendages, which is how it had experienced itself until then. What can be called the subjectivization of an externalization is what produces, according to Lacan, the entrance of the self into the order of the Imaginary. The self must be "technologically" (that is through a "tool" such as a mirror) represented in order for the self to be "formed."

The abject, Kristeva notes, does not even appear as an object. "What does not yet appear to me as thing," she writes, is a source of horror because "laws, connections and even structures of meaning govern and condition me" (Kristeva, 1982: 10). As Tina Chanter argues, the abject is "neither object nor subject." It "designates those unthought, excluded others, whose borderline (non)existence secures the identity of those who occupy authoritative positions in relation to dominant discourses" (Chanter, 2006: 88). She gives a flurry of social examples of the abject, including "mothers, daughters, and wives whose unpaid physical and psychic labor could not be recognized by Marxist class theory" as well as "racialized minorities that perform paid labor within the home." These are people, who are, in the words of Gayatri Spivak, "double occluded." The "occlusion" of women whose unwaged labor and domestic labor vis-à-vis a broadly leftist politics is "epistemic" in addition to being material. "Dominant discourses," writes Chanter, "operate in ways that gain legitimacy for themselves by maintaining the fantasmatic completion of some bodies only by requiring abjection of others, and then denying the completion thereby effected" (Chanter, 2006: 90).

In policy debates concerning welfare, any subject other than the *liberal* subject is abject. As Wendy Brown explains, the subject of liberalism is one who is "presumed to be morally if not ontologically oriented toward autonomy, autarky and individual power" (Brown, 1992: 19). According to the "origin myth of liberalism," men exit the "state of nature" voluntarily to "procure rights" in society. They, Brown notes, "do not establish the state to protect or empower individual inside families" (Brown, 1992: 18). Much in the vein of social contract theory, the individual's natural liberty is understood as "traded" into the state for a form of security (Brown, 1992: 8).

The private sphere, then, is considered originary. It is where "comfort and regeneration" occurs. But, as Brown notes, it is "inherently bound to the male position and privileges bourgeois characterizations of universal freedom and equality" (Brown, 1992: 18). For women, under the liberal state, the private sphere does not provide these things as the family is understood as simply "natural." It is "prepolitical and ahistorical," unproblematically universal. Hence, the woman is the "primary worker and signifier of the family," as she is "naturally" better suited to reproductive work. The "family" is a natural entity that the state needs to support and maintain through protective codes (Brown, 1992: 17).

Oddly enough, these codes are actually constraints, functioning as "key technologies in regulating privileged women as well as in intensifying the vulnerability and degradation of those on the unprotected side of the constructed divide between light and dark, wives and prostitutes, good girls and bad ones" (Brown, 1992: 9). Following Brown, we can say that state powers are "neither gender-neutral nor neutral with regard to race and class." Moreover, the state does not merely "address private needs or issues but configures, administers, and produces them" (Brown, 1992: 30).

Those persons "recognized and granted rights by the state are walking freely about civil society, not contained in the family" (Brown, 1992: 19). Women, in the private sphere, are only able to achieve identity inside the family, as Barbara Welter demonstrated in her work on "the cult of true womanhood" (Welter, 1966). They are constrained in the prospects of recognition within the liberal state as they "lack the stuff of liberal personhood—legal, economic and 'civil personality'" (Brown, 1992: 19).

It is here that the state in capitalism truly emerges. While indeed Engels' pronouncements regarding the securing of private property rights and relations of production hold true, there is the added detail of what those relations of production consist of, which, in the contemporary context, includes sexuality, contraception, abortion, control of women's reproductive capacities. The state thus perpetuates a "masculinist state," propped up by a "gendered welfare and unemployment benefits system and the absence of quality public daycare, the specifically capitalist sexual division of labor" (Brown, 1992: 22). The liberal state therefore "ontologizes" women in a particular manner, relegating those that do not fit within its definitional confines abject (Brown, 1992: 9).

And thus, it struggles to explain, within its epistemology, facts that demonstrate unequal suffering such as: one-fifth of all women are officially poor and two out of three poor adults are women. Or, the poverty rate for children under six being 25 percent with 47 percent of that consisting of African American children, and 40 percent Hispanic children. Approximately one-half of poor "female-headed" households are on welfare; over 10 percent of all U.S. families thus fit the profile of being headed by women (Brown, 1992: 10).

Politicians and policy analysts, when faced with such facts, still assume the transcendental status of the free, masculine subject, "who simply moves from isolated to collectivized conditions, as opposed to a subject who is differentially produced by these respective conditions" (Brown, 1992: 29). But as scholars who have studied poverty and the "underclass" in the United States have demonstrated repeatedly, in addition to structural barriers to employment, the "truly disadvantaged," as the sociologist Wilson has dubbed them, are not simply unable to exercise the types of rationality and exhibit the logical behavior of liberal subjects. This subjectivity is not transcendental; in it is not available to all. In fact, most people receiving welfare are unable to function as free, individual subjects due to care responsibilities, multiple jobs, and other structural and cultural reasons. It is not for a lack of desire or will. They are not, as Brown and others have discussed, deficient liberal subjects. To address poverty by assuming liberal subjectivity is not only to fail to address the problem of poverty but to help produce abjection through the constitution of an ideal subject of the state.

The construction of an ideal, liberal subject forges a hierarchy of moral deservedness, which is assessed through economic rationality, irrespective of the sphere of social life, even sexuality. Melinda Cooper analyzes the example of the U.S. government's response to the AIDS epidemic in her discussion of the latent family values of neoliberalism. She convincingly argues that the state's response to AIDS embodied a neoliberal approach wherein sex could be "analyzed as a market" with "prices" that represent value but also risk. What is most interesting in this analysis is how certain forms of familial ties are privileged over others.

To do so, she presents the work of Richard Posner and Tomas Philipson, economists whose work was influential in the governmental response to the AIDS epidemic, in particular informing decisions around healthcare. For them, normative judgements about sexuality were "counterproductive to the smooth functioning of markets" (Cooper, 2017: 169). Instead, they encouraged seeing sexuality in terms of markets with a "negative externality" (Cooper, 2017: 171). Within the context of the AIDS epidemic, sex is therefore an "exchange of pathogens that generates social costs beyond the strict bounds of the consensual transaction." But if, as in all markets, there are only rational actors, then we can assume that "such risk-takers have reasoned that the immediate rewards of pleasure maximization are greater than the long-term costs of infection and have acted accordingly." The risks of HIV transmission are therefore "fully internal" to the "market" of unsafe sex or intravenous drug use, which means that the risk and cost should be "privately assumed by those who participate in them." "As long as it poses no substantial social costs," Posner and Philipson write, "the freedom to take sexual risks should never be limited or regulated by state paternalism, but nor should it be reinsured by the state in the form of subsidized health care, public education programs, or federally funded research" (Cooper, 2017: 172).

In this line of argument, the state has no business meddling in sexual activity. Part and parcel is the idea that the state should not be expected to insure the "intimate and personal costs of private transactions." In other words, government should not be directly involved in matters considered private. But that does not mean that the state could not influence behavior in order to reduce risk to it. For Posner and Philipson, the perfect compromise was to promote marriage (Cooper, 2017: 173). By promoting same-sex marriage, the state could reduce the "exorbitant costs of promiscuity in the gay male community," which was the population most associated with HIV and AIDS in the early days. In their estimation, marriage would help internalize the cost of AIDS biomedically and economically. The burden of care— both emotional and physical—would be placed onto a spouse. In identifying marriage as "a substitute for social insurance and the most efficient means of minimizing the social costs of healthcare." They end up "[restoring] the private family and its legal obligations of care to a foundational role in the free-market order" (Cooper, 2017: 174).

For Cooper, this is moralism under the guise of economic rationality. The "attendant moral categories of personal responsibility and fault" of the debate around welfare could be seen here. The Reagan-era infatuation with the virtues of voluntarism over the social state was now translated into the "self-care" and discourses of "freedom" from the government (Cooper, 2017: 179). The Clinton-era reform to welfare, which restricted public assistance to single mothers, making "marriage promotion" and "family responsibility" key aspects, could now be applied to discussions of same-sex marriage (Cooper, 2017: 210). The small amount of social insurance that existed would only go to those already adhering to certain requirements of marital and familial status. "The call to recognize same-sex marriage," Cooper forcefully argues, "thus becomes a demand for inclusion within a family wage system that is itself in terminal decline" (Cooper, 2017: 211).

Cooper's analysis speaks to the way in which states act in extraordinary ways to produce forms of citizenship in order to enact ideologies, thus policing the boundaries of the individual's care network and of social bonds. By interpreting sexuality as an "externality," that is, outside of the realm of the market, constructed in the logic of neoliberalism, as the privileged form of sociality, the supposed "consequences" of so-called private acts, such as sex, is understood as "personal responsibility." The family is constituted as an extension of the private; therefore, the family takes on attendant risk of private acts not the state. The state, then, not only *assumes* that the free masculine subject is transcendental as in the case with welfare provisions but it frames citizenship in a particular mode of subjectivization, so as to construct isolation out of collective conditions, as Cooper shows.

Conclusion

So, what does this mean for understanding social suffering?

Most obviously, it shows that the state operationalizes social theodicy by constructing a "just world," in which people get what they deserve (Lerner, 1980). As Daniel Sullivan argues, just worlds ensure a "basic sense of personal control." Theodicies help convince the individual that "their life projects may be successfully pursued despite the apparent possibility of encountering undeserved calamities" (Sullivan, 2013: 110).

The work on the welfare state assessed above shows that this is accomplished through ideological means and policy. Without a convincing theodicy, as Nietzsche warned, nihilism would predominate. Modernity therefore paints suffering as "a result of unfortunate natural forces that are sometimes outside of the realm of human control and moral understanding" (Sullivan, 2013: 109). This is seen as protecting individuals from both nihilistic disorientation—resulting from uncertainty about the value of one's goals—and despair—resulting from an inability to achieve one's "culturally sanctioned goals." By chalking up misfortune to "natural causes," modernity attempts the fine balance of "[focusing] individuals on the uncertainty and contingency of existence and culturally sanctioned paths to value" while also maintaining the self's stability. Modernity's task was to defer nihilism by providing a sufficient explanation of suffering that would not result in feelings of guilt or inadequacy—not exactly an easy task. As Sullivan points out, the cost of reducing guilt or inadequacy is the increase of uncertainty and anxiety. But too much of the latter threatens social integration. Without an overarching "social ethics" that functions as a guide "for valued individual action while maintaining social integration," the potential for disenchantment in the sense of dissatisfaction or, what Bernard Stiegler identifies as, "disaffection" (Stiegler, 2012) is high (Sullivan, 2013: 111).

As mentioned briefly in the Introduction, Merton noted back in the 1930s, social structure and social reproduction is tied to anomie. In terms that he famously laid out, institutional norms and cultural goals needed to be aligned in order for there to be full conformity. However, as he so insightfully pointed out, the reproduction of the social order and the withholding of anomie is not dependent upon conformity but rather simply the adherence to the cultural goals. This seems like a recapitulation of the culturalist reading of theodicy that sees suffering as having be merely explained without any guide for action. But, in the case of Merton's example of this relationship between social structure and anomie(which became the basis for the sociology of deviance and strain theory), there is a clear sense that the cultural goal (of money-making) already influenced the activity of those he called "innovators," which included drug dealers and members of organized crime. When reading Merton against the grain, the takeaway is precisely that the social order need not ask so much from its adherents for its perpetuation. All it needed to transmit were cultural values *not necessarily* norms.

Today, it seems that to ensure adherence and perpetuation, values and norms are made to be adhered to all the while there is growing disaffection. As Stiegler observes:

> Disenchantment, when carried to extremes, may have allowed capitalism to conquer the entire world, but it eventually leads to the loss of the capitalist spirit. Now I believe...that a capitalism totally deprived of spirit, that is, in the end, of motivation, or in other words of motives for living, of what I have just called the kingdom of ends—such a capitalism, having lost its spirit or its mind, is not possible...I believe, on the contrary, that capitalism is very profoundly threatened by itself...
>
> The destruction of spirit leads to the loss of all hope, but also to the loss of the very possibility of constituting horizons of expectation of a *we*. This is the result when capitalism—in order to penetrate every market and to exploit every possibility revealed by industrial innovation, at the same time continuously disrupting social structures, that is, those systems of collective individuation through which psychic individuals find their place—succeeds in destroying every barrier to the circulation of commodities.
>
> (Stiegler, 2012: 131)

In calling this contemporary condition "the Antigone complex," Stiegler notes that disenchantment has led to a feeling of fatalism in contradistinction to nihilism. As a result, the very possibility of sociality has eroded. If that is the case, we may be on the verge of something unimagined by even Nietzsche—a world of suffering and abjection that, while it still affects, needs no explanation. It is one made up of normalized disorientation and despair.

References

Asad, T., 2011. Thinking About the Secular Body, Pain, and Liberal Politics. *Cultural Anthropology*, 26 (4), 657–675.

Barbour, I.G., 1997. *Religion and Science*. Revised, Subsequent edition. San Francisco, CA: HarperOne.

Berger, P.L., 1990. *The Sacred Canopy: Elements of a Sociological Theory of Religion*. Reprint edition. New York, NY: Anchor.

Bourdieu, P., 2000. *The Weight of the World: Social Suffering in Contemporary Society*. Stanford, CA: Stanford University Press.

Brown, W., 1992. Finding the Man in the State. *Feminist Studies*, 18 (1), 7–34.

Chanter, T., 2006. Abjection and the Constitutive Nature of Difference: Class Mourning in Margaret's Museum and Legitimating Myths of Innocence in Casablanca. *Hypatia*, 21 (3), 86–106.

Cooper, M., 2017. *Family Values: Between Neoliberalism and the New Social Conservatism*. New York, NY: Zone Books.

Das, V., 1997. Sufferings, Theodicies, Disciplinary Practices, Appropriations. *International Social Science Journal*, 49 (154), 563–572.

Dollimore, J., 2003. *Radical Tragedy: Religion, Ideology and Power in the Drama of Shakespeare and His Contemporaries*. 3rd edition. Durham, NC: Duke University Press Books.

Douglas, M., 2002. *Purity and Danger: An Analysis of Concepts of Pollution and Taboo*. London; New York, NY: Routledge.

Douthat, R., 2020. When You Can't Just 'Trust the Science'. *The New York Times*, 19 Dec.

Fassin, D., 2013. The Predicament of Humanitarianism. *Qui Parle: Critical Humanities and Social Sciences*, 22 (1), 33–48.

Frost, L., and Hoggett, P., 2008. Human Agency and Social Suffering. *Critical Social Policy*, 28 (4), 438–460.

Fuller, S., 2011. Theodicy Sociologised: Suffering Smart in the Twenty-First Century. *Irish Journal of Sociology*, 19 (1), 93–115.

Gillespie, M.A., 2009. *The Theological Origins of Modernity*. Chicago, IL: University of Chicago Press.

Goldberg, D.T., 1993. *Racist Culture: Philosophy and the Politics of Meaning*. 1st edition. Oxford, England; Cambridge, MA: Wiley-Blackwell.

Kleinman, A., and Kleinman, J., 1996. The Appeal of Experience; The Dismay of Images: Cultural Appropriations of Suffering in Our Times. *Daedalus*, 125 (1), 1–23.

Kleinman, A., Das, V., and Lock, M.M., eds., 1997. *Social Suffering*. 1st edition. Berkeley, CA: University of California Press.

Koyre, A., 2012. *From the Closed World to the Infinite Universe*. Scotts Valley, CA: CreateSpace Independent Publishing Platform.

Kristeva, J., 1982. *Powers of Horror: An Essay on Abjection*. Reprint edition. New York, NY: Columbia University Press.

Langer, L., 1997. The Alarmed Vision: Social Suffering and Holocaust Atrocity. In: A. Kleinman, V. Das and M.M. Lock, eds. *Social Suffering*. Berkeley, CA: University of California Press, 47–66.

Lerner, M., 1980. *The Belief in a Just World: A Fundamental Delusion*. 1980th edition. New York, NY: Springer.

Lindbeck, A., 1996. *Incentives in the Welfare State: Lessons for Would-Be Welfare States*. Stockholm: Institute for International Economic Studies.

Matthews, D., 2016. 'If the Goal Was to Get Rid of Poverty, We failed': The Legacy of the 1996 Welfare Reform. *Vox*. Retrieved July 22, 2022 https://www.vox.com/2016/6/20/11789988/clintons-welfare-reform#earlyhistory/.

Morgan, D., 2002. Pain: The Unrelieved Condition of Modernity. *European Journal of Social Theory*, 5 (3), 307–322.

Morgan, D., and Wilkinson, I., 2001. The Problem of Suffering and the Sociological Task of Theodicy. *European Journal of Social Theory*, 4 (2), 199–214.

Schaefer, R., 2021. Secular Justifications of the World. A Neo-Weberian Typology of Cosmodicies. *Social Compass*, 68 (1), 81–97.

Semuels, A., 2016. The End of Welfare as We Know It. *The Atlantic*. 1 Apr.

Standing, G., 2017. *Basic Income: And How We Can Make It Happen*. 1st edition. London: Penguin Press.

Stein, D., 2014. Full Employment for the Future. *Lateral*,(3). Available from: https://csalateral.org/issue/3/full-employment-for-the-future/

Stiegler, B., 2012. *Uncontrollable Societies of Disaffected Individuals: Disbelief and Discredit, Volume 2*. Cambridge: Polity.

Sullivan, D., 2013. From Guilt-Oriented to Uncertainty-Oriented Culture: Nietzsche and Weber on the History of Theodicy. *Journal of Theoretical and Philosophical Psychology*, 33 (2), 107–124.

Surin, K., 1983. Theodicy? *Harvard Theological Review*, 76 (2), 225–247.

Turner, B.S., 2011. Max Weber and the Spirit of Resentment: The Nietzsche Legacy. *Journal of Classical Sociology*, 11 (1), 75–92.

Weber, M., 2009. *From Max Weber: Essays in Sociology*. Abingdon, Oxon: Routledge.

Welter, B., 1966. The Cult of True Womanhood: 1820–1860. *American Quarterly*, 18 (2), 151–174.

Wilkinson, I., 2001. Thinking With Suffering. *Cultural Values*, 5 (4), 421–444.

Wilkinson, I., 2004. The Problem of 'Social Suffering': The Challenge to Social Science. *Health Sociology Review*, 13 (2), 113–121.

Wilkinson, I., 2006. Health, Risk and 'Social Suffering'. *Health, Risk & Society*, 8 (1), 1–8.

Wilkinson, I., 2012. With and Beyond Mills: Social Suffering and the Sociological Imagination. *Cultural Studies ↔ Critical Methodologies*, 12 (3), 182–191.

Wilkinson, I., and Kleinman, A., 2016. *A Passion for Society: How We Think About Human Suffering*. Berkeley, CA: University of California Press.

Wilson, W.J., 1997. *When Work Disappears: The World of the New Urban Poor*. New York, NY: Knopf.

6

FROM HERO TO CELEBRITY

Fame, familiarity, and redemption

Introduction

Critics and social commentators of all political stripes have described the current era as defined by a "new celebrity species." What separates the new from the old is the context—social, cultural, and, undoubtedly, technological. "In the 21st century," the cultural critic Rachel Syme writes, the celebrity emerges out of a concomitant "rise of social media and smartphones." In the language of a podcast devoted to celebrity culture, the world of fame is made up Whos and Thems. A Who can be an influencer, a former teen idol, an actor with a bit role in the Marvel Cinematic Universe, YouTube stars, and peripheral members of the royal family. Compared to Whos, the Thems are more traditional, and thus more high-profile. Anyone could recognize a Them:

> Rihanna is a Them; Beyoncé is a Them; Julia Roberts, Dwayne Johnson, and Oprah are Thems. These are people for whom the fame machine still functions in the old-fashioned way—through high-powered publicists and manicured feeds, Oscar campaigns and major-arena tours.
>
> (Syme, 2021)

But, as Syme notes in her appraisal of the podcast *Who? Weekly?*, the gap between a Who and a Them used to be quite big, but "the proliferation of Internet platforms has led to confusion."

This is because "fame"—her word—has a "shorter half-life than ever." And as a result, how celebrity is understood has dramatically changed in the last two decades, Syme argues. She goes on, "Fame always took work…But, historically, stars went to great lengths to obscure their exertions." Stars were "Thems, idealized figures whose everyday doings—Brad Pitt goes to the grocery

DOI: 10.4324/9781003110859-8

store! Jennifer Lopez rents a film at Blockbuster!—we cared about because they otherwise seemed unreal." But something has changed, as now we "constantly encounter people who are trying, hard and transparently, to become famous, not through distance but through aggressive proximity." Content creators abound on TikTok, YouTube, Instagram and other platforms. Syme concludes that the quickening tempo of fame has as much to do with "the shifting ways in which we invest in them" as anything else. Pointing to fraying attention spans, she points out that fandoms are becoming fickler, and bringing with it, counterintuitively, a *greater* "allure of fame" as it can now so easily be lost. Syme's cultural analysis, as ever, is spot on.

In linking the dynamic shifts in celebrity culture, technology, and society more broadly, Syme sits within a thrust of scholarship and criticism on celebrity that identifies celebrity *culture*, from this perspective, as a bellwether of a larger discourse around cultural change. In particular, celebrity culture has historically been seen as part of a "worrying" movement toward the "[privileging of] the momentary, the visual and sensational over the enduring, the written and the rational" (Turner, 2013: 4). In this reversal of the Platonic injunction of the *Phaedrus* to be skeptical of text, the rise of the celebrity is viewed as an instance of the domination of what the American historian Daniel Boorstin called "the image." To care about what someone other than a friend or family—an all-but stranger—is seen to be a "compensation for a loss of community" in contemporary society.

Likewise, it is also seen as the epitome of commodification. Celebrity is a product of not only cultural processes but economic ones, a fact easily supported by all of the promotion, publicity, and advertising involved. While this may seem rather obvious from a contemporary perspective, it is from a historical lens, relatively new. A celebrity is not simply that a person with an "innate or 'natural' quality" that happened to have been discovered organically. There is a fame *industry*. Equally, there are media that prop this form of celebrity up, made up of journalists, feature writers, and publicists, all of whom reinforce the "star quality" or "charisma" of the celebrity. All of this contributes to the notion that today, a celebrity's fame "does not necessarily depend on the position or achievements that gave them their prominence in the first instance" (Turner, 2013: 1). As a matter of fact, there may not have been a "first instance" at all.

In these sorts of analyses, celebrity culture is viewed as having undergone significant change itself while also embodying a larger socio-cultural shift. Syme cites the past two decades, with the year 2000 and the advent of social media as a watershed. But as scholars of celebrity studies have pointed out for just as long, the very idea of a "celebrity" had in fact marked a shift in the history of another figure—the hero (Drucker and Cathcart, 1994; Frisk, 2019).

The idea of a continuum from the figure of the "hero" to that of the "celebrity" can be traced to the publication of *The Image: A Guide to Pseudo-events in America* in the early 1960s. There, Boorstin decries the "thicket of unreality" resulting from the "illusions that flood our experience" through the media of the time—radio, television, newspapers, and so on (Boorstin, 1992: 3). For him, among all the constituent elements of the celebrity industry, it was public relations and advertising that was responsible for collective self-deception. Americans, by demanding more (of what? one wonders but this will be discussed further below), had laid the foundations for a media landscape that sated this desire for not only more but also bigger, better, and more vivid. In short, Boorstin claims "the image" is an alternative world—one of our own making, born of a distinctly American penchant for "extravagant expectations" to the point of "going beyond the limits of reason or moderation" (Boorstin, 1992: 3).

The advertising industry exploded in the post-war period in America (Ewen, 2001). As Stuart Ewen writes, "modern advertising must be seen as a direct response to the needs of mass industrial capitalism" (Ewen, 2001: 31). In particular, "advertising offered itself as a means of efficiently creating consumers and as a way of homogeneously 'controlling the consumption of a product'" (Ewen, 2001: 32). Herbert Marcuse precisely notes that advertising excelled at producing "false needs," which are "superimposed upon the individual by particular social interests in [people's] repression" in order to drive consumer demand. "The result then," he argues, "is euphoria in unhappiness." Hence, the "need" to relax, have fun, and consume, all are "in accordance with the advertisements." More to the point, Marcuse mentions the deployment of sexuality in advertisements, resulting in the eroticization of commodities. To boot, sex is, as he puts it, "integrated into work and public relations," making it more susceptible to "controlled satisfaction" (Marcuse, 1964: 5). The presence of sexuality in advertisements does not point toward liberation but rather *liberalization*, that is, its channeling into socially constructive (namely, capitalist and exploitative) forms. It is the pleasure principle being absorbed into the reality principle in the Freudian phrasing that Marcuse made so famous.

We can point to two ways in which Marcuse and Boorstin are utterly dissimilar. Most obviously, Marcuse's politics run counter to that of Boorstin, whose politics are often characterized by scholars as "neoconservative" (Steinfels, 2013). In addition, Marcuse's indictment of "advanced industrial societies" like the United States at the time underscores "too much" control, to put it rather simply. In other words, "repressive desublimation" is what happens to sexual desire when it has been overdetermined by the advertising industry. The unleashing of sexuality represses rather than liberates. What separates Boorstin from Marcuse, however, is his diagnosis of the problem of contemporary America as a lack of moderation. Americans want more of everything and thus construct a "world-picture" that substitutes America with an illusory one. We have come to prefer the exaggerated image over sober reality. Rhetorically at least, Boorstin claims Americans are not getting enough of reality while Marcuse, to the contrary, contends that they, and their desires, have given way to reality.

Yet, it is on this point regarding the status of "reality" that their parallels are most obvious. It is clear that there is, for both, a detectable narrative of decline, what one commentator calls a "politics of cultural despair." The role played not only by the proliferation of advertising but the very media on which ads appeared—radio, print, and television—were also responsible for this reality. Hence, in the view of this commentator, "the entirety of" *The Image* is "[close] to Herbert Marcuse's *One-Dimensional Man*(1964) and the Frankfurt School's criticism of the triumph of technology and the emptiness of mass culture" (Whitfield, 1991: 306–307). Since at least the 1960s then, there has been some degree of agreement that the celebrity culture of the 20th century was unique due to developments in media and technology. This is indeed the basis for Chris Rojek's claim that celebrity culture had "colonized everyday life" (Rojek, 2004). Though not explicitly stated, it is the media–technological means that have spurred this colonization.

Of note here is how the critique of modernity overlaps with the history of tragedy already covered above. In brief, the idea that the disenchantment of the world has made tragedy defunct parallels the story of celebrity replacing the hero due to commodification. This is attributable to what Eva Illouz identifies (rather suspiciously) as "cultural exhaustion," whereby culture is "no longer capable of creating heroes, binding values, and cultural ideals…replacing this content with a narcissistic self-concern" (Illouz, 2008: 2 Emphasis added).

For those who subscribe to this story of cultural declension, Kim Kardashian, the perfector of the "selfie," is emblematic of this era of "narcissistic self-concern," and is thus "famous for being famous" (Vara, 2013), a paraphrasing of "well-known for well-knownness," which appears in Boorstin's *The Image*. Kardashian is often put forth as the face of the "new celebrity species." In a brief article in *The New Yorker* called "The Celebrity as Product," the magazine's then-business editor, Vauhini Vara, details a new website that sets up meetings with celebrities for a fee. To meet the singer Shakira will cost $15,000. To have lunch with Mike Tyson is $50,000. Vara uses this development to speak to larger shifts in celebrity culture, speaking in disapproving ways of increasing commodification. She finds the fact that there was a website offering hangouts for exorbitant amounts "off-putting." Contemporary celebrity culture focuses on the private lives of individuals, and "in particular, the most banal elements of those lives." "On Twitter," she writes, "we hear directly from Kim Kardashian about the sneakers that have been delivered for her fiancé, Kanye West, and from Miley Cyrus about her heartbreak over Lou Reed's death." Now, there's a website that "formalizes the status of celebrities as products by, literally, allowing them to sell their personal time and attention" (Vara, 2013).

In spite of the fact that she is barely mentioned, Kardashian's photo is the lead image. There is of course the easy explanation, having to do with the magazine needing to garner clicks and a readership, and thus following the logic of contemporary celebrity. Leaving aside the ironic contradiction of the nature of that explanation, one could also make the point that Kim Kardashian, and the Kardashian family more broadly, is the genuine symbol of celebrity culture today. This, however, nevertheless entails a critique of the way in which Kim Kardashian has attained celebrity status, which, according to many critics today, has influenced not only celebrity culture but the culture of social media generally. More specifically, a line of critique against the Kardashians has been that they, with how Kim got famous initially (through a sex tape, which some say was premeditated and orchestrated by her mother Kris Jenner), have had a deleterious effect on young girls especially, among whom Kim as well as her sisters and half-sisters are popular. In fact, one of the major points of blowback has been that the Kardashians "were the prototypes for the uncanny cyborg look that has…colonized social media…[refashioning] femininity into a computer prompt: enhance, enhance, enhance" (Desk, 2020). And thus, Kim is seen as emblematic of the confusion of authentic and the artificial, launching an era of "cheapened" celebrity that "entangle" us in a "snare," rendering us hopeless to the "fascinating, and reproducing individuals known, if only for their known-ness" (Grout, 2019).

This brief foray into Kim Kardashian offers a momentary glimpse into the critique of contemporary culture. For its critics, celebrity is now democratic; it is available to too many people. Through social media, anyone can be a celebrity. One does not need a talent or to display any sort of courage. Put simply, one can become simply famous without being a hero. It is a celebrity bereft of respect. To be famous today is not to earn it but to simply be called one.

From hero to celebrity

As with the oversimplified identification of Kardashian with contemporary celebrity culture, Boorstin's deployment of the phrase—"well-known for well-knowness"—was meant to point out the fact that America in the 1960s had constructed a technological world-picture that had become the repository of grand expectations, resulting in an illusory situation where "people expected so much more than the world could offer" (Boorstin, 1992: 4). Upon reflection, Boorstin's message in *The Image* was largely that America was "over its skis." Boorstin's critique was characterized not only by moralism but, more relevant for this chapter, was characterized by an argument about how people have never been "more the masters of their environment," yet they were "more deceived and disappointed" (Boorstin, 1992: 4) than ever. In making this world, we "deceive ourselves" (Boorstin, 1992: 5). The images that "we have put in place of reality" have taken hold in our minds (Boorstin, 1992: 6). Our worlds, therefore, are made up of "pseudo-events."

One of Boorstin's examples is that of a 30-year-old hotel that wishes to raise its prestige. A PR firm would say that the hotel should mark its 30th birthday with a celebratory event. And in doing so, it would promote the hotel's longevity and its assertion that it is generally a good hotel. In addition, photographs of the celebration would make the event an event. As Boorstin writes, "it is the occasion itself that gives the hotel the prestige to which it is pretending" (Boorstin, 1992: 10). By making an event reportable, the hotel makes the experience real. "Pseudo-events" are, put simply, made for media. They are not spontaneous but planned, planted, or incited. Their "success" is measured by how widely it is reported (Boorstin, 1992: 11). Pseudo-events are more dramatic than real events. They are also easier to disseminate. They can be repeated at will. Their occurrence is planned for our convenience(Boorstin, 1992: 39).

Pseudo-events have such currency because of what Boorstin calls the Graphic Revolution, alluding to the shift in media, technology, and society that makes easier the ability to make, preserve, transmit and disseminate precise images. With these new techniques, such as photography, which make direct images of nature, "verisimilitude takes on a new meaning" (Boorstin, 1992: 13). Both the techniques for vividness and the appetite for it, coalesced in the early 19th century, when the modern increase in supply and the demand for news began (Boorstin, 1992: 12). In turn, the press became "The Fourth Estate," and took its seat as "the tribune of the people" (Boorstin, 1992: 16).

The institutionalization of the press had a profound effect on news in framing reality. With television, there is the live element, which provides the effect of "being-there" (Couldry, 2004). "Liveness," as Nick Couldry argues, offers a "potential connection to shared social experiences as they are happening" (Couldry, 2004: 355). To describe something on radio, television, or the Internet as "live" is to deploy a category that naturalizes the idea that "we achieve a shared attention to the 'realities' that matter for us as a society" through media toward two ends (Couldry, 2004: 356). The first is that the audience, through liveness, gains access to something of a broader, central significance. This event is happening now and must be worth accessing as it is happening. The second is that the audience of the event, the "we" who have gained access to the event, are not a random group but representative of a particular social group. Lastly, it is based on the idea that media is the "privileged means for obtaining that access" (Couldry, 2004: 356).

This epistemological authority afforded by the broadcasting of live events, Boorstin notes, was leveraged by the Kennedy administration, for instance, when it began a practice that is now standard in the White House—a live press conference with the White House press pool (Boorstin, 1992: 16). Decades prior to that, another Democratic president, Franklin Delano Roosevelt, began the practice of delivering the famous fireside chats on radio (Boorstin, 1992: 20). For Boorstin, these are pseudo-events par excellence. While the presence of the president in a somewhat "casual" setting, and speaking off the cuff, is meant to exude spontaneity, these events are still largely "performances where men in the news simply act out more or less their prepared script" (Boorstin, 1992: 19). By the sheer fact of their choreography, these means of reporting are "institutionalized" news leaks. They are "planned ways of emitting information" rather than the product of an enterprising muckraker (Boorstin, 1992: 33).

While pseudo-events are planned, Boorstin makes clear that they are distinct, and even the opposite of, propaganda. Although pseudo-events such as live press conferences and fireside chats are both predicated on presumed intimacy, propaganda relies on "emotional appeal." Pseudo-events depend on "ambiguous truth." They do not create outright falsehoods. They engage in what could be described as selective information disclosure. Unlike propaganda, which blurs the line between "sham and reality," pseudo-events, according to Boorstin, are rooted in constructing "false assumptions" about reality (Boorstin, 1992: 36). We cannot say that we are being fooled. In fact, it would not be entirely inaccurate to say that we are being "informed" (Boorstin, 1992: 36). Hence, pseudo-events are animated by an "honest desire to be informed" and "have all the facts." They "appeal to our duty to be educated" whereas propaganda "appeals to our desire to be aroused" (Boorstin, 1992: 34). Propaganda, Boorstin writes, "oversimplifies experience" whereas "pseudo-events "overcomplicate it" (Boorstin, 1992: 35).

For Boorstin, the celebrity was the *human* embodiment of the pseudo-event (Boorstin, 1992: 46). Unlike heroes, for which the prototype was the "war hero," the celebrity has "greatness thrust upon them" (Boorstin, 1992: 45). The war hero "achieved greatness" but the celebrity is *made* famous (Boorstin, 1992: 46). Greatness, as Boorstin makes clear, was the precondition for fame. There was no fame without greatness. But in the contemporary era, greatness is obsolete as fame can now be "manufactured." Since 1900, when the process of fame-manufacture had been "discovered," fame as a hallmark of greatness became increasingly obsolete. Well-knownness could now be fabricated.

Quite interestingly, Boorstin draws parallels with secularization, stating, "God-made heroes are no longer" (Boorstin, 1992: 47). To map the decline of the hero onto this sort of narrative is to put forth an argument of disenchantment, in particular, the declining significance of myth. And while the obvious sociological counterpart would be Weber, just as significant would be the parallel with the argument put forth by Walter Ong. Drawing on the Plato's *Phaedrus*, Ong's work concerns the advent of writing in particular and its "restructuring of consciousness." Plato's invective against writing positions writing as "inhuman" and "external." It is a thing, a manufactured product, and has worrying ontological powers. It "[pretends] to establish outside the mind what in reality can only be in the mind." Writing's dehumanizing effect also extends to its effect on memory. With the use of writing, one does not need to remember anything since it has been written down. Likewise, Plato argues that text is unresponsive. It cannot speak back and "defend itself." The natural give and take between persons is not prioritized.

And here, the importance of dialogue in Socratic metaphysics becomes clear. While the "Socratic dialogue" is often discussed in the context of pedagogy (in the form of the "Socratic method") it can be traced to a Socratic ontology of souls. For Plato's Socrates, true communication occurs between souls, which can only happen through speech. Orality requires the physical co-presence of those in dialogue. It requires active listening. The achievement of meaning is more obviously social. With text, the exchange is asynchronous. One writes and then waits for a response that relies on the interlocutor's own interpretation of the text. Writing, therefore, "interiorizes experience," as Ong puts it, separating "the word from the living present." The dynamism of sound is otherwise quieted (Ong, 2000: 83).

Hence, when Boorstin suggests that the secularization of celebrity can be attributed to the Graphic Revolution, in which a hero could be "mass-produced" through media and public relations, he means to speak to the *visuality* of pseudo-events. But unlike the live press conferences of modern politicians, modern celebrity depends on other-than-rational means. The modern imperative to know is certainly there but, in addition, a different sensorial dynamic is at play—hero-worship. As Boorstin writes, "the zestful search for heroes, and the pleasure in reverence for heroes remain, the heroes themselves dissolve" (Boorstin, 1992: 48).

In detailing the differences between a hero (a Big Man) and a celebrity (a Big Name), Boorstin notes that a key element of the hero is that he (usually) is self-made. By this, Boorstin means to point out that the human figure that is given the title of hero (whether real or imaginary) has been known to show greatness in some form of achievement. The hero, put simply, is someone who has performed some great deed (Boorstin, 1992: 49). But what has changed in the contemporary era is not that there are fewer exceptional individuals that perform greatness but rather the "passion for human equality has carried great distrust of individual heroic greatness" as a result of the rise of democracy and science. And thus, Boorstin identifies a decline in the cultural *appetite* for heroes and heroic greatness.

Hero-worship, after all, does seem anathema to democracy. Even the heroes of American history (at least according to the conventional history taught in American schools), such as Benjamin Franklin, George Washington, and Abraham Lincoln, Boorstin notes, were admired due to their embodiment of "popular virtues" (Boorstin, 1992: 50). The myth of George Washington and the cherry tree in addition to Lincoln's nickname of "Honest Abe" are not about, for instance, military feats in the case of Washington or some legislative accomplishment in the case of Lincoln but honesty, a characterstic not beyond the reach of ordinary Americans. As Boorstin notes:

> We revere them, not because they possess charisma, divine favor, a grace or talent granted them by God, but because they embody popular virtues. We admire them, not because they reveal God, but because they reveal and elevate ourselves. (Boorstin, 1992: 50)

In identifying such a change in the relevance of a particular cultural framework or narrative, Boorstin is actually making a larger, historical point having to do with what sociologists in the middle of the 20th century referred to as "mass society." The rise of mass society meant the decline of "folk" (Boorstin, 1992: 56):

> The folk had a universe of its own creation, its own world of giants and dwarfs, magicians and witches. The mass lives in a very different fantasy

world of pseudo-events. The words and images which reach the mass disenchant big names in the very process of conjuring them up.

(Boorstin, 1992: 57)

Mass society entails the *production* of subjectivity. It assumes a degree of conformity. Theoretically, the idea of "the mass" emerges from an intellectual tradition that emphasizes the power of social forces, including ideology and class, on individual worldviews. This perspective, that environmental influences (sociology) were responsible for internal maladjustments (psychology) can even be seen in the literature of the time. There are no heroes in the work of Williams, Miller, Hemingway, and Faulkner. Their central figures, Boorstin claims, are victims. They suffer from circumstances (Boorstin, 1992: 52–53).

It is telling that Boorstin points to the tragic figures of works that are often called "modern tragedy" to describe the decline of heroes. These characters, especially Willy Loman of *Death of a Salesman*, are everyday characters; their flaws are mundane. They are not that different from those of the audience or reading public. The choice of examples sits logically within Boorstin's greater argument that views the rise of celebrity as a symptom of the decline of heroism. There is no longer anything resembling specialness in a massified culture. In the vein of the Frankfurt School, Boorstin seems to bemoan the end of a "high culture" full of heroes in an era of industrialized culture.

It is no surprise then that Boorstin writes that "in a democracy, anyone can become a celebrity." Pointing specifically to "the news," as long as one can get into the news and stay there, he can become a celebrity, including "entertainers" and athletes (Boorstin, 1992: 60). The celebrity, as a "substitute" for a hero, is simply a person "known for his well-knownness." While a hero's main feature is a virtue, for a celebrity, it is personality (Boorstin, 1992: 65). It is no wonder that their fame does not fill us with meaning since they are "receptacles into which we pour our own purposelessness" (Boorstin, 1992: 61). Their fame, in this regard, is cheap, rooted in our mere familiarity with them—a feat that is accomplished, "induced and reenforced by public means," by which he undoubtedly means the media. It is realized by making celebrity a creature of gossip, public opinion, magazines, and newspapers (Boorstin, 1992: 63). Familiarity, therefore, is a passing and passive form of knowledge. Fame, on the contrary, resembles admiration.

As a consequence of the displacement of fame by familiarity, Boorstin asserts:

There is not even any *tragedy* in the celebrity's fall, for he is a man returned to his proper anonymous station. The tragic hero...was a man fallen from great estate, a great man with a tragic flaw. He had somehow become the victim of his own greatness. Yesterday's celebrity, however, is a commonplace man who has been fitted back into his proper commonplaces not by any fault of his own, but by time itself.

(Boorstin, 1992: 63 Emphasis added)

In effect, Boorstin suggests that celebrities cannot evoke tragedy because they are too close to us, ordinary people. Heroes, who are the proper subjects of tragedy, are supposed to be situated *outside* the social order as Carlyle had proposed in his classic *On Heroes, Hero-Worship and the Heroic in History* (Frisk, 2019: 91). But celebrities, as they are simply "stand in[s] for the heroes we no longer have," cannot be endowed with greatness, a precondition in Boorstin's mind, for tragedy. Indeed, if celebrities are just "a more-publicized version of us," then we are looking ourselves as "models" (Boorstin, 1992: 74). The great sin of mid-century American culture was not only excess but narcissistic self-delusion.

The most relevant question pertaining to tragedy is what the retention of the term to describe lives of celebrities says about the contemporary era, in spite of Boorstin's claim that they could never be dubbed "heroes." The partial answer presented in this chapter, following Rojek, is that it is not the paucity of heroes but, in some ways, their proliferation that has allowed tragedy to be in circulation as a cultural narrative. Thus, when examining the media discourse of celebrity deaths, for instance, we can see that there is a rhetorical reliance on the trope of redemption. The notion of redemption acts to connect "tragedy" to celebrity culture in an era where there is "achievement famine," a "condition in which the demand for fame is distributed more generally than the means of attainment." Whereas Boorstin highlights the lack of heroes to worship, Rojek identifies something slightly different, which is the lack of opportunity to live a "heroic life." In other words, whereas for Boorstin, the decline of heroism in celebrity culture has to do with the rise of the PR machine and media, for Rojek, it signals a larger shift in everyday life, which he calls "non-heroic life."

Heroic life is necessarily counterposed to everyday life (Frisk, 2019: 95). The everyday life for most people is filled with "routine, reserve, and dependence" (Rojek, 2012: 106). Excitement and satisfaction are hardly ever found in the sublimated way of living in contemporary capitalism under the "reality principle." For Rojek, the "PR-Media Hub" responds to an extant "widespread demand" for a heroic life by "exaggerating incident, emergency and risk in the lives of celebrities" (Rojek, 2012: 107). And thus, "the heroic life of celebrities relieves the burden of responsibility of ordinary people to cast aside the non-heroic life and challenge the status quo." It is a "means of handling the emotional impasse of this state of affairs." It is a way of using "vicarious engagement" that "enables ordinary people to live out epic struggle through the heroic roles and humanitarian campaigns of celebrities" (Rojek, 2012: 107). Celebrity culture, in sum, "[fills]the vacuum left by the waning of organized religion," a compensatory response that amounts to a mere "echo of idolatry" (Rojek, 2012: 120). While we may think we live in "an anti-, post- or hyper-heroic age," in which "heroism has lost meaning with modernization," there is evidence to suggest that "claims of a corrosion of heroism are (at best) exaggerated" (Frisk, 2019: 98). The argument here is not so much that Rojek is right (that indeed heroism is alive and well) or wrong (that heroism is dead) but that heroism is able to survive through its attachment to "tragic redemption." This is clear in how heroism was used to frame the deaths of two recent figures—Princess Diana and Kobe Bryant.

Tragic celebrity deaths

At first glance, Princess Diana and Kobe Bryant seem like an odd pairing to demonstrate the retention of certain aspects of heroism. After all, they are public figures, whose respective rises to fame do not overlap. Their "fields" are quite different. One was a member of the British royal family; the other was a professional basketball player. One is a white Anglo-Saxon. The other is African American. Yet, in spite of these differences, we can see that both Diana and Bryant have commonalities in their tragic narratives. When investigating the coverage of their deaths (Diana's in 1997 and Bryant's in 2020), we can glean some insight into how tragic themes—in particular, redemption—are folded into discussions of heroism and celebrity.

As mentioned above, Princess Diana has a unique place in the study of celebrity, often viewed as the transitional figure between the old guard (of heroism) and the new guard (of celebrity). Scholars have pointed to her within various lines of inquiry, including the changing status of the British monarchy, motherhood, and also the culture of grief (Brown et al., 2003; Elliott, 2020; Walter, 1999). The reaction to her death (as well two other passengers including her partner Dodi Fayed), as a result of a car accident in a tunnel in Paris while being chased by paparazzi, spurred national debate in the U.K. regarding the role of the monarchy in public life but also the nature of celebrity. As Harris puts it, the entire tragedy put into relief the struggle between two types of celebrity that Diana had embodied. She was at once "warm, accessible, [and] empathetic," photographed alongside sick children, victims of war, and AIDS patients, and also a member of the royal family with all that that entails (Harris, 1998: 282). Diana, before her death, but especially after, was "remade" into a "people person," that is, an "emotional equal, our peer," whose "entire life" was cast as a "debate between spontaneity and protocol," between "relating" and "expressing" and "frigid, upright civility" (Harris, 1998: 283).

Many scholars argue that Diana's "super-ordinary" status was supported by a global visual culture in which her life was covered by media. The narrative of having been born a lady and later becoming a princess could only be buttressed by a mediated visibility that bred familiarity, rather than exceptionality. For instance, James Thomas posits that Diana's common touch could only be facilitated through "para-social interaction" that simulated "intimacy at a distance." Through media events that preceded her death, including her marriage and subsequent public appearances, the public was conditioned to learn and express "feelings that were similar to those of normal friendships" (Thomas, 2008: 369). As Thomas argues, the disentangling of the "authentic" and the "mediated" were nearly impossible in her case (Thomas, 2008: 363).

Nicholas Mirzoeff's assessment is that Diana was a "celebrity punctum," deploying the Barthesian language of visuality. Along with Jacqueline Kennedy Onassis, Diana, as a public figure, compelled a "personal attraction" to her, "[cutting] into the viewer" (Mirzoeff, 2009: 240). It was the visual nature of Diana's celebrity that "our involvement" with her included "our desire to expose [her] secrets and see what [she] do not want us to see" (Mirzoeff, 2009: 242). The never-ending tabloid coverage of her whereabouts fed into what Mandy Merck calls the "delusions of intimacy" with Diana (Merck, 1998: 8).

Part and parcel of the visuality of Diana is what Elizabeth Wilson points to as the narrative of "the fallen woman" (Wilson, 1998: 114). The fallen woman is, in the 20th century, the "confused woman." It is a tragic trope that sees women finding themselves in and then breaking free from restrictive relationships. No matter the variation, Wilson notes, "underneath it is the same." The most obvious example is found in operatic narrative structure, in which a typical arc begins with a woman, out of love or desperation, breaks her marriage vows, finding herself in "a no-(wo)man's land of social ambiguity." In her own way, Diana's fate was that of "not having a clear social group or clear social role":

> In one way, Diana had fewer choices than most of us, owing to her attachment to the world of international royalty where, it seems, women are still defined overwhelmingly in terms of marriage and their relationship to men. Diana's predicament after her divorce illustrated the ambiguity of all women's lives, was a paradigm of contemporary confusions. There is really no consensus whether women should concentrate on being mothers or go out to work, whether they are still oppressed by men, or have overtaken them and now threaten masculine identity.
>
> (Wilson, 1998: 115)

The story of Diana fits within a long-standing Western tradition of "doomed love," which includes *Romeo and Juliet*, *Tristan and Isolde* among others (Wilson, 1998: 116).

Even for the French cultural critic Francoise Gaillard, who suggests that Princess Diana's death did not appear "scandalous" because of the fact that Diana was not a hero but rather a celebrity, admits that it mirrored "tragic destiny." Diana's death was almost as if she owed it to us, as a form of repayment of a debt of her being celebrated:

> Part of the implicit contract between these celebrated people and ourselves, their devoted admirers, is that they give us our money's worth of passion, intrigue and drama. The price can be heavy; but celebrity has become a consumer product, so it is paid.
>
> (Gaillard, 1998: 162)

Gaillard identifies what lies underneath this drama is the expectation of such. While it may be the case that she calls Diana a celebrity—and decidedly not a hero—because of her reliance on image, Gaillard nevertheless concedes the fact that the image must be buttressed by this "contract." Diana, in her estimation, "did nothing at all" to gain prominence and that, as a celebrity, she did not "deserve her glory." She was "the ultimate embodiment of celebrity precisely because, being associated with no memorable deed or exploit, her image could serve as universal referent" (Gaillard, 1998: 164). From her wedding to Prince Charles to her death, Diana's life seemed to embody "misfortune in its tragic dimension, beyond human understanding," as Gaillard puts it, "therefore not so much something to identify with as an invitation to let go, to overflow, to pour out a suffering too long contained":

> Our state is very similar to the passive resignation to misfortune we imagine characterizes women in traditional societies, forever weeping and wailing, except that we longer know how to cry as they do. The sight of a tiny Rwandan orphan or an Algerian farmer butchered with his family leaves us dry-eyed; we no longer know how or why to weep. For although these days all that happens is experienced in the fatalist spirit proper to natural catastrophes, most of the scenes of horror that come to us through our small screens are still, despite everything, haunted by this specter of politics. And although we no longer know what to make of this specter, it pollutes our suffering with vague feelings of guilt. But Diana's death served as an overflow conduit for all the unshed tears.
>
> (Gaillard, 1998: 165)

As Harris suggests, Diana straddled both sides of the transition from a "religious culture" whose subject needed to be saved to "a therapeutic culture" whose subject needed to be pleased. Diana was *of* a standoffish and impersonal nobility (heroes) but also submitted to the demands of a democratic culture that personalities turn the public into confidants (celebrities). Diana, as Harris describes her, lowered herself from the pedestals on which we usually place them (Harris, 1998: 283). She gave the public "the solace of being seen, being listened to, and, maybe, of being known" (D'Addario, 2017).

And for this, she was punished, made to pay with her life.

While the discussion of her status as a hero or celebrity among cultural critics and scholars alike seems to remain within the realm of the analytic confines of celebrity studies and what this says about the state of contemporary media culture, at the margins, there is a detectable presence of the question of the role of tragedy. In many ways, whether Diana can be considered a hero or a celebrity hinges on the possibility of tragedy today. This is unfortunate as it too neatly aligns with narratives of modernity that rely on theories of disenchantment, reducing "the tragic" to some vague notion of "religiosity." But much like easy theories of secularization, it assumes a dynamic of replacement, where large-scale, socio-cultural change can only be seen in a discontinuous manner. This overly simplistic story appears to motivate much of the writing on Diana. But there is a narrative substrate that even allows for her death to be viewed within tragic terms, especially when it comes to the identification of the role of the paparazzi, and the broader public's appetite for news and images of Diana. One piece written on the occasion of the 20th anniversary of the American magazine *The Atlantic* sums up the conventional wisdom of Diana's death in this way:

> The press, the logic went (the photographers, in particular), were at least partially to blame for the car accident that took her life. The paparazzi, frenzied by Diana's new relationship with Dodi Fayed, had chased her into that tunnel in Paris; they had encouraged Fayed's chauffeur, Henri Paul, to speed up in an effort at evasion; the effort failed in the most tragic way possible. The jury at the 2008 inquests into the deaths of Diana and Fayed found the paparazzi to be a contributing factor in those deaths. In 2007, Phil Hall, who had been the editor of the News of the World during Diana's life, put it bluntly: "A big Diana story could add 150,000 sales," he said. "So we were all responsible."
>
> (Garber, 2017)

Diana's death could only be seen as tragic because she was "so revered, so belittled, so sanctified, so victimized." Tony Blair's bestowment of the title "the People's Princess," perfectly captured the contradiction of her status as both hero and celebrity; or her way of retaining some qualities of "achieved celebrity" (closer to the classical conception of the hero) while also having the identity of the "ascribed celebrity" as a royal (Rojek, 2004). Her fallibility and the circumstances of her death are what allowed for her to be what should have been oxymoronic—a people's princess. Likewise, the late basketball player Kobe Bryant presents another case study, in which the death of a public figure significantly impacts the understanding of their life as "tragic."

Today, Kobe Bryant is viewed by basketball fans as a "GOAT." Short for "Greatest of All Time," Kobe—known by his first name much like "Diana"—is a five-time National Basketball Association (NBA) champion, a three-time Olympic gold medalist, Most Valuable Player Award winner, and an inductee of the Naismith Memorial Basketball Hall of Fame. Bryant is credited as the face of the post-Michael Jordan era (the 2000s) of the NBA, whose star power and greatness on the court solidified the global popularity of the sport, which Jordan inaugurated in a previous era(the 1990s).

His sudden death in a helicopter crash in January 2020 drew widespread shock. This was in no small part due to the fact that along with Bryant, there were eight other passengers, including his 13-year-old daughter Gianna, her basketball teammates, and fellow parents. They were on their way to a basketball tournament. The helicopter had flown into the side of a hill; the pilot had apparently been unable to see the horizon due to the cloud cover in the San

Fernando Valley. TMZ, the online tabloid outfit, was the first to report on social media that ""KOBE BRYANT, DAUGHTER GIGI DIE IN HELICOPTER CRASH …" (Wise, 2021).

In the aftermath, there were condolences from across the sports world but also from the broader public. The death of children was something that many people across different walks of life could find sad. Yet, in much of the discourse, an overwhelming use of "the tragic" was in relation to Kobe's life, in particular, and his reputation for aspiring to greatness. The most closely reported and authoritative article detailing the exact events leading up to the crash—what in journalistic slang would be a "tick-tock" (Burns and Allen, 2009)—is titled "Kobe Bryant's Tragic Flight." Published in *Vanity Fair*, and written by Jeff Wise, the article focuses on the technical aspects of flying a helicopter as well as all of the decision that go into flying in adverse weather conditions and also the pressures of having a celebrity client whose identity is largely defined by an unrelenting demand for greatness:

> Every flight has a safety margin, a multilayer cushion that protects it from a crash. Among the components are backup parts for crucial aircraft systems, multiple safeguards to prevent the aircraft from hitting things, and procedures to ensure a pilot doesn't miss any crucial steps. Island Express [the company hired by Bryant] had a procedure in place to ensure that its pilots stayed within conservative safety parameters. Called the flight risk analysis tool, it was an electronic checklist of 69 items that would tally up a number of points indicating the risk factor. If the visibility was below VFR minimums, for instance, the system would add nine points, and so on. If the score totaled higher than 45, then the pilot could not fly without first consulting management.
>
> Enough of those conditions applied on January 26 that the form instructed pilots to write down what they would do if they couldn't complete the flight as planned, and to discuss the situation with the director of operations or the chief pilot. The Los Angeles Police Department had grounded its helicopters.
>
> But Bryant needed to get through, and [the pilot] had an out. He was Island Express's chief pilot. So he skipped writing down his backup plans, left critical risk factors unchecked, and hit Submit. He was good to go.
>
> (Wise, 2021)

This juxtaposition of adherence to safety protocol and Bryant's demanding reputation continues, with the article drawing analogies between flying a helicopter "above the clouds" to Bryant's "unquenchable drive to rise above":

> At 17, in 1996, he became the first professional guard to skip college and be drafted straight into the NBA. As an established superstar, he dubbed himself "The Black Mamba" to convey a sense of superhuman speed,

precision, and danger. This autonym, Bryant would later explain, was also a self-protective reaction to the backlash that followed his arrest in 2003 for the sexual assault of a front-desk clerk in a Colorado hotel. The criminal charges were later dismissed, but a civil settlement with the accuser included Bryant's apology, and the event dogged him; sponsors dropped him, and he struggled to answer questions about the incident. Now, coasting swiftly and high over Los Angeles suited his Black Mamba alter ego and lifted him far above the public criticism he sometimes received.

Here, we are meant to understand Bryant's penchant for getting around Southern California via helicopter as part of the "Mamba Mentality."

The Mamba Mentality was something Bryant had come up with himself. After the settlement of his sexual assault accusation, Bryant sought to revamp his image and began to engage in a project of self-mythology. At the core of such a project was a new alter ego, "the Black Mamba" (Lee, 2020). Bryant himself told *The New Yorker* that he drew from the Quentin Tarantino film *Kill Bill*, in which "black mamba," the snake, was an assassin's alias. Known for its agility and aggressiveness, Bryant stated that the snake was "the perfect description of how I would want my game to be"(McGrath, 2014). But in addition to the admiration for the qualities of the snake, Bryant also harkens back to being accused of sexual assault:

> After the Colorado incident [the accusation of sexual assault], I had every major sponsor drop me, except for Nike…So I'm sitting there thinking, What am I going to do now? My vision was to build a brand and do all these things…[My] name just evokes such a negative emotion. I said, 'If I create this alter ego, so now when I play this is what's coming out of your mouth, it separates the personal stuff, right?' You're not watching David Banner—you're watching the Hulk.

Part and parcel of the "Black Mamba" moniker is what he calls the "Mamba Mentality," which describes a certain attitude or psychology around hard work and drive. In a book he wrote called *The Mamba Mentality: How I Play*, Bryant describes his workouts as "biblical":

> Over the years, my routine might have changed some but my philosophy never did. If something has worked for other greats before you, and if something is working for you, why change it up and embrace some new fad? Stick with what works, even if it's unpopular.
>
> (Bryant, 2018)

In another section, Bryant describes his work ethic:

> From the beginning, I wanted to be the best.

I had a constant craving, a yearning, to improve and be the best. I never needed any external forces to motivate me.

…

I didn't need that extra push to be great. From day one, I wanted to dominate. My mindset was: I'm going to figure you out…. And to do way more than anyone else.

That was the fun part for me.

But in addition to his "excellence as a player" and "love of the game," the "Mamba Mentality" also referred to his "greatness as a father," as James Bingaman notes (Bingaman, 2020: 4). Bingaman is specifically making reference to the hashtag #GirlDads that began to circulate on Twitter after a segment on ESPN's SportsCenter by anchor Elle Duncan, who recounted her one and only encounter with Bryant. Upon meeting Bryant while eight months pregnant, she recalls that he said that he would have five more girls if he could after learning that she was expecting a girl. (He already had three daughters at the time). "I'm a girl dad," he told her.

This phrase "Girl Dad" subsequently dispersed online and became attached to many posthumous analyses of Bryant's life and career. A segment on the newsmagazine program *Entertainment Tonight* featured numerous photographs and video clips of Bryant and his daughters, but especially Gianna, who had promise as a basketball player, to carry on his legacy. There were interviews with his former teammates who gave testimony to how devoted Bryant was to Gianna's basketball development (*Kobe Bryant, the 'Girl Dad'* 2020). A subsequent segment on SportsCenter by Duncan is called "#GirlDad: How Kobe Bryant's love for his daughters sparked a movement." Duncan states, "With two simple words, the world found a way to pay tribute to the legend, through their daughters." The Los Angeles Dodgers outfielder Mookie Betts appears and states, "Kobe impacted me as a Girl Dad by just showing that girls can do the same thing that guys can do. They can have the same mindset" (*#GirlDad: How Kobe Bryant's love for his daughters sparked a movement | SportsCenter* 2020).

All of this amounts to what Marc Stein in *The New York Times* described as Bryant's "brilliant and complicated legacy." The Mamba Mentality, while it signified an unrelenting drive to greatness and an equally passionate devotion to his daughter's basketball development, could have easily been understood as too much. In fact, in the *Vanity Fair* piece, the writer implies that Bryant's reputation for perfection motivated the pilot's risky decision-making. These elements of Bryant's public image alone did not enable the tragic frame and his redemption. It was, in fact, also what happened *after* the crash.

As mentioned, the gossip site *TMZ* was the first to report news of the crash and the death of all its passengers. While the report was not wrong, it was too early, as the LA County sheriff had not yet notified the family members, including that of Bryant. Alex Villanueva, the LA County sheriff, called out TMZ by name. As *The New York Times* notes, news organizations have difficulty, in this fast-paced climate, gauging how fast to report a story. Breaking news garners clicks, and thus the "drive to be first" at times sits "above sensitivity toward victims and members of their family." This is especially in reporting on "tragedies" (Schrotenboer, 2022).

In addition to the *TMZ* incident, Bryant's family also had another indignity they suffered at the hands of first responders and law enforcement. Employees of the county sheriff's office and the fire department allegedly took and shared photos of Bryant and his daughter after they were killed in the crash. Documents revealed in the suit filed by his widow, Vanessa Bryant, alleges that a sheriff's deputy showed "graphic crash-scene photos on his phone at a bar two days after the accident." This was confirmed by the sheriff's office's own internal investigation which revealed crash-scene images were found on 28 devices in its office (Schrotenboer, 2022). Similarly, the fire department also had employees that had shared images of the crash site and its victims.

As David Rowe notes, "victimhood" in the contemporary United States is rarely afforded to black men athletes. In his analysis of fellow basketballer Magic Johnson's announcement of his HIV diagnosis, he notes that Magic, who was a beloved figure in the sports world, was able to merit human compassion in spite of the moralism of American culture by becoming "the face of the virus," producing numerous public service announcements and acting as a spokesperson for safe sex. However, as Rowe notes, Magic was not seen as an "innocent victim" but rather a "guilty victim." As the "tragedy" of Magic could not be attributed to the "malign outcome of arbitrary fate" since he contracted HIV sexually, Magic was, for decades, still spoken of with reservation (Rowe, 1994: 16).

Bryant, as a fellow African American man and Laker, could have also been framed as a "guilty victim," especially in the wake of the sexual assault trial that he settled out of court. Moreover, with the risky flight pattern taken by the pilot being attributed, in part, to Bryant's demanding reputation, the crash could have been discussed as contributed to by Bryant himself. However, as the discourse of #GirlDad emerged, Bryant took on the status of "noble victim," which Weaver and Jackson point out, approximates the ideal tragic hero. Mothers, who experience the death of a child, are the example *par excellence* of such a tragic heroism (Weaver and Jackson, 2012: 434). Bryant, as someone who died along with his daughter and whose death was exploited in a media-hungry culture, was able to be mediated as a victim in this way.

Like Princess Diana, Bryant also suffered at the hands of "media." The mediatization of Kobe's death and its aftermath aided in the framing of his life as tragic with him positioned as a victim of tabloid culture and the larger appetite in the culture of pseudo-events. Their demise was due to celebrity culture more broadly.

Redemption against tragedy

For both Princess Diana and Kobe Bryant, their deaths resulted in a reframing of their lives as tragic, which I try to suggest in this chapter as not necessarily tied to their status as heroes but rather to the way in which their public images were able to achieve some degree of redemption. The relationship between redemption and tragedy is traditionally characterized by a certain sequence whereby "tragedy" is suffering of some sort, after which the hero gains redemption. As in the case of Job, the suffering is considered tragic when it is deemed unjust. But for Diana and Kobe, their deaths were the preconditions of redemption.

Redemption, when used with regards to individuals, is defined along the lines of "righting a wrong" or the admission of wrongdoing and taking personal responsibility. The discourse of redemption is usually couched in religious, specifically Christian, language. Thus, redemption and salvation are often equated with one another. Jesus is frequently referred to as "the Redeemer," who saves us from sin.

In today's celebrity culture, the rise and fall structure of individual celebrities is a common "media framing" made up of "three stations," which Lenn Goodman likens to chapters in a story: "discovery and rise, tragic fall, comeback and redemption" (Goodman, 2010: 511). As Lieve Gies notes, "downfall and disgrace is the mainstay of the celebrity narrative." A turn in a celebrity's fortunes is "part of a cycle of ascent followed by downfall and descent." This, in turn, becomes the groundwork for a "process of redemption" that, according to Rojek, often takes the form of "public confession,", which describes a "*ritualized* attempt by a fallen celebrity to reacquire positive" status, "[requesting] for public absolution" (Gies, 2011: p. 353 Emphasis added).

As Meyer notes, however, redemption in contemporary, post-religious societies is quite difficult to achieve. There is not a "specific person or body to apologize" (Meyer, 2019: 6). Job had Jehovah; Oedipus had the gods. Redemption, while spoken of in an individualized manner, is a social process of "restoring balance" and the reinstitution of the "established operation of a system" (Meyer, 2019: 6). Today, for celebrities, this occurs among and through media rather than a cleric or judicial body; they must be tried by "the court of public opinion."

Catherine Palmer notes redemption follows a "hermeneutic structure." In researching the narratives of redemption from athletes with a history of alcohol abuse, Palmer finds that this structure was composed of "celebration, punishment, redemption and self-discipline" (Palmer, 2016: 171). As she writes, "sporting careers map onto particular narrative arcs or discursive patterns that lend themselves neatly to their reproduction in other forms of popular culture such as film, television or tabloid media." This stands in a dialectical relationship with common "life scripts" (Palmer, 2016: 174), that are rooted in a narrative of restitution. As the sociologist Arthur Frank puts it famously, "yesterday I was healthy, today I'm sick, but tomorrow I'll be happy again" (Palmer, 2016: 171). For this reason, Palmer reckons that athletes are "paradigmatic heroes."

And here, we see that Palmer too links the possibility of redemption with heroism. But what contemporary celebrity culture facilitates is the rise and fall hermeneutic structure of figures like Princess Diana and Kobe Bryant without a resolution. In fact, their ultimate falls are the condition of redemption. What sort of "heroes" are Princess Diana and Kobe Bryant and what sort of redemption did they achieve?

The American cultural context offers important perspective. As Glenn D. Smith Jr has written, "no society has worshipped the celebrity figure as intently as Americans have" (Smith, 2009: 222). Celebrity in America follows an even more specific narrative or "hermeneutic structure." The "climb to fame" is most often a "rags to riches" story, "with the polished final image presented to fans as an embodiment of the American values of individual struggle, responsibility, and financial success." The celebrity then is not merely an image of a self but also the embodiment of a cultural myth, which in the case of the United States, is that of the American Dream. The values of "individual struggle, responsibility, and financial success" (Smith, 2009: 223) fuel a larger ideology of "romantic individualism" that, at its core, follows a linear, upward trajectory or an "arc" (Smith, 2009: 229), where "one's humble beginnings can be left behind and by accumulating large amounts of wealth, secure a position at the next level of society" (Smith, 2009: 230).

Redemption in this context is rather specific then, retaining the linearity of Christianity, but also detached from any sort of institutional religiosity, and closer to *civil* religiosity (Bellah, 2009). Redemption therefore is both specifically post-Christian in a sense but also generalizable in American culture. It is part of a distinctly American cultural narrative that provides "Americans of many different persuasions with a common language or format for making sense of an individual life," as Dan McAdams writes. "Even when we resist seeing our lives as conforming to this pattern," he goes on, "we are deeply (often unconsciously) cognizant of the pattern, and we must ultimately come to terms with it" (McAdams, 2008: 20). This pattern consists of a protagonist being chosen early on for a "special destiny." The awareness of the protagonist's chosen status comes with another—a consciousness that "the world is not fair and that many other people suffer greatly" (McAdams, 2008: 22). This theodictic insight, McAdams argues, veers toward a specific interpretation of suffering as merely a step in a bigger story of "atonement, recovery, emancipation, enlightenment, upward social mobility, and/or the actualization of my good inner self." "As the plot unfolds," for the protagonist, "I continue to grow and progress. I bear fruit; I give back; I offer a unique contribution. I will make a happy ending, even in a threatening world" (McAdams, 2008: 20).

McAdams, as a psychologist, thus identifies the redemptive self as rooted in a "life story," a narrative of the self that provides "coherence and purpose." As he notes, "it is less an objective rendering of what really happened in life and more a personal myth, part fact and part fiction, selected and edited to function as a narrative of personal identity" (McAdams, 2008: 21). These stories not only express certain aspects of our identities but also "speak to and for culture," saying "as much about the culture wherein they are told as they do about the teller of the story" (McAdams, 2008: 21). As Weber puts it, redemption, in any context, "expresses a systematic and rationalized 'image of the world'" as it offsets the "irrationality of 'fate'" through the introduction of "the idea of a vague and deterministically conceived 'destiny'" (Weber, 2009: 283). Put simply, redemption is rooted in a specific kind of theodicy.

For McAdams, American subjectivity more broadly can be understood as redemptive. Rooted in the ideals of "romantic individualism," the redemptive self presumes "the good and productive life" to be "the heroic actualization of the inner self." To live well is to "live freely." It is to "manifest one's inner destiny." This redemptive self can be found in the forms of the cultural and literary canon of America—"from the spiritual autobiographies written by 17th-century Puritans to the 19th-century African-American slave narratives"—as well as contemporary forms of popular culture, including "self-help manuals, business guides, Hollywood movies, People magazine, best-selling fiction, prime-time entertainment, and episodes of the Oprah Winfrey Show" (McAdams, 2008: 21). Redemption therefore sits at the core of the American idea that we are the "chosen people" selected to live out a particular destiny.

McAdams' notion of the "redemptive self" speaks not only to American subjectivity but also to how celebrity is understood in contemporary contexts as "cultural signifiers" with the "ability to tell a larger story" (Black, 2017: 213). This "larger story," if we follow McAdams, is that "the good is inside us" but the world outside is bad, "and in need of redemption." And thus:

> If I am especially favored in a difficult world, then it becomes my calling to exert some positive impact on that world. I need to use my gifts in a positive way. I need to give something back.
>
> (McAdams, 2008: 23)

But McAdams' larger point speaks to the *limits* of redemption as it often comes at the *expense* of tragedy. For him, redemption undermines the power of tragedy. Redemption proffers a "decided lack of ambivalence about moral and ethical values in life stories." As McAdams writes:

> The redemptive self may reflect important shortcomings and blind spots in Americans' understandings of themselves and the world. Is it not arrogant, for example, to imagine one's life as the full manifestation of an inner destiny?… The *story* may have a kind of arrogance about it, even if the *person* living it seems humble and nice.
>
> (McAdams, 2008: 25)

It is the cultural narrative of redemption that leads to a phenomenon like "American exceptionalism." It expresses an attitude consisting of: "I am blessed with the truth; I will share the truth with you; I will liberate you to see the truth the way I see it; you will follow my path, which is the right path; you will follow my path even if you do not want to" (McAdams, 2008: 25).

Redemption is limited in the sense that it acts as a "moral framework" through which to see the universe of human action. As McAdams writes, "human beings are moral agents, to be sure, but not every action or event makes sense… Sometimes we are just lucky, or unlucky. Fate, happenstance, blind chance, serendipity—tragedy teaches us that lives sometimes turn on these capricious factors" (McAdams, 2008: 26). Moreover, it questions "the belief that any particular individual is blessed with an innocent and good inner self that is destined to achieve good things":

> Tragedy gives fuller expression to the ambivalence and multiplicity of human lives than do many other narrative forms. It looks with skepticism upon the kind of ideological certitude celebrated in the redemptive self. Surely, it is good for people to have strong moral principles. But many would say that the principles need to be flexible, and need to change as the world changes. The tragic hero anguishes over the moral complexities in the world. He or she does not settle for simple truths and pat answers.
>
> (McAdams, 2008: 26)

Thus, it may be said that the retention of tragedy in celebrity culture is precisely as an antidote to the certitude and "strength" of the redemptive dominant culture of the day. McAdams notes, after all, that "[p]eople often identify moments of greatest intimacy in their lives as those times when they shared with others deep sadness and pain." They report that "shared suffering bonds them to others in a powerful and enduring way. It may also be true that others are easier to like and to know when they admit to their own vulnerabilities and flaws. Tragedy suggests that we are all flawed, and it rejects the notion that selves can ever be perfected. The redemptive self can sometimes seem impenetrable and aloof" (McAdams, 2008: 26).

It is clear that when "the tragic" is used in connection to celebrity deaths, "redemption" is undoubtedly its preferred synecdoche. In fact, the retention of tragedy in a disenchanted celebrity culture that confuses Whos and Thems is predicated on the cultural narrative of redemption, which, in McAdams' estimation, *undermines* the tragic. The redemptive self of which he warns being impenetrable and aloof may not be such a worry as true redemption is not so readily available. It could very well be that contemporary celebrity culture is bringing forth a complicated and contradictory realization: neither tragedy nor redemption is available as theodicy.

References

#GirlDad: How Kobe Bryant's love for his daughters sparked a movement | SportsCenter, 2020.
Bellah, R.N., 2009. *Beyond Belief: Essays on Religion in a Post-Traditional World*. Berkeley, CA: University of California Press.
Bingaman, J., 2020. "Dude I've Never Felt This Way Towards a Celebrity Death": Parasocial Grieving and the Collective Mourning of Kobe Bryant on Reddit. *OMEGA - Journal of Death and Dying*, 86, 364–381.
Black, J., 2017. The Reification of Celebrity: Global Newspaper Coverage of the Death of David Bowie. *International Review of Sociology*, 27 (1), 202–224.
Boorstin, D.J., 1992. *The Image: A Guide to Pseudo-Events in America*. New York, NY: Vintage Books.

Brown, W.J., Basil, M.D., and Bocarnea, M.C., 2003. Social Influence of an International Celebrity: Responses to the Death of Princess Diana. *Journal of Communication*, 53 (4), 587–605.

Bryant, K., 2018. *The Mamba Mentality: How I Play*. New York, NY: MCD.

Burns, A., and Allen, M., 2009. The Art of the 'Tick-Tock'. *POLITICO*. Retrieved July 29, 2022 (https://www.politico.com/story/2009/12/the-art-of-the-tick-tock-030248).

Couldry, N., 2004. Liveness, "Reality," and the Mediated Habitus from Television to the Mobile Phone. *The Communication Review*, 7 (4), 353–361.

D'Addario, D., 2017. How Princess Diana Created a New Era of Celebrity. *Time*, 25 Aug.

Desk, T.S., 2020. How 'Keeping Up With the Kardashians' Changed Everything. *The New York Times*, 9 Sep.

Drucker, S.J., and Cathcart, R.S., 1994. *American Heroes in a Media Age*. Bonn: VNR AG.

Elliott, A., 2020. *Routledge Handbook of Celebrity Studies*. 1st edition. London: Routledge.

Entertainment Tonight. 2020. *Kobe Bryant, the "Girl Dad."*

Ewen, S., 2001. *Captains of Consciousness: Advertising and the Social Roots of the Consumer Culture*. New York, NY: Basic Books.

Frisk, K., 2019. What Makes a Hero? Theorising the Social Structuring of Heroism. *Sociology*, 53 (1), 87–103.

Gaillard, F., 1998. Diana, Postmodern Madonna. *In*: M. Merck, ed. *After Diana: Irreverent Elegies*. London; New York, NY: Verso, 159–168.

Garber, M., 2017. The Enduring Fictions of Princess Diana. *The Atlantic*, 24 Aug.

Gies, L., 2011. Stars Behaving Badly. *Feminist Media Studies*, 11 (3), 347–361.

Goodman, L.E., 2010. Supernovas: The Dialectic of Celebrity in Society. *Society*, 47 (6), 510–515.

Grout, H., 2019. The History of Celebrity Is a History of the Concept of Self. *Aeon*. Retrieved July 22, 2022 (https://aeon.co/essays/the-history-of-celebrity-is-a-history-of-the-concept-of-self).

Harris, D., 1998. The Kitschification of Princess Diana. *Salmagundi*, Spring/Summer (118/119), 279–291.

Illouz, E., 2008. *Saving the Modern Soul: Therapy, Emotions, and the Culture of Self-Help*. Berkeley, CA: University of California Press.

Lee, A., 2020. Why Kobe Bryant Gave Himself the Nickname 'Black Mamba'. *CNN*. Retrieved July 22, 2022 (https://www.cnn.com/2020/01/27/us/black-mamba-kobe-bryant-spt-trnd/index.html).

Marcuse, H., 1964. *One-Dimensional Man*. Boston, MA: Beacon Press.

McAdams, D.P., 2008. American Identity: The Redemptive Self. *The General Psychologist*, 43 (1), 20–27.

McGrath, B., 2014. The Fourth Quarter. *The New Yorker*, 24 Mar.

Merck, M., ed., 1998. *After Diana: Irreverent Elegies*. London; New York, NY: Verso.

Meyer, A.R., 2019. Redemption of 'Fallen' Hero-Athletes: Lance Armstrong, Isaiah, and Doing Good While Being Bad. *Religions*, 10 (8), 486.

Mirzoeff, N., 2009. *An Introduction to Visual Culture*. 2nd edition. London; New York, NY: Routledge.

Ong, W.J., 2000. *The Presence of the Word: Some Prolegomena for Cultural and Religious History*. New Haven, CT: Yale University Press.

Palmer, C., 2016. Drinking, Downfall and Redemption: Biographies and 'Athlete Addicts'. *Celebrity Studies*, 7 (2), 169–181.

Rojek, C., 2004. *Celebrity*. London: Reaktion Books.

Rojek, C., 2012. *Fame Attack: The Inflation of Celebrity and Its Consequences*. 1st edition. London: Bloomsbury Academic.

Rowe, D., 1994. Accomodating Bodies: Celebrity, Sexuality, and 'Tragic Magic'. *Journal of Sport and Social Issues*, 18 (1), 6–26.

Schrotenboer, B., 2022. 'Unable to Reach a Resolution:' Vanessa Bryant's Lawsuit Remains at Impasse With County. *USA TODAY*, 12 Apr.

Smith, G.D., 2009. Love as Redemption: The American Dream Myth and the Celebrity Biopic. *Journal of Communication Inquiry*, 33 (3), 222–238.

Steinfels, P., 2013. *The Neoconservatives: The Origins of a Movement: With a New Foreword, From Dissent to Political Power*. New York, NY: Simon & Schuster.

Syme, R., 2021. "Who? Weekly" Explains the New Celebrity. *The New Yorker*, 31 May.

Thomas, J., 2008. From People Power to Mass Hysteria: Media and Popular Reactions to the Death of Princess Diana. *International Journal of Cultural Studies*, 11 (3), 362–376.

Turner, G., 2013. *Understanding Celebrity*. 2nd edition. Los Angeles, CA: SAGE Publications Ltd.

Vara, V., 2013. The Celebrity as Product. *The New Yorker*, 1 Nov.

Walter, T., 1999. *The Mourning for Diana*. Oxford: Berg.

Weaver, R., and Jackson, D., 2012. Tragic Heroes, Moral Guides and Activists: Representations of Maternal Grief, Child Death and Tragedy in Australian Newspapers. *Health Sociology Review*, 21 (4), 432–440.

Weber, M., 2009. *From Max Weber: Essays in Sociology*. Abingdon, Oxon: Routledge.

Whitfield, S.J., 1991. The Image: The Lost World of Daniel Boorstin. *Reviews in American History*, 19 (2), 302–312.

Wilson, E., 1998. The Unbearable Lightness of Diana. *In*: M. Merck, ed. *After Diana: Irreverent Elegies*. London. New York, NY: Verso, 111–126.

Wise, J., 2021. Kobe Bryant's Tragic Flight. *Vanity Fair*, 25 Jan.

7

TRAGEDY OF THE COMMONS

Genre and collective agency amidst climate change and the COVID-19 pandemic

Introduction

Luc Boltanski asks, "On what conditions is the spectacle of distant suffering brought to us by the media morally acceptable" (Boltanski, 2005: xv)? He posed this question in 1993, a year when "the global Internet" had an estimated "15 million computer users" (The Size and Growth Rate of the Internet in 1993: History of Information 2022). Just only a year prior, in 1992, the term "surfing the internet" had been coined. In 1994, the year following the publication of *La Souffrance à distance: Morale humanitaire, médias et politique*, the White House, under President Bill Clinton, had gone online for the first time (Pew Research Center, 2014). There is no doubt that Boltanski is speaking from a "media situation" (Kittler, 1999) rather tame compared to that of the current one. For Boltanski, the politics of suffering and witnessing came out of an Arendtian moral vision that saw the physical distance between "the unfortunate" and the spectator problematic. It created "pity" not "justice," as he so famously put it.

But in saying this, Boltanski seems to equivocate in his explanation of the technological conditions under which "distant suffering" emerges. To spectate suffering, he is quick to note, is not simply a "technical consequence of modern means of communication." He argues this while also admitting that "the power and expansion of the media have brought misery into the intimacy of fortunate households with unprecedented efficiency" (Boltanski, 2005: 12). These "instruments" can only "convey a representation" but not "an action" (Boltanski, 2005: 17). Indeed, while trying desperately to avoid "technological determinism," Boltanski nevertheless argues that "certain reports or televised current events" can be "all the more problematic the further away the unfortunate is and the more possibilities of action open to the spectator are, as a result, uncertain"

DOI: 10.4324/9781003110859-9

(Boltanski, 2005: 23). The dichotomy he sets up, between "representation" and "action," is an instance of the larger division he draws between "fiction" and "reality." Televised events render the spectator "utterly powerless," with "the horizon of action" receding into the distance. The suffering ends up closer to "fiction" than "reality" (Boltanski, 2005: 23). For Boltanski, this constitutes the immorality of distant suffering. When mediatized in such a way, suffering, while very real, becomes closer to fiction due to the lack of the possibility of "commitment" or "action."

A limitation of Boltanski's argument is the lack of specificity in his discussion of "media." Do all representations of suffering operate similarly? Should there be a distinction made between image and text? What about the advent of television and 24-hour cable news? What about the democratization of internet and the explosion of various streaming platforms with the attendant rise of misinformation?

Among these, there is the question of genre, upon which representational forms often draw. This is especially relevant to media coverage of specific events. As the sociologist Ronald Jacobs shows, in relation to what is colloquially known as the "L.A. Riots," an eventual "tragic frame" came to dominate newspapers and television shows. He argues that news media, at the time, had to construct a tragic narrative in order to discuss "race and civil society" in the wake of the not-guilty verdict of the police beating of Rodney King. Hence, for Jacobs, the *genre* of tragedy functions as a discursive security blanket for news media, allowing an American society normally reticent to tackle issues of race and racism to do so.

Jacobs defines genre as simply the style, category, or type in reference to a cultural object. Developed in large part in literary studies and film studies, genre analysis relies a great deal on the study of "basic plot structures," and how they "influence public expectations and social outcomes." For social scientists, in particular, genre is a way of connecting the "underlying meaning structure of a narrative to its productive and reception" (Jacobs, 2001: 225). In other words, to study genre in a social manner, we must see how plot and character development affect expectations and character identification. Genre then is a way of constructing structures of recognition, and, in effect, forming and organizing an "interpretive community" but also a social group more generally.

In the case of the L.A. Riots, Jacobs notes that in the initial coverage of the uprising, there was a "surprising amount of narrative diversity and openness toward the lifeworld understandings of inner-city urban blacks." This only lasted for a short time, however. It eventually resulted in the prevalence of "increasingly despondent and resigned interpretations":

> These more tragic narratives edged out the possibility of a hopeful, romantic understanding of the events, and, in the process, reinforced a sense that talk about matters of racial concern was a hopeless waste of time. As a

consequence, tragedy has become the dominant cultural legacy of the 1992 Los Angeles uprising.

(Jacobs, 2001: 224)

In tracking how "the tragic genre became the most powerful representational form for talking about race and civil society during the 1990s" in America, Jacobs suggests the following typology of "tragic stories."

1. the tragedy of urban neglect and historical repetition
2. the tragedy of politics
3. the tragedy of racial division and legal paralysis.

(Jacobs, 2001: 224)

He argues that these sorts of stories "prime" the audience to think about the issues of race as tragic. Specifically, the audience anticipates "standard narrative features" such as "tragic flaws from the potential heroes, expecting failure or catastrophe as the ultimate end of the story, and adopting the mood of somber isolation." This amounts to a "cultural agenda-setting," as Jacobs calls it, influencing "the kinds of stories individuals tell to themselves and others, and helping them to develop a more general understanding of how they should orient to the world around them" (Jacobs, 2001: 226). In structure, Jacobs' argument parallels that of McAdams "redemptive self" mentioned in the previous chapter.

In the case of the L.A. riots, the tragic frame constructed an expectation of "failure and resignation." To frame the riots tragically would be to think: little, if anything, had changed in American race relations. For Jacobs, this pessimism was rooted in finding historical continuity "so deep as to be unchangeable," a view that he attributes to "the tragic genre":

> By describing American racial history as the repetition of the same sequence of events, media narratives such as these suggested natural causal forces beyond the control of individuals or groups. Upon reaching the end of the tragic story, the putative freedom of individuals had been narrowed to a process of causation; the life created and the choices made had become inevitable, even as a comparison had been made with the uncreated potential life lost.

(Jacobs, 2001: 228)

In short, Jacobs' criticism of the tragic framing of the L.A. riots is the preclusion of the possibility of political progress or collective action. It promotes a stance that amounts to giving up. Since urban neglect and racism are longstanding historical realities, there is no point, according to the picture Jacobs paints, in trying to change or address these issues.

We do not need to go much further into Jacobs' work as his disdain towards tragedy is obvious. For him, there is an "inevitability" in tragedy. And when this definition of tragedy is mapped onto politics, there is the likelihood of it

resulting in a kind of paralysis, a succumbing to the "causal and cyclical movement of history" (Jacobs, 2001: 231):

> But the 1992 Rodney King narrative told the story of racial division
> through the tragic plot device of a "paradise lost," in which the civic ideals
> of legal impartiality and discursive neutrality were no longer possible. The
> not guilty verdicts in the first trial of the police officers charged with beat-
> ing Rodney King brought the recognition that white racism threatened
> legal impartiality. Two additional trials—the trial of the four men accused
> of beating Reginald Denny, and the federal trial of the Los Angeles police
> officers charged with beating Rodney King—dramatized even further the
> danger of racial division for the legal institutions of civil society.
>
> (Jacobs, 2001: 232)

Jacobs would prefer a "balance" of representational forms in interpreting the
L.A. riots, drawing on a genre other than tragedy (Jacobs, 2001: 236).

In classical Durkheimian fashion—unsurprising for a proponent of American
cultural sociology, Jacobs argues that tragedy is simply one form of "collective
representation." But is "by no means the only one" (Jacobs, 2001: 236). Why
media—again, most certainly just television news and newspapers—would lean
so heavily on a tragic narrative is rather simple: because it effectively offers cohesion. Using the following sort of plot structure aids in recognition: "an increase
in narrative tension, followed by a release of that tension through the use of
highly schematized and ideological plot devices" (Jacobs, 2001: 237):

> When narratives of crisis end in tragedy, as they did in the aftermath of the
> 1992 Los Angeles uprising, they encourage the audience to adopt a mood
> of resignation and somber isolation, an attitude which acts as a conservative
> brake against the potentially progressive belief that civic engagement and
> participation are worthwhile things. Tragedy encourages a mechanistic
> ordering of events that tends to discredit agency and contingency in favor
> of structural determinism and cyclical repetition, encouraging the reader
> to adopt the resigned acceptance of an evil…This weakens the cultural
> motivation for participating in the public sphere, which is based on an
> active conception of democratic legitimacy, demanding that the world be
> ordered according to some coherent notion of the good society.
>
> (Jacobs, 2001: 238)

We can see rather clearly that the source of Jacobs' consternation around tragedy
is the potential for anti-democratic sentiment:

> By emphasizing the inevitability of fate, the acceptance of evil in the world,
> and the necessity of achieving transcendence or redemption through a con-
> templative and mythic "flight from the world," unchecked tragic discourse

discourages collective mobilization, public engagement, and motivation to work through difficult public problems.

(Jacobs, 2001: 238)

In the case of the L.A. riots, but perhaps more broadly for Jacobs, the representational form of tragedy, and, specifically, narrative emplotment inherent in tragedy, is the chief dynamic of "media" in framing specific issues and/or events. One could go so far as to say that there is an elision of media and genre, a tendency found in other parts of the social sciences like communications.

We can see for instance in a study by Turnage on the tragic framing of what is known as the "Duke Rape Case." In 2006, an African American woman, hired as an exotic dancer for a party informed the police that she had been raped by three white members of the Duke University lacrosse team. The lacrosse team was subsequently suspended by the university and three players were charged and indicted for rape. But after a year and a half, the North Carolina attorney general cleared the players of any wrongdoing, concluding that the local attorney general was guilty of misconduct (Liptak, 2007).

In her study of what she calls the "social drama" of the case, Turnage argues that the discourse surrounding the case adopted the "tragic frame." Drawing on Burke in particular, Turnage argues that the discourses of both the prosecution and the defense use the language of "the scapegoat" in order to paint one side as wrongfully vilified. In portraying one's own side as "the scapegoat," both the prosecution and the defense could claim that they were being blamed to "restore order" and "purge guilt." In other words, it was a rhetorical strategy to claim that the community was out to simply get blood so that it could restore a "frayed town-gown relationship" (Turnage, 2009: 149). As a result of the conflicting tragic frames, the attribution of a *single* "scapegoat" was, regrettably in her view, not possible.

In the immediate aftermath of the announcement of the indictment, the lacrosse team, which served as a proxy for the "gown" crowd, was positioned as the scapegoat. The history of unruly and illegal behavior, and the disrespect that the largely white, upper class campus crowd had shown the African American "locals" came to be mapped onto this case in a significant way. When the charges against the players were dropped, this dynamic was reversed—with the exotic dancer labeled as an "agent of false accusations." The local community was seen as the agent of prejudice (Turnage, 2009: 143). But without a firm consensus on an ultimate scapegoat, tensions lingered.

For Turnage, this could have been avoided if another framing had dominated—the comic frame. The comic frame offers the possibilities of "transcendence" as it "invites rhetors to look at themselves and their own involvement in the controversy at hand." This claim goes onto, without substantiation, another that asserts that instead of scapegoating, a comic frame supports "mortification." Rather than blaming others, mortification is the purging of guilt through self-blame. By conceptualizing "responsibility" in this way, the comic frame's end is "not passiveness," as Burke states, "but maximum consciousness" as it "would involve a recognition of some issue or issues within the social order that need to be resolved without overthrowing the social order itself" (Turnage, 2009: 151).

Turnage's argument for the comic frame interestingly relies on a defense of the social order. The tragic frame, she seems to imply, would force communities not to "transcend the social problems" they face but rather question the arrangements of the social order as such. It would seem that agents, according to Turnage, could only "accept their individual culpability" if they saw the social order as worth maintaining. Hence, for Turnage, culpability is tied to an investment in the social order (Turnage, 2009: 153).

When "civil repair" is bound to commitment to the social order as in Turnage's argument, the question of justice is elided. What if the given social order is incapable of addressing wrongs as its foundational norms and values have inequality baked in?

The relationship between agency and responsibility in relation to the social order is problematically posed in other discussions of tragic and comic framing as well. In Foust and Murphy's study of global warming discourse in U.S. elite and popular press coverage, the tragic is a constituent part of what they deem the "apocalyptic framing" of environmental issues, which emphasizes "a catastrophic end-point that is more or less outside the purview of human agency" (Foust and Murphy, 2009: 151):

> Certain versions of this frame may stifle individual and collective agency, due to their persistent placement of "natural" events as catastrophic, inevitable, and outside of "human" control. Analyzing them could help explain why some individuals take a fatalistic attitude toward, or consider their agency very small in comparison to, the challenge of climate change.
>
> (Foust and Murphy, 2009: 152)

According to them, an apocalyptic frame usually takes on a narrative that stipulates some sort of "catastrophic telos somewhere in the future." This seemingly inevitability renders "human choice... superfluous, a final Judgment that forecloses all individual judgments" (Foust and Murphy, 2009: 152). And indeed, much like Jacobs, they suggest that the tragic frame paints the social order as beyond repair. However, unlike Jacobs, this is a matter of temporality, as the world's collapse is imminent. There is little hope for intervention. Hence, they conclude, the tragic framing of the apocalyptic is characterized by "resignation." It is an ending foretold.

For them, the tragic framing of the apocalypse is a kind of metaphysics. It is "following the divine will and behaving in ways decreed by God" (Foust and Murphy, 2009: 154). A frame, therefore, is not simply a representational form based on generic elements such as plot or character but a set of "familiar and highly ritualized symbolic structures" that not only organize content but put forth certain pathways of meaning while promoting others. Thus, in line with

Jacobs, the frame within Foust and Murphy's work "shapes how readers may define problems, attribute causes, and evaluate solutions" (Foust and Murphy, 2009: 153). They demonstrate this with a rhetorical analysis of global warming discourse:

> A number of discursive features constitute global warming tragically: verbs which express the certainty of catastrophic effects, a lack of perspective or shortening of time from beginning to telos, and analogies which equate global warming with foretold apocalyptic outcomes. Each feature forecloses human agency or frames climate change as a matter of Fate. Within the tragic variation of apocalypse, global warming (not other "natural" or divinely ordained events or processes, such as a steady decline to extinction which inevitably befalls all earthly species) is viewed as the demise of humanity.
>
> (Foust and Murphy, 2009: 157)

The words "is," "will," and "could" call attention to variations in human agency, according to their close reading. When a particular article or news item states that "the catastrophic telos of climate change *is* happening or *will* occur," it reduces, according to them, the potential for human intervention. In describing "predicted events through present-tense verbs," media that use the tragic frame "[heighten] the deterministic effect" of global warming.

In addition to temporality, another axis is revealed—the human and "extra-human." Global warming, when framed tragically, is posited as somehow driven by "cosmic forces" beyond the realm of human action. It is almost "Fated." According to them, "this makes it difficult to hold humans accountable for pumping greenhouse gases into the atmosphere." It could "[alleviate] humans of responsibility for creating, or at least contributing to, climate change." It could even "reduce the responsibility for combatting it" (Foust and Murphy, 2009: 152).

In another moment of resemblance to Jacobs, Foust and Murphy argue that there needs to be "balance" in the coverage of global warming in order to promote human agency. The natural counterpart would be the comic frame. Within a comic frame, global warming is experienced by readers as occurring in a more "manageable time period." It does not result in resignation but rather inspires the audience "to take steps to make change." It is "charitable, but not gullible." That is because comedy, they say, "unifies communities and promotes possibilities." It gives them some way of influencing their fate. But, as they note, this may be only because it "[appeals] to hegemonic values rather than, for instance, fundamentally challenging the neo-liberal logic which justifies the exploitation of the earth" (Foust and Murphy, 2009: 163).

So, their recommendation to "rhetors" is to avoid "ultimatums"—if we do not act, it will spell disaster. They say instead of "threatening the public," rhetors should present the current crisis as "an opportunity to avoid potential disaster for our families and communities" (Foust and Murphy, 2009: 153). To influence the global warming narrative, they should "stress human agency" across everyday life such as adjusting heating and cooling practices, using mass transit, cycling, walking, and working from home as well as political pressure for alternative, sustainable energy (Foust and Murphy, 2009: 164). In principle, this argument stands to reason. But when delving into their analysis, it is not all that convincing. One example of what they deem to be "comic framing," highlights the use of words such as "possible" while noting that the "permanent inundation" of New York City, as a result of rising sea levels, for example, is not likely to occur in "our grandchildren's lifetimes, or even their grandchildren's" (Foust and Murphy, 2009: 161). Thus, it would be more agentive and even accurate to omit this detail. While it may give a marginal degree of agency to humanity, one wonders whether the readership of *The New York Times* would interpret "possible" any differently. Certainly, it seems unlikely that the "comic frame" (which seems not all too different from how the authors define the "tragic frame" in terms of language and rhetoric) would inspire action. Nevertheless, as Foust and Murphy as well as Jacobs seem to argue, the tragic framing of events *evacuates* agency (Foust and Murphy, 2009: 164).

As we can see from the brief discussion of recent scholarship on the tragic frame, there is, notwithstanding slight differences, a consensus that it is deleterious to human agency. But this line of argument relies on a simplified understanding of media dynamics, one that is, at first glance, close to Stuart Hall's notion of "encoding/decoding." As Hall points out, messages are communicated through socially embedded meanings. Hence, an event must be a story—a narrative recognized by most in a given social group—before it can become communicative. The messages must always be "translated" into social structures through "rules." These rules are rooted in "recognizable types," whose content and structure are then "easily encoded" through symbols and tropes. The ease of the audience's "decoding" is thus a reflection of the symbols and tropes already embedded and naturalized in the social world. Hall describes this as a "visual competence" (in film and television). These "conditions of recognition" are shared by members of a culture as a function of hegemony. Hegemony not only defines a culture's "mental horizon" but births the "universe of possible meanings of a whole society or culture." This in turn carries an epistemological legitimacy, "[appearing] coterminous with what is 'natural'" or "taken for granted" in the social order (Hall, 2007: 397).

What Hall recognizes and these scholars *miss*, however, is that meanings are embedded in society and culture. The success of recognition relies on the distribution of a specific sort of understanding of tragedy and comedy. But it is not clear whether the tragic narrative is all that widespread or whether tragedy is defined hegemonically. As the previous chapter argued, certain aspects of tragedy, such as redemption, may act as a synecdoche. For scholars to argue that a tragic framing inculcates resignation and even threatens the social order, then, is to suggest that the audience recognizes, as Hall suggests, tragedy in a similar way through shared codes. In their haste to condemn tragedy, Foust and Murphy misstate its influence as a signifier. As Roland Barthes says about myth, when it becomes "form," that is, a signifier, "only the letter remains." He goes on: "There is here a paradoxical permutation in the reading operations, an abnormal regression from meaning to form, from the linguistic sign to the mythical signifier... there is no fixity in mythical concepts: they can come into being, alter, disintegrate, disappear completely" (Barthes, 1972: 117).

When media adopts a tragic frame in covering large-scale social problems, are they giving up hope for "human agency" necessarily or are they articulating new realities wherein the limits of *individual* human agency have been made clear? In an era where changes to the climate and the impact of pandemics can only be addressed through collective action, it seems that there is a shift in how "tragedy" and "tragic," as signifiers, are operating in media, especially in coverage pertaining to climate change and COVID-19.

In her analysis of the coverage of the 2008 drought in the Murray-Darling Basin in Australia, Eva-Karin Olsson puts forth the idea of "responsibility framing" (Olsson, 2009: 226). As she notes, responsibility framing relies on blame games that, in turn, depend on a clear ascription of the crisis to exogeneous factors or to endogenous ones (Olsson, 2009: 229). *The Australian*, the only national paper with daily circulation, had framed the drought of the Murray-Darling Basin, which provides water to three million Australians, tragically. Instead of using a "responsibility framing," *The Australian* resorted to the language of tragedy, reporting that politicians were seen as "facing a tragic choice." They either "[let] the lower lakes of the river acidify or flooding the lakes with seawater in order to prevent acidification and consequently changing the entire ecosystem." This decision was framed as "irreversible":

> The framing of the situation as a tragic choice set the tone of the reporting and underlined both the complexity and the urgency of the situation. The framing, in which available alternatives were all attached to major irreversible changes in ecosystems, posed new challenges to crisis communication insofar as it questioned the traditional underpinning of crisis communication as a means to returning to "normalcy."
>
> (Olsson, 2009: 232)

In other words, there would be no way for politicians and other actors to easily quell the concerns of the public by stating that there was a "normal" to return to if they acted one way or another. Here, tragedy is thus defined by a "damned if you do, damned if you don't" situation. To leave the basin as-is would be untenable. Likewise, to take steps to fill it in would also mean doing some sort of potential harm. To call this framing "tragic," says Olsson, is to acknowledge the difficulty of "calculating the incalculable." To use another phrase attributed to Ulrich Beck, the tragic is necessitated by the "unintended consequences" of all choices.

The drought and the subsequent water crisis in the Murray-Darling Basin was seen as an example of a climate change-induced "compounded crisis" with ripple effects affecting ecology, society, economics, and politics. It is seen, by some, as "the developed world's first climate change crisis." In Olsson's estimation, the drought met the criteria of a "critical discourse moment" in media coverage of global warming, whereby "a new sense of urgency" was attached (Olsson, 2009: 227). However, what is complicated, as Beck notes, is that because of the "erosion of the traditional distinction between crises as 'man-made' and 'acts of God'," ascertaining responsibility in the climate crisis is increasingly difficult as nature no longer has the mysterious and metaphysical status of an enchanted world. Thus, nature has "moved from being understood as an uncontrollable force to an object that can be controlled by scientific and technological advances" (Olsson, 2009: 228–229). It is, by extension, difficult to assign blame or responsibility to a single party or a set of actors, such as in war. Climate change, and associated extreme weather events, is due to the "combined effects of the actions" of many individuals and parties (Olsson, 2009: 229).

This was also clear in the summer bushfires of 2019 and 2020, to take another example from Australia. Known as "Black Summer," this period consisted of 24 million hectares being burned and directly causing 33 deaths directly and almost 450 more from smoke inhalation. An analysis by some of Australia's top scientists states that the annual area of burned by fire across the country had increased by 48,000 hectares per year over the last 30 years. They also note that the three of the four extreme forest fires since they started keeping records 90 years ago have occurred since 2002. Fire season is also "growing" in the sense that it was no longer relegated to spring and summer. It now extends into fall and winter. "These trends are almost entirely due to Australia's increasingly severe fire weather and are consistent with predicted human-induced climate change," they proclaim (Dowdy et al., 2021).

Media coverage of these fires occurred almost instantaneously. In fact, one of the most widely circulated photographs of 2020 was of a silhouette of a kangaroo racing passed a mailbox in the foreground with a structure (most likely a house) totally engulfed in flames. Taken in Lake Conjola in New South Wales by photographer Matthew Abbott, the photograph ended up in *The New York Times*, coming "to symbolize the destruction wrought by the wildfires in Australia" (Abbott and Shimabukuro, 2020). Even while the fires were still raging, articles attempting to figure out "why the fires in Australia are so bad" were being published. But the answers, in part, were quite clear. As one article reported:

> Even as emissions continue to soar, the country, currently governed by a conservative coalition, has found it difficult to reach a political consensus on energy and climate change policy. Those politics, in part, are influenced by Australia's long mining history and its powerful coal lobby.
>
> (Parsons et al., 2020)

This kind of stark analysis was also extended to criticism of Rupert Murdoch, the Australian media magnate, whose "standard-bearing national newspaper, *The Australian*, has also repeatedly argued that this year's fires are no worse than those of the past." But scientists suggest that this is patently false, "noting that 12 million acres have burned so far, with 2019 alone scorching more of New South Wales than the previous 15 years combined" (Cave, 2020).

In the aftermath, news analysis that took stock of the fires framed them as "tragic." For instance, an article discussing a documentary called *Australia Burns: Silence of the Land* (2021) poses the question: "Was humanity, in fact, to blame?" after an opening paragraph that details the historic nature of the bushfires. According to the article, the film is asking, "whether such fires could ever be explained as *random* tragedy that some suggested they were, or if they were instead a planet at breaking point, a cry for help from Mother Nature, and a preview of an inevitable and devastating future" (Myers, 2021 Emphasis added).

The question of blame consists of a false dichotomy between tragedy and a cry for help from Nature. The distinction between tragedy and a planetary breaking point is born out of an idea about tragedy that is misguided but commonplace. Tragedy, and in particular the tragedy of climate change, in this article, is random. When drilling down on "random," we can make two points. On the one hand, we can say that randomness in this usage, while not exactly the formal definition of "made, done, happening or chosen without method or conscious decision" nor the informal definition of "unfamiliar or unspecified," does come close enough to both in order to be justified. Although inexact, "random," here, signifies something more like "out of human control." On the other hand, we can say this is precisely the problem with this sort of adjectival modifier of tragedy. To characterize tragedy, especially that of the bushfires and climate change more broadly, as "random" is precisely to make the error that somehow events are "tragic" because no single individual had consciously decided to start the bushfires.

But this usage is not altogether unusual in Australian media. A similar description is found in a more recent article from *7News* that recounts the bushfires. It calls the Black Summer of 2019 and 2020 an "'indiscriminate and random' tragedy" (Bannister and Turnbull, 2022). It quotes Phil Mayberry, a resident of New South Wales, who says "(The bushfires) were so indiscriminate and random, we were simply lucky our building wasn't affected" (Bannister and Turnbull, 2022). All the while, local municipalities in New South Wales have recorded "36 declared natural disasters" since 2016. It therefore begs the question whether these bushfires were random in the sense that it was "unfamiliar." That's clearly not the case as they were being tracked by local communities.

As Dr. Joelle Gergis, a climate scientist who appears in the film, notes:

there was nothing "natural" about the extent of the fires and their ferocity. While they could be attributed to any number of causes, the conditions that fueled the fires were indisputably and ashamedly the result of climate change.

(Myers, 2021)

Humans, however, mostly function to authentically recount moments where they are victims of the devastating toll of the fires. The slight degree of "responsibility" given to humans is in relation to the disregard of the knowledge and techniques of Aboriginal people in dealing with fires. Cultural burns, the article states, "have played a critical role in mitigating the threat posed by fire on the continent for thousands of years" (Myers, 2021). Hence, with the exception of cultural burns, much of the tragic frame with regard to the Black Summer of 2019–2020 refers to the individual human victims of climate change without real reference to the perpetrators, or the agents, of climate change. As the previous chapters of this book have argued, this is due to a specific definition of tragedy that asserts a clear delineation of agency and responsibility between victims and perpetrators.

New lines of solidarity: cosmopolitanism vs cosmopolitics

In the past several decades, development in social and critical theory has forced a rethinking of this idea of tragedy, especially as it pertains to responsibility and risk of climate change. Scholars like Bruno Latour, Ulrich Beck, and Isabelle Stengers—broadly under the heading of "cosmopolitics"—have put forth a new way of conceptualizing solidarity in light of a new planetary reality that takes seriously how much climate change has forced us to rethink agency and responsibility.

Beck's famous risk society thesis places "the ecological crisis" as one of the core examples of what he called "reflexive modernity." The ecological crisis, he argues, is one of the triggers of an "awareness of the necessity of a new reflexive self-determination." As a result of the intensifying levels of threats and unintended consequences associated with "techno-industrial development" in what Beck calls "first modernity," there is now a greater recognition of "the necessity of a new reflexive self-determination," especially as it pertains to the "foundations of social cohesion" and also the "conventions and foundations of 'rationality'." With specific reference to the "ecological crisis," the accelerated modernization over the course of the 20th century resulted in environmental degradation and contributed to climate change. This "negative" consequence of what was surely supposed to be an era of post-Enlightenment Progress revealed, according to Beck, a "conflict inside modernity over the foundations of rationality and the self-concept of industrial society" (Beck et al., 1994: 10). Second, or reflexive, modernity consisted of addressing the limitations of modernity. It was "modernity" taking a look at itself and exercising a degree of "self-criticality" (Beck et al., 1994: 11).

Beck therefore expands on his research on risk society to suggest that today, various risks—economic, epidemiological, and environmental—traverse national borders, creating opportunities for people to transform existing political institutions beyond the logic of nationalism. The ecological crisis is "global, local and personal at the same time." Risk, therefore, *demands* a new transnational politics, which he calls "cosmopolitanism" (Saito, 2015: 444).

With the "security fictions" of industrial, nation-based society demystified (Beck et al., 1994: 12), there must be, according to Beck, a "conceptual reconfiguration of our modes of perception" in this reflexive modernity. It requires a "global sense, a sense of boundarylessness." In calling this "the cosmopolitan outlook" (Beck, 2014: 2), he argues for a shift in perception that comes out of "the experience of crisis in world society." There must be "an awareness of the interdependence and the resulting 'civilizational community of fate' induced by global risks and crises, which overcomes the boundaries between internal and external, us and them, the national and international" (Beck, 2014: 7). And thus, Beck's conceptual language moves to that of "*world* risk society" in describing not so much a given "community" but a latent one formed out of "shared global risks." It comprises "people's reflexive attempts to create transnational civil societies and public spheres so as to debate and cope with global risks effectively." This "cosmopolitan form of politics" is where Beck sees potential in "[extending] political participation and solidarity" (Saito, 2015: 444).

With this awareness comes to a larger realization that the "boundaries separating us from others" are not absolute. There is an "irreversible sameness [that] opens a space of both empathy and aggression." Beck goes on to explain that this "is a consequence both of pity and of hatred." On the one hand, there is a pity because "the (no longer heterogeneous) other becomes present in one's feelings and experience." On the other hand, there is "hatred…because the walls of institutionalized ignorance and hostility that protected my world are collapsing" (Beck, 2014: 8). In deploying the tragic language of "pity" in describing the cosmopolitan outlook, Beck seems to make a complex historical point that in second, reflexive modernity, "what takes center stage is the historically irreversible fact that people, from Moscow to Paris, from Rio to Tokyo, have long since been living in really existing relations of interdependence" (Beck, 2014: 9). It is not that the risks have brought people together but that they have made these extant lines of connectivity clear.

The language in Beck's theory of cosmopolitanism, which in addition to "pity," includes "empathy," and "fate," evokes a tragic register. The conjoining of a singular cosmos is what, for Beck, facilitates a buy-in of sorts of global citizens to the tragedy of the ecological crisis. In using this language, it is apparent that Beck means to forge lines of solidarity across national lines in particular. By tying our fates together, he reckons a community is formed.

Yet, it is precisely with the supposed universality of the "cosmos" that Bruno Latour takes umbrage. Latour finds that, in Beck's work, there is a "givenness" to "nature, the world, the cosmos." It is, as he puts it, "simply there." And because humans share basic characteristics, the world, for everyone, "at baseline," is the same (Latour, 2004: 453). This, for Latour, wreaks of "mononaturalism."

Mononaturalism, this idea that we live in a single cosmos is outdated, and even perhaps never was, argues Latour. "It's impossible," he writes, "for us now to inherit the beautiful idea of cosmopolitanism since what we lack is just what our prestigious ancestors possessed: a cosmos" (Latour, 2004: 453). Instead, what is necessary, in light of the *disappearance* of a single, homogeneous world, is a cosmo*politics*.

A cosmopolitics, Latour asserts, must then "embrace, literally, everything— including all the vast numbers of nonhuman entities making humans act" (Latour, 2004: 454). He calls for the use of William James' term "pluriverse." This is then not only a mere description of reality but a normative claim, an imperative to see it in a specific for a specific purpose. It is, in other words, it is a call—a vision:

> A common world is not something we come to recognize, as though it had always been here (and we had not until now noticed it). A common world, if there is going to be one, is something we will have to build, tooth and nail, together. The ethnocentrism of sociologists is never clearer than when they paper over the threat of multiple worlds with their weak notion of cosmopolitanism.
>
> (Latour, 2004: 455)

Put simply, Latour's criticism of Beck's position is that cosmopolitanism, as a tragic vision, is too ineffective in these times of crisis. It is limited in its understanding of what sorts of entities can impact human life, especially as it pertains to climate change and global pandemics.

Latour shares many aspects of his theory of cosmopolitics with Isabelle Stengers, who contends that the Beckian "cosmos" is Kantian. The cosmos in this conceptualization is a "good common world," which, in its accomplishment, would lead to "perpetual peace." While Beck, as a liberal, which Latour casts him as, seems to strive for such a world, Stengers, to the contrary, does not. In fact, as she writes, "the idea is to precisely slow down the construction of this common world, to create a space for hesitation regarding what it means to say 'good'" (Stengers, 2005: 995). Cosmopolitics, as opposed to cosmopolitanism, refers to an "unknown" cosmos, constituted by "multiple, divergent worlds, and to the articulations of which they could eventually be capable" (Stengers, 2005: 995). In leaving open the possibility of what this cosmos looks and feels like, Stengers points out that a cosmos of cosmopolitics "[affirms] the inseparability of ethos, the way of behaving peculiar to a being, and oikos, the habitat of that being and the way in which that habitat satisfies or opposes the demands associated with the ethos or affords opportunities for an original ethos to risk itself" (Stengers, 2005: 997). In calling *this* cosmos "etho-ecological," Stengers objects to Beck's notion of the cosmos as that which puts things into equivalence. Rather, the cosmos of cosmopolitics puts things into equality. Equality, she writes:

...does not mean that they all have the same say in the matter but that they all have to be present in the mode that makes *the decision* as difficult as possible, that precludes any shortcut or simplification, any differentiation a priori between that which counts and that which does not.

(Stengers, 2005: 1003 Emphasis added)

When speaking of "the decision," Stengers is discussing social action of any kind. Any sort of action, in such a cosmopolitical context, must be difficult, that is, without simplification. As it is an "intra-action," its potential effects on other entities will most certainly be felt.

We can see glimpses of this sort of cosmopolitics when looking at the COVID-19 pandemic.

As of this moment, there are over a million Americans that have died from COVID-19. This means that more Americans have died of COVID-19 than in two decades of automobile accidents or in the wars in Iraq and Afghanistan combined. There have been more deaths during the pandemic than from HIV during the four decades of the AIDS epidemic, as Ed Yong reports in *The Atlantic* (Yong, 2022). Not to mention, it is clear that the one million deaths are most likely an underreported number. When *The New York Times* in its May 24, 2020 edition, filled its front page with the names of 100,000 who had been reported as dead, it described their loss as "incalculable." "Now the nation hurtles toward a milestone of 1 million. What is 10 times incalculable?.," Yong poignantly asks. The tone of Yong's question, equally befuddled and fatalistic, is carried through in more recent articles in the *Times* dealing with the pandemic several years on. In one piece, the opening line of the piece reads, "The magnitude of the country's loss is nearly impossible to grasp." Yet, the very next sentence suggests that "experts say deaths were all but inevitable" (White *et al.* 2022).

The scale of the pandemic's destruction in terms of death is what many writers and publications have focused on to express the tragedy of COVID-19. But this is not limited to overall deaths but extends to specific axes of inequality, the most obvious being age and race. Three-fourths of the total deaths were made up by the nation's oldest residents, aged 85 and older. Among the rest, Black and Hispanic people died at a much higher rate than whites. "The virus," the *Times* notes, "did not claim lives evenly, or randomly." Working-class people were "five times more likely to die of COVID than college graduates." Also, "within every social class and educational tier, Black, Hispanic, and Indigenous people died at higher rates than white people" (White *et al.* 2022). Yong gives a very illustrative hypothetical: "If all adults had died at the same rates as college-educated white people, 71 percent fewer people of color would have perished" (Yong, 2022).

People living in urban environments were also disproportionately affected as well. As David Hayes-Bautista, a professor of medicine and the director of the Center for the Study of Latino Health and Culture at the University of California, Los Angeles, made a note, "more crowded housing might also have contributed to higher transmission rates, hospitalizations and deaths in Black and Hispanic families." Another explanation had to do with structural concerns such as density. In pointing out that New York City was hit harder than any other city in the country, the article drops a major figure—a New Yorker was dying of COVID every two minutes in March and April 2020. According to epidemiologists, this is due to the city's density but also its interconnectedness, acting as a global hub of commerce and tourism. City officials and politicians pointed at the federal government, whose messaging was inconsistent, making it difficult to garner public adherence to disruptions such as lockdowns and school closures. People of color also make up a large proportion of the "nearly 80 percent of workers ages 20 to 64 who died of COVID in 2020 worked in industries designated as essential, according to data obtained by a team of researchers led by Yea-Hung Chen, an epidemiologist at the University of California, San Francisco." The following 11 sectors were exempt from stay-at-home orders: food services, health care, construction, transportation, agriculture and manufacturing, and they were "almost twice as likely to die from COVID as others the same age."

Regionally speaking, while urban centers such as New York City were the symbols of the ravages of the pandemic in its early days in 2020, it was the American South that has "experienced the highest death rates from COVID of any region." As the *Times* reports, this had to do with the fact that it had some of the lowest vaccination rates in the United States. The average death rate fell everywhere in the country after the availability of vaccines except for the South, where it rose by 4 percent. The South is also where the proportion of adults with at least three or more chronic health conditions is higher than in any other part of the United States. Among these, many are risk factors specific to COVID-19. Diabetes, for instance, is a major one, with several studies suggesting that 30 to 40 percent of all COVID-related deaths involve diabetics.

From these pieces of information, one could easily think that the effect of the pandemic is indeed quite calculable, and already accounted for statistically. In the middle of 2022, there are plenty of statistics linked to COVID-19. Yet, as Yong points out, there is still widespread "fatalism," which has been "stoked by failure." Under the Trump and Biden administrations, the U.S. government floundered in its attempt to control the virus, ultimately shifting "responsibility for doing so on to individuals." The "incalculability" of the pandemic's effects as expressed in certain journalistic outlets in the United States has less to do with rational calculation and more to do with tragic incalculability in terms of human agency and understanding. Hence, 100,000 deaths and a million deaths are both equally "incalculable."

This is befuddlement shot through in how political blame is framed as well. Among those interviewed in these articles, there were some who blamed President Trump by name. A widow who lost her husband to COVID mentioned the former President but also pointed to federal health officials, who sought to quell concern in early March 2020 and therefore did not recommend mask-wearing early enough in her estimation. But as much of the analysis makes clear, it was not the role of individual politicians and public health officials alone. The fact is there was something institutional and cultural about the United States' response to the pandemic that resulted in such disastrous consequences.

In an article comparing the United States and Australia in their respective responses to the pandemic, Australia bureau chief for *The New York Times* Damien Cave argues one "lifesaving trait that Australians displayed from the top of government to the hospital floor, and that Americans have shown they lack: trust, in science and institutions, but especially in one another" (Cave, 2022). Cave seems to point to the fact that while otherwise rather comparable, the United States and Australia differ in what would otherwise be called "solidarity." Australia's death rate is a 10th of the United States'. It was easier to get Australians to abide by measures such as social distancing, movement restrictions, mask-wearing, and vaccinations than it was for health officials and political leaders in the United States. Cave refers to global surveys, reporting that Australians agree that "most people can be trusted"—a trend not exhibited by their American counterparts. But this "compliance" is not simply a matter of cultural difference. It runs deeper into what he calls "interpersonal trust," which he defines as "a belief that others would do what was right not just for the individual but for the community." It is tempting for an American journalist like Cave to fall into the trap of the much-mythologized "mateship," which is understood as the bond between equal partners or close friends. This "national trait," Cave suggests, was able to be "turn[ed] into action" (Cave, 2022). As he dramatically puts it:

> In the United States, hospital executives were lining up third-party P.P.E. vendors for clandestine meetings in distant parking lots in a Darwinian all-against-all contest. Royal Melbourne's supplies came from federal and state stockpiles, with guidelines for how distribution should be prioritized.

But the social norm of rule-following in Australia is not detached from a material base. As Cave goes on to point out, "studies show that income inequality is closely correlated with low levels of interpersonal trust. And in Australia, the gap between rich and poor, while widening, is less severe than in the United States" (Cave, 2022). Meanwhile, the United States has failed at persuading Americans to get vaccinated and boosted. Nearly a third of people in the United States have not been fully vaccinated (meaning, two shots). Seventy percent of the population has not gotten a booster (White et al. 2022). If we are to follow Cave's logic, this disparity can be chalked up to a difference in levels of solidarity. While Australia is able to garner and maintain it amongst its population, the United States cannot. It amounts to a kind of collective tragic flaw.

But as I hope the previous chapters of this book have made clear, tragedies, especially social ones, are hardly ever rooted in the singular flaws of individual characters. In the social drama of the pandemic in the United States, it is a confluence of factors that resulted in such poor outcomes for what is still the richest country in the world. And these factors were *not* unknown prior to the arrival of the virus into the United States sometime at the end of 2019. As many analysts have repeated ad nauseum, the pandemic intensified and exacerbated extant inequalities and deficiencies. Public health officials therefore do not frame the pandemic as presenting "new" challenges as such. As Dr. Mitch Katz, the head of HHC (New York City's public hospital system) admitted as much, when he says, "I don't think any of us understood the scale of it" (White et al., 2022). In suggesting that the scale of the matter was not understood, Katz is expressing the sheer difficulty faced by those heading institutions not only in terms of space but also time. It is about representability and understanding.

The fraught link between representation and tragedy can also be explored in climate change. As Zoë Lescaze points out about climate change, it "is a different kind of crisis, one that requires a different kind of art":

> This is a catastrophe in which we are all complicit and all at risk. The scale is simply too vast for any didactic artistic critique to feel adequate. As a species with relatively short lives and even shorter attention spans, humans struggle to grasp the long-term scope of an evolving emergency they will not live to experience in full. The most effective protest art, then, does not confront us with evidence we've already proven perfectly willing to ignore. Instead, it broadens the narrow ways in which we tend to conceive of time and our position within larger ecologies, without necessarily mentioning climate change by name. The resulting works are not demands for immediate action but ones that expand our psychological capacity to act.
>
> (Lescaze, 2022)

Lescaze's words here are aspirational as much as they are descriptive. But what is significant about her comments is the specific place of visuality in helping people to "grasp" the scale of an "evolving emergency of climate change." This, she argues, is what can (and should) expand the capacity to act rather than rehash evidence that we have been exposed to frequently. The COVID-19 pandemic in America can be said to exemplify this idea of the "evolving emergency" as well. We can return to Ed Yong's reporting for evidence of this. "The threat—a virus," he says, "is invisible, and the damage it inflicts is hidden from public view":

> With no lapping floodwaters or smoking buildings, the tragedy becomes contestable to a degree that a natural disaster or terrorist attack cannot be. Meanwhile, many of those who witnessed COVID's ruin are in no position to discuss it.

He quotes the sociologist Lori Peek, when he writes that the pandemic "feels so big that we can't put our arms around it anymore." Likewise, the pandemic seems to be ongoing. For us "to grapple with the aftermath of a disaster, there must first be an aftermath":

Thinking about it is like staring into the sun, and after two years, it is no wonder people are looking away. As tragedy becomes routine, excess deaths feel less excessive. Levels of suffering that once felt like thunderclaps now resemble a metronome's clicks—the background noise against which everyday life plays.

The tragedy of the COVID-19 pandemic in the United States is ungraspable. It is a story as old as America's "chronically underfunded public-health system that struggled to slow the virus's spread." It is simply the newest episode of "the packed and poorly managed 'epidemic engines' such as prisons that allowed it to run rampant." It is the newest upgrade to "an inefficient health-care system that tens of millions of Americans could not easily access and that was inundated by waves of sick patients." And it is the final movement in the symphony of "a shredded social safety net that left millions of essential workers with little choice but to risk infection for income."

When the pandemic is understood (or not) as "tragic" in such a way, it leaves governments to "[frame] the crisis as solely a matter of personal choice, even as [they] failed to make rapid tests, high-quality masks, antibody cocktails, and vaccines accessible to the poorest groups." This is the case not only in the United States but across the poorer, global South, with a greater proportion of people unvaccinated. It "shifts the burden to the very groups experiencing mass deaths to protect themselves, while absolving leaders from creating the conditions that would make those groups safe," according to Courtney Boen (Yong, 2022).

Rethinking the commons in the context of tragedy

Bruno Latour in March 2020 made the claim that the responses to the virus—"confinement," he calls it—would be a "dress rehearsal" for the "next crisis." It is not simply that we will all need to stay at home in order to exercise solidarity and save the planet so to speak. But, as Latour puts it, "the reorientation of living conditions is going to be posed as a challenge to all of us, as will all the details of daily existence that we will have to learn to sort out carefully." The health crisis, by which he means the COVID-19 pandemic, "prepares, induces and incites us to prepare" for the next crisis, or more precisely climate change.

Of course, climate change is an ongoing crisis. It is not "next" in any meaningful sense. Yet, Latour's point stands. The pandemic reveals, in part, a potential playbook for climate change. Better put, the pandemic and climate change offer similar "sudden and painful realizations," the most obvious of which are that "the classical definition of society—humans among themselves—makes no sense." Latour, in his signature way, argues:

> The state of society depends at every moment on the associations among many actors, most of whom do not have human forms. This is true of microbes—as we have known since Pasteur—but also of the internet, the

law, the organization of hospitals, the logistics of the state, as well as the climate.

(Latour, 2021: 25)

Another realization is that there are no "natural phenomena." Even pandemics, which are obviously driven by a virulent infectious agent, act in a specific way in local contexts. The same virus—be it HIV, influenza, or coronavirus—can act differently in Melbourne, Singapore, New York, or London. Likewise, the effects of climate change are not felt identically across the world. Rising sea levels are more dangerous for Palau than they are for Switzerland (Latour, 2021: 26; Welle, 2022). As Latour reminds us, these are not simply "natural" differences.

Lastly, Latour reminds us that the state *can* act. It, for various reasons, does not choose to in the case of climate change. Latour even asks us to engage in a bit of a thought experiment:

> Imagine that [French President] Macron came to announce, in a Churchillian tone, a package of measures to leave gas and oil reserves in the ground, to stop the marketing of pesticides, to abolish deep ploughing, and, with supreme audacity, to ban outdoor heaters on bar terraces. If the gas tax triggered the yellow vest's revolt, then imagine the riots that would follow such an announcement, setting the country ablaze.
>
> (Latour, 2021: 27)

The crisis of COVID-19 is that humans—as humanity—are fighting against a virus that is "killing us without meaning to." However, in the case of climate change, "the situation is tragically reversed." The "pathogen" that has resulted in "the living conditions of all the inhabitants of the planet is not the virus at all—its humanity" (Latour, 2021: 27)! What Latour evokes is a kind of "tragedy of the commons."

Often, Garret Hardin's classic article from *Science* of all places is viewed *wrongly*, as David Harvey argues, as a statement *in favor of* private property, in particular, in its relationship to the use of land and resources. It is often wrongly put forth as "irrefutable justification for privatization." He makes the point that this is, in part, due to the metaphor of cattle that Hardin uses. In Hardin's article, the example of cattle is specifically used in reference to those owned privately by individuals concerned with maximizing their utility that graze on common land. For Hardin, the "tragedy" is that the commons—the grazing land that was not owned privately up until the 16th century in England—would be decimated due to overuse. The ecologist Hardin, it would seem, was suggesting that public ownership results in environmental degradation.

For Harvey, it is abundantly clear that the problem is that the cattle are privately owned and that the individuals in the example offered by Hardin were simply out to maximize utility. But the widespread misreading of the concept of the "tragedy of the commons" cannot be explained simply by the impreci-sion of this metaphor. According to Harvey, the issue stems from an active and, even ideological, misunderstanding of Hardin's argument. Hardin was mostly concerned with population growth not so much grassland. Much in line with Malthus, Hardin feared that population growth would destroy the global com-mons. Authoritarian population control was the only solution (Harvey, 2011: 101). Hence, Hardin's argument was, in some respect, an argument *for* the commons.

Recently, the work of Nobel-prize-winning economist Elinor Ostrom on governing the commons has been the most influential in terms of countering the Hardinian view. Yet, in Harvey's estimation, it suffers the same "scale problem." In Ostrom's work, which consists of case studies demonstrating instances where "individuals can and often do devise ingenious and eminently sensible ways to manage common property resources (CPR) for individual and collective ben-efit." In doing so, Ostrom aims to break through the intractable dichotomy in the thinking on the commons: between private property rights and centralized regulation. By showing contemporary and historical evidence of appropriators directly negotiating each other, Ostrom is aiming to show that resources must either be regulated top-down or subject to libertarian market conditions.

While undoubtedly sympathetic to Ostrom's overall aim to moving away from private property, Harvey points out that her examples are small-scale. Managing resources at one level, "such as shared water rights between one hundred farmers in a small river basin, do not and cannot carry over to problems such as global warming or even to the regional diffusion of acid deposition from power sta-tions." Plus which, good solutions at a local level may not scale up to make for good solutions at the global level:

> This is why Hardin's metaphor is so misleading: he uses a small-scale exam-ple to explicate a global problem. This, incidentally, is also why the lessons gained from the collective organization of small-scale solidarity economies along common-property lines cannot translate into global solutions with-out resort to nested hierarchical forms of decision making.
>
> (Harvey, 2011: 102)

In sum, Hardin's and Ostrom's views on the commons revert to some sort of enclosure. Both take "natural resources" as the frame through which to view the commons. But, as Hardt and Negri point out, some commons are not sub-ject to the logic of scarcity like water or grass. Their view of "the common," in the singular, involves not only the product of labor but also the means of future production. It consists of the earth but also the languages, social practices, and modes of sociality that we create. These various modes of being in the world are common and cannot be destroyed or depleted.

The problem is precisely due to the terms under which the commons have been discussed. Namely, it is the framing of individual private property rights as the best means to fulfill common interests. The equation of private property with the common good, at least in liberal thought, has always involved some sort of state-like regulatory institution that bears down on the market. When citing liberal theorists like Smith or Locke, many supporters of private property (including those who do so implicitly such as development theorists) do not realize that both Smith and Locke defend the market as the ultimate mediator of collective labor through some sort of theory of socialization. As Harvey explains:

> Market exchange socializes that right when each individual gets back the value he or she has created by exchanging it against an equivalent value created by another. In effect, individuals maintain, extend, and socialize their private property right through value creation and supposedly free and fair market exchange. This is how the wealth of nations is most easily created and the common good best served.
>
> (Harvey, 2011: 104)

A major problem here is that liberal theory presumes that markets can be fair and free. Moreover, those who fail to produce value in such a way have no claim to the property. Hence, when Marx takes on the labor theory of value, he does so by showing not only that the labor market is unfair and unfree as it is set up for the generation of surplus value but also that the factory system collectivizes the labor process:

> If there were any property right to be derived from this form of labor-ing, then surely it would have to be a collective or associated rather than individual one. The definition of value-producing labor, which grounds Locke's theory of private property, no longer holds for the individual but is shifted to the collective laborer.
>
> (Harvey, 2011: 105)

Harvey's point is that "value," generated by "socially necessary labor time," is in fact "the capitalist common." The "universal equivalency" to measure it is money:

> The common is not, therefore, something extant once upon a time that has since been lost, but something that, like the urban commons, is continuously being produced. The problem is that it is just as continuously being enclosed and appropriated by capital in its commodified and monetary form.
>
> (Harvey, 2011: 105)

The "tragedy of the commons," here, is "similar to that which Hardin depicts, but the logic from which it arises is different." Put simply, without regulation, individualized capital accumulation will destroy two basic property resources of the commons that buttress all production: the worker and the land. Harvey's pro-posal is to socialize surplus production and distribute common wealth. Indeed, this would require, as even Harvey admits, a new way of thinking and also new visions of "being in common."

Recently, scholars have put forth various new definitions of the commons. For Ash Amin and Philip Howell, the commons must be thought of as "a practice or process" (Amin and Howell, 2016: 2). This is distinct from the commons as "public provisions and protections" (Amin and Howell, 2016: 6). It is not merely about the welfare state, for instance. It is about rethinking "relationality." As Silvia Federici has pointed out, "community" too often means something exclusionary. The commons should be something that approximates "a quality of relations, a principle of cooperation and of responsibility to each other and to the earth, the forests, the seas, the animals" (Amin and Howell, 2016: 11). The commons must not depend on shared identity or homogeneous culture. "Rather," Jeremy Gilbert argues, "they will be related primarily by their shared interest in defending or producing a set of common resources, and this shared interest is likely to be the basis for an egalitarian and potentially democratic set of social relationships" (Amin and Howell, 2016: 11). And thus, the tragedy of the commons does not stem from a lack of trust and reciprocity, as both Hardin and Ostrom seem to argue (Velicu and García-López, 2018: 56) but rather, as Harvey makes clear, from a limited understanding of being.

With Velicu and Garcia-Lopez, the tragedy of the commons can be read as a challenge to renew relational politics through the lens of mutual vulnerability. For them, following the work of Judith Butler, "commoning" is the term used to describe subjectivity that acknowledges the non-autonomy of becoming. The commoner becomes one through the very relationship of being "bound" to another. Most interestingly, they argue that, as "effects of power," commoners are blind to themselves. They reproduce the very power relations that gave birth to them, they are often opaque to themselves. What sustains them therefore undoubtedly limits them. In this sense, "commoning" is an ongoing struggle both "within" and "against" power and agency. As Velicu and Garcia-Lopez put it, this is the "double valence" of power, subjection and agency (Velicu and García-López, 2018: 63–64). Given this, the "commoner" is not so much a "fully formed alternative/communal subjectivity" but rather relationally constituted. "Who 'we' are," they argue, "is a social construct (an ego, identity(ies)) which helps us survive in a world of complex relations, norms and political-economic structures." Not only do we not know ourselves but the idea is that we can never hope to. This is not only because of the psychoanalytically inflected theory of subjectivity in Butler but also because, as Velicu and Garcia-Lopez argue, "we embody our proximities or relations–often unchosen–both within and 'against' ourselves" (Velicu and García-López, 2018: 62).

This Butlerian critique of the stable self is not a defense of vulnerability for its own sake. Rather, it is a critique of enclosure all the way down, including that of the self. In defending the commons, Ostrom still smuggles in an enclosure of relations. To say that the commons require trust and cooperative rules to prevent overuse is to imply that it needs rational, communicative (e.g., Habermasian) subjects with "clear boundaries or identities." These relations often take the form of "exchange." This is, to put it simply, the commons of Ostrom. But what Velicu and Garcia-Lopez are arguing for is a commons based on shared and partial blindness of ourselves, to use Butler's terminology. Put otherwise, they wish to argue for a commons seeping with vulnerability and dependency. Fragility and dependency can also be "an empowering relational condition of humanity, a terrain of 'agency'" (Velicu and García-López, 2018: 66).

While Hardin sees the commons as vulnerable to exploitation by those who take advantage of it, others have tried to counter this by stating tragedy is not inevitable. Ostrom, for example, treats the issue essentially as a matter of communication. Cooperative institutions could help reduce the likelihood of the overuse of resources. But "critical commons scholars argue that institutions are an end-of-pipe solution and seek to address the structural problems that produce enclosures and vulnerability." The real tragedy is enclosures and displaced commoners, which would be addressed by building commoning alternatives. "These ideas," argue Velicu and Garcia-Lopez, "help us de-naturalize the 'tragedy' narrative as a taken-for-granted vision of individuals; more so, they help us shed a different light on the issue of vulnerability" (Velicu and García-López, 2018: 64).

Conclusion

Reading the tragedy of the commons through the lens of relationality and solidarity points us to reimagining action and scale within the context of tragedy more broadly. As Peter Hitchcock and Christian Haines wonder:

> Perhaps every story of the commons is also a story of downfall—a narrative of reversal (*peripeteia*) in which the will to monopolize the social discovers its own incapacity, its inability to secure accumulation against the dispossessed. What could be more tragic than the rule of law (or the capitalist order of propriety) toppling to the desires of unruly commoners? *Then again, perhaps the only tragedy of the commons is its belatedness. Think of all the time that commoners have lost to the fairy tale of scarcity, that bogeyman used to frighten children into believing that freedom and private appropriation are one and the same thing.*
>
> (Hitchcock and Haines, 2019: 64 Emphasis added)

Tragedy, in the sense of inaction and fatalism, is premised farcically on scarcity that is generated.

The main method by which scarcity has been enforced in the history of capitalism is the enclosure. The enclosures movement is how nearly all of the agricultural land in Britain came to be owned by just a tiny sliver of the population (1 percent). As a result of ongoing legislation beginning in the 1600s, land known as "commons" became privatized by fiat. Before enclosures, there were shared pastures where landless villagers grazed their animals. These villagers were mostly tenant farmers, who, unlike sharecroppers, had their own animals and tools. What they lacked was land. Therefore, tenant farming was conducted cooperatively, using what is called an "open-field system, cultivating crops on narrow strips of land." Likewise, commoners had "rights of pannage, of turbary, of estovers, and of piscary—rights to run their pigs in the woods, to cut peat for fuel, to gather wood from the forests, and to fish." In other words, commoners had the "rights to subsistence…to live on what they could glean from the land." This was the system for 700 years prior to the enclosures movement. The commons were therefore a "resource reserved for those with the least," as the writer Eula Biss describes it (Biss, 2022).

The history of enclosures, in this regard, is then a history of the unequal distribution of risk and vulnerability through the forced removal of the individual from the collective. It is the story of the artificial control of supply to manipulate demand. It is the fixing of the social cost of living together, making it payable by the most vulnerable. In brief, it is cartelism presented as ethics. The tragedy of the commons is the failure to recognize the tragedy of acting alone in the world. It is the misappropriation of responsibility. It is in fact the tragedy of enclosure and enclosed selves.

References

Abbott, M., and Shimabukuro, M., 2020. In One Photo, Capturing the Devastation of Australia's Fires. *The New York Times*, 10 Jan.

Amin, A., and Howell, P., 2016. Thinking the Commons. *In*: A. Amin, and P. Howell, eds. *Releasing the Commons*. London: Routledge.

Bannister, M., and Turnbull, T., 2022. 'Indiscriminate and random': Two Years on from the Devastating Black Summer Bushfires. *7NEWS*. Retrieved July 23, 2022 (https://7news.com.au/news/bushfires/indiscriminate-and-random-two-years-on-from-the-devastating-black-summer-bushfires-c-5160827).

Barthes, R., 1972. *Mythologies*. London: Macmillan.

Beck, U., 2014. *Cosmopolitan Vision*. Cambridge: Polity.

Beck, U., Giddens, A., and Lash, S., 1994. *Reflexive Modernization: Politics, Tradition and Aesthetics in the Modern Social Order*. Redwood City, CA: Stanford University Press.

Biss, E., 2022. The Theft of the Commons. *The New Yorker*, 8 Jun.

Boltanski, L., 2005. *Distant Suffering Morality, Media and Politics*. Cambridge: Cambridge University Press.

Cave, D., 2020. How Rupert Murdoch Is Influencing Australia's Bushfire Debate. *The New York Times*, 8 Jan.

Cave, D., 2022. How Australia Saved Thousands of Lives While Covid Killed a Million Americans. *The New York Times*, 15 May.

Dowdy, A., Cook, G., Knauer, J., Meyer, M., Canadell, P., and Briggs, P., 2021. Australia's Black Summer of Fire Was Not Normal – and We can Prove It. *The Conversation*. Retrieved July 23, 2022 (http://theconversation.com/australias-black-summer-of-fire-was-not-normal-and-we-can-prove-it-172506).

Foust, C.R., and Murphy, W.O., 2009. Revealing and Reframing Apocalyptic Tragedy in Global Warming Discourse. *Environmental Communication*, 3 (2), 151–167.

Hall, S., 2007. *Encoding and Decoding in the Television Discourse.* CCCS Selected Working Papers. London: Routledge.

Harvey, D., 2011. The Future of the Commons. *Radical History Review,* 2011 (109), 101–107.

Hitchcock, P., and Haines, C.P., 2019. Theses on the Commons. *The Minnesota Review,* 2019 (93), 62–67.

Jacobs, R.N., 2001. The Problem With Tragic Narratives: Lessons from the Los Angeles Uprising. *Qualitative Sociology,* 24 (2), 221–243.

Kittler, F.A., 1999. *Gramophone, Film, Typewriter.* 1st edition. Stanford, CA: Stanford University Press.

Latour, B., 2004. Whose Cosmos, Which Cosmopolitics? Comments on the Peace Terms of Ulrich Beck. *Common Knowledge,* 10 (3), 450–462.

Latour, B., 2021. Is This a Dress Rehearsal *Critical Inquiry,* 47 (S2), S25–S27.

Lescaze, Z., 2022. How Should Art Reckon With Climate Change? *The New York Times,* 25 Mar.

Liptak, A., 2007. Prosecutor Becomes Prosecuted. *The New York Times,* 24 Jun.

Myers, K., 2021. 'Australia Burns: Silence of the Land' Is a Call to Action. *Guide.* Retrieved July 23, 2022 (https://www.sbs.com.au/guide/article/2021/11/04/australia-burns-silence-land-call-action).

Olsson, E.-K., 2009. Responsibility Framing in a 'Climate Change Induced' Compounded Crisis: Facing Tragic Choices in the Murray—Darling Basin. *Environmental Hazards,* 8 (3), 226–240.

Parsons, A., Goldman, R., and Abbott, M., 2020. Why the Fires in Australia Are So Bad. *The New York Times,* 1 Jan.

Pew Research Center, 2014. *World Wide Web Timeline.* Washington, DC: Pew Research Center: Internet, Science & Tech.

Saito, H., 2015. Cosmopolitics: Towards a New Articulation of Politics, Science and Critique. *The British Journal of Sociology,* 66 (3), 441–459.

Stengers, I., 2005. The Cosmopolitical Proposal. *In*: B. Latour and P. Weibel, eds. *Making Things Public.* Cambridge, MA: MIT Press, 994–1003.

The Size and Growth Rate of the Internet in 1993: History of Information [online], 2022. Available from: https://historyofinformation.com/detail.php?entryid=2547 [Accessed 23 Jul 2022].

Turnage, A.K., 2009. Scene, Act, and the Tragic Frame in the Duke Rape Case. *Southern Communication Journal,* 74 (2), 141–156.

Velicu, I., and García-López, G., 2018. Thinking the Commons Through Ostrom and Butler: Boundedness and Vulnerability. *Theory, Culture & Society,* 35 (6), 55–73.

Welle, D., 2022. German Foreign Minister Annalena Baerbock Calls for Global Response to Climate Change in Palau [online]. *DW.COM.* Available from: https://www.dw.com/en/german-foreign-minister-annalena-baerbock-calls-for-global-response-to-climate-change-in-palau/a-62416528 [Accessed 23 Jul 2022].

White, J., Harmon, A., Ivory, D., Leatherby, L., Sun, A., and Almukhtar, S., 2022. How America Lost One Million People. *The New York Times,* 14 May.

Yong, E., 2022. How Did This Many Deaths Become Normal? *The Atlantic,* 8 Mar.

8

TOWARD A TRAGIC SOCIAL SCIENCE

Responsibility, critique, and thinking diffractively

Introduction

This book has argued for the contemporary relevance of the tragic, specifically its significance for theorizing in the social sciences, in hopes of acting as notes toward an approach that rejects wholesale the primacy of human rationality and control. Moreover, it sought not only to make a case for a re-engagement with tragic literature in the Western tradition but also to expand the definition of "the tragic" beyond the literary and philosophical and to include theodicy, which would help remind us of its vital role in the formation of social science. By establishing tragedy's relationship to theodicy, the book suggests that there are lessons that are especially pertinent in a world that not only explains misfortune and evil in a previous era but also aims to think about ideas for how to live in the current world of uncertainty. And thus, there is an ethical component (though perhaps not a normative one) in the preceding pages.

One of the key aspects of tragic ethics, Nussbaum argues, is the expansion of what we would think of as part of human life. It requires the "refining our perceptions of the complex 'material' of human life" (Nussbaum, 2001: 378). Human life consists not only of human beings but also their actions. As Charlotte Witt argues, challenging the boundaries of human life necessarily impacts understandings of responsibility. It eschews "culpability" for "accountability" (Witt, 2005: 70). To be accountable is not only accepting responsibility but also means to "confront the questions of identity and self-understanding that are raised by the unintended nature and outcome of one's actions." Culpability, on the contrary, is largely a *legal* category. It operates in terms of reward and punishment as well as praise and blame. It is, for this reason, regulatory. Culpability assumes that action is voluntary, that action has its causal origin in the human being. There is, within the logic of culpability,

DOI: 10.4324/9781003110859-10

full intentionality. The agent knows "the relevant facts concerning the circum-stances surrounding the action."

But, this level of knowledge, tragedy reveals, is almost impossible (Witt, 2005: 71). In tragedy, human actions may arise out of "internal sources, yet our internal motivations are complex and are not simple expressions of our natures." The sources of the action may be internal but this is in the context of "a kind of internal agent passivity in the face of overwhelming desire or anger" (Witt, 2005: 72). Humans are not necessarily flawed; they simply err, which Stephen Halliwell locates "in the space between guilt and vulnerability to arbitrary mis-fortune" (Witt, 2005: 78).

Vulnerability, as Butler and those inspired her work maintain, can be the basis of a radical form of kinship and, in turn, human relationality more broadly. In her famed analysis of Antigone, Butler argues that Antigone "refuses" the command of Creon, who has forbidden her to perform the duties of "family" by giving a proper burial for (and crucially, *grieving*) her brother (Butler, 2002: 11). Butler describes as love, as Antigone "refuses" the law that itself refuses public recognition of her loss. Her enactment of kinship is to grieve. There is no life that cannot be grieved. There is no loss that is not grievable (Butler, 2002: 24). For Butler, this is a radical form of kinship, one not in its ideal form but rather in a state of "deformation and displacement." It

> puts the reigning regimes of representation into crisis and raises the ques-tion of what the conditions of intelligibility could have been that would have made her life possible, indeed, what sustaining web of relations makes our lives possible, those of us who confound kinship in the rearticulation of its terms?
>
> (Butler, 2002: 24)

Butler's articulation of kin as a "sustaining web of relations" that "makes our lives possible" is usually interpreted in critical and queer theory as part of a larger critique of the heteronormative, bourgeois family. In fact, this part of her analysis includes some choice words for Kath Weston's work on "families we choose" (Weston, 1997) and sociologist Orlando Patterson's work on slavery and social death (Patterson, 2018). In demonstrating that both scholars respectively rely on the heteronormative, patriarchal family as the model of the family, Butler pushes for a renewed sociality, thinking of "relations" and "life" (and tragic ethics) in more expansive ways.

A potential repercussion of the widening of the web of social relations occas-sioned by a tragic ethics, I wish to argue, is the broadening notion of "responsi-bility." The philosopher Hans Jonas presents a typology of responsibility in three parts. In traditional, ethical theory, the first and "the most general condition of responsibility is causal power." Action makes an impact on the world. This assumes that, second, the acting is under the agent's control. In doing so, third, the agent "foresees its consequences." But Jonas points out that there are two senses of responsibility at play here. There is a sense of accountability, meaning, that one is responsible for one's deeds. But in addition there is the responsiblility for certain objects, which commit "an agent to particular deeds concerning them" (Jonas, 1985: 90). The former sense Jonas describes as "the mere fact of accountability." Without "the agent's consent," it is nothing but a "precondition of morality but not yet itself morality" (Jonas, 1985: 92). For Jonas, the imperative of responsibility is based simply on *things* mattering rather than states of will:

> By engaging the will, the things become ends. Ends may sometimes be sublime—by what they are, and even certain acts or lives may be so; but not the formal rule of the will whose observance is for any chosen end, or act, the condition of being a moral one, or, more precisely, of not being an immoral one.
>
> (Jonas, 1985: 89)

It is important to recognize that Jonas' perspective is ecological. The vulnerability of nature—undoubtedly a crucial node in the web of relations that sustain human life—"alters the very concept of ourselves as causal agency in the larger scheme of things." It is this ecological perspective, which takes for granted the causal nature of human life that Jonas articulates a particular theory of responsibility, which does not "[fall] into a narrow anthropocentric view (Jonas, 1985: 136). In Jonas' estimation, all human action is causal. By this, he means to emphasize its "cumulative character: their effects keep adding themselves to one another, with the result that the situation for later subjects and their choices of action will be progressively different from that of the initial agent and ever more the fated product of what was done before" (Jonas, 1985: 7). This is, as he explains, a departure from traditional ethics, which takes as given the basic situation between persons. Actions that occur within the confines of an interaction are "noncumulative," in other words, ahistorical.

But in what we would today call the era of the Anthropocene, "the nature of human action has changed and with it the focus of ethical theory." As we are now "threatened by catastrophe from the very progress of history itself," Jonas surmises that we cannot trust an "immanent 'reason in history'" or a "self-realizing 'meaning' of the drift of events" to save us (Jonas, 1985: 128). The juggernaut of modernity, which Jonas characterizes as "the forward rushing process"—Giddens' "runaway modernity" (Giddens, 2002)—needs to be taken in hand or else we risk "[shivering] in the nakedness of nihilism in which near-omnipotence is paired with near-emptiness, greatest capacity with knowing least for what ends to use it."

The task, therefore, is to be clear-eyed about the "new kind of human action" that results from the degree of "collective technological practice." We must be clear about not "the sheer magnitude of most of its enterprises" but also "the indefinitely cumulative propagation of its effects." In light of a reality in which "technical civilization" has become "almighty," Jonas argues that the "overruling

duty of collective human action" must shift to "care for the future of mankind…
since man has become dangerous not only to himself but to the whole of the bio-
sphere" (Jonas, 1985: 136). Likewise, the scale of ethics, he argues, has changed
from individual morality to collective responsibility (Jonas, 1985: 122).

The strong normative component of his work comes from what he sees as the
destruction of the sacred by "technical civilization" and the "scientific enlightenment." As he puts it, it is moot whether we can ever restore such a "category."
But without it, what sort of ethics are even capable of coping with the "extreme
powers which we possess today and constantly increase and are almost compelled
to wield." Jonas reveals himself to be quite conflicted in this regard. He admits
that only the sacred "with its unqualified veto" can quell the "computations
of mundane fear and the solace of uncertainty." But with "religion in eclipse,"
ethics cannot shirk its primary task (Jonas, 1985: 23). To induce an ethical orientation of collective responsibility in such an era of "scientific enlightenment" is
to create what I would call a *partial* re-enchantment. For Jonas, while "technical
civilization" is no doubt "almighty," "secularization is here still half-hearted."
There is an opportunity, he states, for some kind of "regulative ideal" that sees
moral conduct "*as if*…it is also [contributing] to the moral advance of the world"
(Jonas, 1985: 127).

Jonas ultimately calls for "a secularized eschatology of the new Adam" that
substitutes "worldly causes for the divine feat that was to work the miracle
of transformation in the religious creeds." For him, "the secular equivalent"
is to socialize production and distribution toward a "classless society" (Jonas,
1985: 179). His attraction to Marxism is rooted in a specific understanding of
the eschatological as future oriented. No doubt an expression of his interest in
Gnosticism and Messianism (similar to Walter Benjamin), Jonas viewed "the
Marxist program" as being a legitimate source of ethics that "aims action pre-
dominantly at the future and thence imposes norms on the present" (Jonas, 1985:
143). This, he maintains, is distinct from utopia, which is characterized by "the
starry-eyed ethics of perfectibility." The ethics of responsibility, on the contrary,
are "sterner" (Jonas, 1985: 201).

The open-ended temporality of the ethics of responsibility is linked to what
the literary critic Frank Kermode famously calls a "sense of an ending." Endings,
he argues, are themselves a form of sense making. Hence, endings are usually
products of narrative based on a tidy structure consisting of beginnings, middles,
and conclusions. But an ending can only result from embracing impending crisis. The anticipation of an end, an eschatology, in other words, is at the heart of
not only *literary* sense-making (especially in fiction) but also making sense of the
world. The "end-feeling," Kermode argues, is absorbed into "the dull mundan-
ities of everyday life" beyond fiction and even beyond literature. This explains
why the death metaphor is mapped onto so many different aspects of life—marriage, chronic conditions, etc. By internalizing death in such a way, the bonds of
terror and anxiety are slipped, according to Kermode's logic. It is to "live within
them" (Garber, 2019).

Thus, to live within tragedy is to anticipate death but in so doing to craft an ethics of responsibility that recasts causality in an expansive manner, acknowledging not only the longue durée of causal agency (taking the cumulative effect of humanity's impact on itself and the world as given) but also the various levels at which agency can operate, even outside of individual, human consciousness. It is also to think beyond endings as resolutions. It may mean to think beyond endings as the impact of one entity to the next could be viewed as continuous. In other words, it is to accept that there may not be meaning in history defined by a singular telos. As Fredric Jameson has couched it, "ends have been sundered from means" (Jameson, 1973: 60) as a result of a "vanishing mediator."

When there is such a "rift between intention and act," Jameson argues, ennui ensues. The sufferer (in this case, all of humanity) resigns to the fact that any sort of action is nothing but a "pure technical performance without intrinsic purpose or value" (Jameson, 1973: 60). We, humans, are "faced with a peculiar impression" that the meaninglessness of life is "in direct proportion" to the control of the environment. "Meaningfulness," therefore, only "remained intact only so long as some portion of that world" held shape. The uses of tragedy are attempts to keep that world together. They serve, to continue with Jameson, as "ideology," or a "cognitive map," a mechanism that situated individual subjects (both consciously and unconsciously) with "the collective social structure" (Jameson, 2020: p. x) within a capitalist mode of production.

Arguably since its inception, social science has held ideology as the main object of critique (Lash 2007; Thompson 1991). Even today, the conceit of critical social science has been to uncover the distortions of an individualist, consumer-oriented society and demonstrate the interlocking fates of the individual and the collective. Hence, the task of social theory, cultural studies, and media and communications studies was to reveal the hidden meaning of social and cultural phenomena—fashion, music, television, cinema, and media more broadly. But, as Jameson notes, the notion of ideology implies "the conception of nature as meaningful." To do social science as ideology critique would also mean an "affirmation not merely of a meaningful system at work in the natural world, but also of human nature as well, one which virtually by definition is normative" (Jameson, 2020: 10).

If we are to get past ideology, then how to do social science *beyond* critique?

Social science beyond critique?

A place we can look to is the new materialism/posthumanities, in which scholars have put forth a "planetary imaginary" that runs counter to the "mechanized worlding" that characterizes dominant geological science and anthropogenic environmental destruction. Under the rubric of "cosmopolitics" or "Gaia," scholars have called for a new "way of worlding" (Sands, 2020: 108) that reflects a "living planet" (Sands, 2020: 105). Gaia, and associated terms, such as the very recent work of Latour on what he calls a "fictional planetarium" (Latour,

2020), rooted in mythology, as Daniella Sands rightly notes, are "articulating non-modern conceptual and practical responses to problems generated by and within modernity" (Sands, 2020: 108).

In so doing, these scholars have also called for a moving beyond "critique."

For Latour and others, including the feminist theorist Rosi Braidotti, concerns about critique stem from a historical association with the Enlightenment, especially its claims around intellectual and political emancipation (Sands, 2020: 113). Critique professes to find the truth of the matter. As literary critic John Michael rightly notes, the practice of close reading or depth analysis is at the very heart of the humanities' (and humanistic social sciences') "critical method." This goes for the Frankfurt School of critical theory to poststructuralist readings to New Criticism and even New Historicism. All of these approaches are founded on a "hermeneutics of suspicion," whereby "techniques of deep or close reading [are] meant to uncover the networks of power and the designs of obfuscation, or the tensions and lapses in structures of signification, or the linguistic patterning of ironies and paradoxes, or the institutional imbrications of complicity or co-optation that constitute the real meaning or actual significance of a text." In other words, the critic functions as "master interpreter," who is able to decipher and reveal a text's "true meaning."

Critique's power, thus, came from its linking of exegesis and emancipation. Its promise stemmed from its purported ability to "help overcome the obfuscations of the world by those powerful forces of the government and the economy interested in controlling the discourses, means, and materials of culture and representation and to reveal the real relationships of power and oppression encoded within...cultural artifacts." This required, of course, a positionality of the critic as "knowing subject" and also the projection of the audience as knowing subjects (Michael, 2017: 253). Thus, critique was viewed as "secular demystification" (Michael, 2017: 254). To secularize *was* to demythologize.

But recently, "the traditional understanding of secularism itself has altered":

> ...[S]ecularism can no longer be understood as the rejection of parochial beliefs and superstitions in favor of catholicisms of science and rationality. In this age, any belief, including the belief in science and rationality, emerges within a context teeming with heterogeneities of contradictory and competing beliefs that do not preclude commitment but disrupt its immediacy, its untroubled possession of its own groundedness. Disenchantment or demystification do not adequately describe the experience of secularization thus understood.
>
> (Michael, 2017: 254)

Without forms of "immediate certainty, including an immediate certainty in the virtues of reason, science and progress," the question is what part can "critique play in a world where a belief in rational discourse as a contribution to progress, enlightenment, and emancipation has ceased to be a belief that the secular critic can naively hold" (Michael, 2017: 255). For Michael, "the moral and social catastrophes of the world increasingly resist narrative enchainment" (Michael, 2017: 255), including the powerful tropes of secular modernity. This occasions a "tragic vision" of a world that responds to the lessened leverage of today's intellectuals in the face of commodity capitalism, neoliberal economics, and empty pieties about nominally "democratic orders" (Michael, 2017: 258).

In the wake of this, Michael argues for a "tragic knowledge" that responds to the end of historical optimism but not the end of hope, as he so eloquently puts it. Tragic knowledge involves "knowing not only who one is but what conduct— what ambitions and aspirations—are proper to one's place," both its limitations and possibilities (Michael, 2017: 259). In a (post-)secular world, this means the rejection of critique as "forensic hermeneutics." The critic as detective is a figure that Michael suggests "embodies fantasies of managed anxiety" (Michael, 2017: 267). Critique can no longer be based on the project of enlightening an audience by deciphering latent codes or meanings.

Instead, what he calls for is "tragic performance" in the form of "translation." By this, Michael argues that critique in a secular world must be an exercise in "meaning making," which is fully aware of the provisional nature and final inadequacy of any meaning accomplished. If one is willing to think of critique in such a way, then the "false security" of critique as a "bringer of enlightenment that divulges the truth and demystifies the world." To perform rather than critique is to be aware of one's limitations—an extension of the ultimate awareness of one's mortality:

> Critical meaning, contingent truth, grows out of various and conflicted lived situations that furnish opportunities for and limitations to critical action, which action can refashion common beliefs and resharpen dulled sensibilities. All this might remind us that our loss of confidence in the ability of critique to discern the happy culmination of history points toward a heightened ethical and political awareness, as tragic knowledge tends to do…. Tragic knowledge is not the grounding of despair or quietism, but is the likely precondition for ethical action and effective political engagement in the secular world.
>
> (Michael, 2017: 269)

Tragic knowledge as translation disavows hubris and disabuses us of the illusion of mastery. It contains no pretense of sovereign power.

With its focus on a goal of mastery, critique has, in Latour's words, "run out of steam" as it has hardly provided a meaningful way out of one of the most trenchant global challenges of the day—the climate crisis (Latour, 2004). To continue to provide facts proving the validity of climate science does little to change the hearts and minds of those in power who are "climate skeptics." Neither does it result in any sort of reversal of climate change itself; it does not lower the temperature and lower sea levels. The continued orientation of "critique" toward scientific facts has lost relevance in this secular era of ethico-onto-epistemological uncertainty. What is needed, in Latour's view, for instance, is a shift from matters of facts to matters of concern (Sands, 2020: 114). Gaia, as a "counter-mythopoetics," is an expression of what Michael calls "tragic performance."

A similar dynamic is seen in the recent theoretical perspectives associated with the concept of "agential realism." Coined by the feminist science studies scholar Karen Barad, agential realism begins from the idea of "diffraction" and thinking "diffractively," which is situated in contrast to "the modern tool and the optics of refraction." Diffraction amounts to a "different form of consciousness that…is attentive to how differences are produced in the world and leave concrete, material marks on bodies, things and environments" (Geerts and Carstens, 2019: 917). In other words, diffraction understands the world in an ontologically immanent manner, where everything in it is entangled. Thus, action in this world thought of "diffractively" is made up of "intra-actions," hence all entities are "ethically responsible" for it and each other. Diffraction, Geerts, and Carstens argue, occasions a different kind of "heuristic" which is open-ended. It sees the knower, the-world-that-is-to-be-known, and knowledge-producing processes as all entangled.

The "entwining of ethics, knowing and being" (Geerts and Carstens, 2019: 920)—ethico-onto-epistemology—engendered by "thinking diffractively" is what "equips us with the tools to think and rethink things, and to reflect upon the consequences of our engagement with the world in a critical and responsible manner" (Geerts and Carstens, 2019: 923). For Geerts and Carstens, this entails "working with and through uncomfortable relations of suffering." This entails recognizing that we are "embroiled in networks of planetary harm" (Geerts, 2016: 253). Thus, *realism* is the proper description of thinking diffractively.

Thinking diffractively

To think diffractively, with suffering, may mean doing social science quite differently. In an article for *The New Yorker*, Elif Batuman asks whether "Greek tragedy can get us through the pandemic." It is a worthy question, especially since the article details the work of an organization called Theater of War Productions, which started by putting on performances of classical Greek tragedies for US military audiences in various parts of the world where American armed forces are stationed. Rather unique about these productions is the presence of a panel made up of active service members, veterans, military partners as well as psychiatrists that speak to how the themes of the play affected them. While initially focused on combat trauma, the organization also puts on productions addressing different forms of trauma—the opioid crisis, gun violence, police brutality, and forth—in the very communities where these traumas are experienced.

In recent years, as Batuman writes, "with trauma roving the globe more contagiously than ever, Theater of War Productions had traded its site-specific approach for Zoom" (Batuman, 2020). The organization has enlisted well-known

Hollywood actors to perform online for frontline healthcare workers, who have been dealing with the trauma of treating patients during the pandemic. Given this, it is unsurprising that people are turning to Greek tragedy. Batuman rightly points out that there was a plague in 430 BC, at the start of the Peloponnesian War. According to Thucydides, the theater in Athens was still operational, leading us to believe that actors and playwrights were "essential workers." Batuman highlights that this is somewhat unsurprising given the connection between ancient theater and therapeutics, pointing to archaeological evidence that found theaters built next to temples.

Batuman discusses the connection between tragedy and therapy in the context of psychoanalysis. Arguably the chief lesson of Oedipus for psychoanalytic theory is that "all adults, with no exceptions, were once babies, and aren't free from the indignities they suffered in this capacity." The importance of childhood in the development of adults is especially important when thinking about trauma of all sorts, and the psychological mechanisms that allows us to "forget that we were so weak and helpless" (Batuman, 2020). Hence, the added shock of trauma is that we are traumatized at all.

In interviewing Bryan Doerries, the founder of Theater of War Productions, Batuman reports that he thinks of Greek tragedy in "functional terms" as a form of ritual integration. Integration is especially needed post-trauma, where victims display "feelings of unremitting physical terror, loss of self, and blockages of memory and language that soldiers experienced in a war." Yet, victims of trauma hardly ever feel listened to. In fact, trauma studies scholars point out that any sort of advancement in the study of trauma is almost always alongside progressive politics that try to give voice to victims, who are otherwise ignored at best and at worst dismissed:

> "It never happened; the victim lies; the victim exaggerates; the victim brought it upon herself; and in any case it is time to forget the past and move on": trauma is inevitably met by the same denials, which are advanced by perpetrators, and accepted by everyone else, because we are all predisposed to identify with power. (By the same token, soldiers come home to realize that "no one wants to know the real truth about war.") Believing victims is a lot more work than believing people who have brought about, or benefit from, the status quo; after all, perpetrators and beneficiaries ask only for our neutrality, whereas a victim asks us to listen to, and empathize with, their long, awful story.
>
> (Batuman, 2020)

As Batuman argues, believing the disempowered requires rethinking some of the "most deeply ingrained ideas" in our culture, such as "it's natural or appropriate for children and women to be subordinated in the family, or for young men to be sacrificed in wars" (Batuman, 2020). It took second-wave feminism for rape trauma to be credible. The same can be said for the antiwar movement of the

1960s and 1970s for combat trauma. One could even extend this to #MeToo and Black Lives Matters, Batuman suggests, as they too reveal long-hidden traumas:

> The reason Greek tragedy works for so many of our social issues is that virtually all the tragedies, like the social issues, dramatize the conservative, contagious impulse to deny trauma: to negate that anyone is a victim or that anything bad is happening. Then someone defies the impulse and screams horrifying stuff that nobody wants to hear, and the spell is broken.
>
> (Batuman, 2020)

In exploring victim-denial, Batuman draws on psychoanalytic theory once again, particularly the work of Alice Miller, whose focus on childhood trauma suggests that speaking out against parental impropriety—what Miller calls "The Fourth Commandment" after "Thou shalt honor thy parents"—is taboo in post-Abrahamic, Western culture. To think that our parents did not love us and perhaps even hurt us is unbearable. Thus, we understand it as shame. Instead of speaking to the realities of our childhood experiences, we blame ourselves. "The first victim we don't believe is ourselves [as children]," as Batuman puts it (Batuman, 2020).

Batuman relates this to what the Frankfurt School called "the authoritarian personality" (Adorno et al., 2019) or what Wilhelm Reich before them dubbed "the mass psychology of fascism" (Reich, 1980). "The worship of power, the silencing of dissent and of logic, and the dehumanization of everyone perceived as weak or other," she writes, "are characteristics shared by authoritarian groups across the ideological spectrum." This widespread tendency to confuse one's "interests" with "the good" is reflective of a culture attached to what Batuman calls the "the moral scaffolding of individual blame and personal responsibility." But as Miller is quoted as saying, "it is not a matter of assigning blame to individual parents … but of identifying a hidden societal structure that determines our lives" (Batuman, 2020).

For Batuman and for the social sciences, tragedy reveals the truth about "structural or systemic problems" during the present crisis. It shows that it cannot be solved by "isolating and punishing individual culprits, leaving the rest of the society pure" (Batuman, 2020). Just as it demonstrates the impossible task of assigning blame to characters for the Theban plague (Oedipus?, Laius?, and the son of the king of Pelops?), it also suggests that removing individuals so that "workplaces aren't toxic to women" or that racism is eradicated by getting rid of racists is foolhardy. Rather, it asks us to "replace the mechanism of blame with that of contagion." In a pandemic, "we don't normally expect whoever gave us a respiratory virus to be punished." Personal responsibility in such a crisis is secondary to a cure. Contagion, therefore, reveals the farcical nature of the idea of choice. In tragedy, hardly anyone has a choice and everyone is to blame. In turn, it beckons the question of complicity, that is, of intra-action. When reckoning with structural crises, which of course social science, and sociology especially, does, "Who is to blame?" is insufficient. It must always also ask, "What is to be done?"

In *Rethinking Tragedy*, Rita Felski called for literary studies to shift toward a "tragic mode" rather than "tragic genre" (Michael, 2017: 14). To do so, she claimed, would be to "recognize the ways in which actions are shaped by forces beyond the individual's control or awareness is not necessarily to deny personhood but to expose the insufficient of modern ideals of autonomy and rationality" (Felski, 2008: 12). It would be to understand the world outside of a dichotomy whereby one side is "helpless" and the other "powerful and evil." To move towards a tragic mode would be altogether "skeptical of a sense of purpose and clarity of judgment." It is to ask for a shirking of a world centered on "moral and metaphysical absolutes" (Felski, 2008: 12).

For social science, it would mean an alternative chronotope, an ethico-onto-epistemology of the world as "not a limitless globe, but a small, fragile and finite place, one planet among others with strictly limited resources that are allocated unequally." It would mean a social science rooted in, in the words of Paul Gilroy "a planetary consciousness of the tragedy, fragility, and brevity of indivisible human existence" (Gilroy, 2005: 75).

References

Adorno, T., Frenkel-Brunswik, E., Levinson, D.J., and Sanford, R.N., 2019. *The Authoritarian Personality.* London: Verso Books.

Batuman, E., 2020. Can Greek Tragedy Get Us Through the Pandemic? *The New Yorker.* Retrieved August 31, 2021 (https://www.newyorker.com/culture/culture-desk/can-greek-tragedy-get-us-through-the-pandemic).

Butler, J., 2002. *Antigone's Claim: Kinship Between Life and Death.* New York, NY: Columbia University Press.

Felski, R., ed., 2008. *Rethinking Tragedy.* Baltimore, MD: Johns Hopkins University Press.

Garber, M., 2019. Apocalypse Is Now a Chronic Condition. *The Atlantic,* 1 Feb.

Geerts, E., 2016. New Materialism [online]. *New Materialism: How Matter Comes to Matter.* Available from: https://newmaterialism.eu/almanac/e/ethico-onto-epistem-ology.html [Accessed 2 Sep 2021].

Geerts, E. and Carstens, D., 2019. Ethico-onto-epistemology. *Philosophy today,* 63 (4), 915–925.

Giddens, A., 2002. *Runaway World: How Globalization Is Reshaping Our Lives.* New York, NY: Routledge.

Gilroy, P., 2004. *Postcolonial Melancholia.* New York, NY: Columbia University Press.

Jameson, F., 1973. The Vanishing Mediator: Narrative Structure in Max Weber. *New German Critique,* 1 (1), 52–89.

Jameson, F., 2020. *Allegory and Ideology.* London: Verso Books.

Jonas, H., 1985. *The Imperative of Responsibility. In: Search of an Ethics for the Technological Age.* 1st edition. Chicago, IL: University of Chicago Press.

Lash, S., 2007. Power After Hegemony: Cultural Studies in Mutation? *Theory, Culture & Society,* 24 (3), 55–78.

Latour, B., 2004. Why Has Critique Run Out of Steam? From Matters of Fact to Matters of Concern. *Critical Inquiry,* 30 (2), 225–248.

Latour, B., 2020. "We don't seem to live on the same planet…"—a fictional planetarium. *In: Critical Zones: The Science and Politics of Landing on Earth.* Cambridge, MA: MIT Press, 193–199.

Michael, J., 2017. Tragedy and Translation: A Future for Critique in a Secular Age. *In:* Elizabeth S. Anker and R. Felski, eds. *Critique and Postcritique.* Durham: Duke University Press, 252–278.

Nussbaum, M.C., 2001. *The Fragility of Goodness: Luck and Ethics in Greek Tragedy and Philosophy.* 2nd edition. Cambridge: Cambridge University Press.

Patterson, O., 2018. *Slavery and Social Death: A Comparative Study, With a New Preface.* 1st edition. Cambridge, MA: Harvard University Press.

Reich, W., 1980. *The Mass Psychology of Fascism.* New York, NY: Farrar, Straus and Giroux.

Sands, D., 2020. Gaia Politics, Critique, and the "Planetary Imaginary". *SubStance,* 49 (3), 104–121.

Thompson, J.B., 1991. *Ideology and Modern Culture: Critical Social Theory in the Era of Mass Communication.* Stanford, CA: Stanford University Press.

Weston, K., 1997. *Families We Choose: Lesbians, Gays, Kinship.* 1st edition. New York, NY: Columbia University Press.

Witt, C., 2005. Tragic Error and Agent Responsibility. *Philosophic Exchange,* 35 (1), 69–86.

INDEX

Printed in the United States
by Baker & Taylor Publisher Services